IMMIGRATION, ET

IN BRAZIL, 1808 TO THE PRESENT

Immigration, Ethnicity, and National Identity in Brazil, 1808 to the Present examines the immigration to Brazil of millions of Europeans, Asians, and Middle Easterners beginning in the nineteenth century. Jeffrey Lesser analyzes how these newcomers and their descendants adapted to their new country and how national identity was formed as they became Brazilians, along with their children and grandchildren. Lesser argues that immigration cannot be divorced from broader patterns of Brazilian race relations, as most immigrants settled in the decades surrounding the final abolition of slavery in 1888, and their experiences were deeply conditioned by ideas of race and ethnicity formed long before their arrival. This broad exploration of the relationships among immigration, ethnicity, and nation allows for analysis of one of the most vexing areas of Brazilian study: identity.

Jeffrey Lesser is Samuel Candler Dobbs Professor of Latin American History and Chair of the History Department at Emory University. He is the author of *A Discontented Diaspora: Japanese-Brazilians and the Meanings of Ethnic Militancy, 1960–1980* (2007), which received an honorable mention for the Roberto Reis Prize from the Brazilian Studies Association; *Negotiating National Identity: Minorities, Immigrants, and the Struggle for Ethnicity in Brazil* (1999), winner of the Best Book Prize from the Brazil section of the Latin American Studies Association; and *Welcoming the Undesirables: Brazil and the Jewish Question* (1994), which won the Best Book Prize from the New England Council on Latin American Studies.

NEW APPROACHES TO THE AMERICAS

Edited by Stuart Schwartz, Yale University

Also published in the series:

IMMIGRATION, ETHNICITY, AND NATIONAL IDENTITY IN BRAZIL, 1808 TO THE PRESENT

JEFFREY LESSER

Emory University

CAMBRIDGE
UNIVERSITY PRESS

CAMBRIDGE
UNIVERSITY PRESS

32 Avenue of the Americas, New York NY 10013-2473, USA

Cambridge University Press is part of the University of Cambridge.

It furthers the University's mission by disseminating knowledge in the pursuit of
education, learning and research at the highest international levels of excellence.

www.cambridge.org
Information on this title: www.cambridge.org/9780521145350

First published 2013

A catalogue record for this publication is available from the British Library

Library of Congress Cataloguing in Publication data
Lesser, Jeff.
Immigration, ethnicity, and national identity in Brazil, 1808 to the present / Jeffrey Lesser.
pages   cm. – (New approaches to the Americas)
Includes bibliographical references and index.
ISBN 978-0-521-19362-7 (hardback) – ISBN 978-0-521-14535-0 (paperback)
1. National characteristics, Brazilian – History – 19th century.   2. National
characteristics, Brazilian – History – 20th century.   3. Immigrants – Brazil – History –
19th century.   4. Immigrants – Brazil – History – 20th century.   5. Brazil – Ethnic
relations – History.   I. Title.
F2510.L48   2012
305.800981–dc23   2012016727

ISBN 978-0-521-19362-7 Hardback
ISBN 978-0-521-14535-0 Paperback

To the memories of my father,

William Morris Lesser, ז״ל

my sogro,

Michael Shavitt, ז״ל

and my mentor,

Warren Dean

CONTENTS

Figures, Tables, and Documents

Figures

TABLES

Documents

Acknowledgments

The idea for this book was generated while eating. Stuart Schwartz, the General Editor of the New Approaches to the Americas series, suggested that I write a volume on immigration but I demurred. Jerry Dávila was also at the meal. He took me aside and told me that I had, yet again, made a wrong decision. To him and Stuart, go my thanks for encouraging me to embark on what has turned out to be an exciting project.

Many institutions and individuals supported me as I worked on this volume. Most of the manuscript was written during a year I spent at the Bill and Carol Fox Center for Humanistic Inquiry at Emory University. My thanks go to Martine Brownley, Keith Anthony, Colette Barlow, and Amy Erbil for their support and generosity. The manuscript was completed at the Raymond and Mortimer Sackler Institute for Advanced Studies at Tel Aviv University, where Professor Abraham Nitzan and Ms. Ronit Nevo made sure I had the time and resources needed to focus on my writing. I particularly want to thank Raanan Rein, who over many years has been my brother in researching, writing, and adventuring.

While at Tel Aviv University, I had the chance to present a draft of the early chapters to the Latin American Studies Seminar coordinated by Rosalie Sitman. She and the members of the seminar were critical in helping me to reorient the book. I also had a chance to present chapters to the Immigration Workshop at the University of Chicago, and my thanks go to Marianna Staroselsky, Dain Borges, and their colleagues for suggestions. Later versions received superb comments from the participants in the Toronto Brazilian Studies Workshop organized by Gillian McGillivray. An almost final version of the introduction was presented to Emory University's Interdisciplinary Workshop in Colonial & Post-Colonial Studies.

Most of the photographs in the books came from the archives of the Ibero-Amerikanisches Institut Preussischer Kulturbesitz in Berlin and the Arquivo Histórico Judaico Brasileiro in São Paulo. My appreciation goes to Ricarda Musser and Gudrun Schumacher at the former and to Roney Cytrynowicz, Eliane Klein, and Sr. Arnaldo at the latter. Koji Sasaki kindly shared his photos and information on Brazilian migrants in Japan and Anna Toss did the same with a photo of Brazilians of Japanese descent. Nelson Bohrer at the Fundação D. João VI de Nova Friburgo generously provide images of immigrant life in Brazil. Aron Lesser negotiated with the security guards on the Rua 25 de Março to take the photographs of the monument discussed in Chapter 5.

Individual chapters of this book were improved immensely because of the comments of Ben Bryce, Clifton Crais, Roney Cytrynowicz, Jerry Dávila, Max Pendergraph, Fabrício Prado, Raanan Rein, Lena Suk, Cari Williams Maes, and Genevieve Zubrzycki. Nate Hofer and Andrea Scionti helped with Arabic and Italian translations, respectively. Grant Mannion worked on the tables and footnotes. Patrick Allitt read an early version of the entire manuscript and was always good-humored in spite of my inability to learn the difference between "of" and "from." Ben Nobbs-Thiessen, Glen Goodman, Thomas Rogers, and David Sheinin read later versions, and their comments improved the book immensely. Phyllis Berk was outstanding both as a production advisor and as a copy editor, in spite of her baseball preferences. Eric Crahan at Cambridge University Press moved the book through the review process during which the anonymous readers made excellent suggestions.

As with most of what I write, the final touches were done in my beloved São Paulo where my family and friends always make life exciting and interesting.

CHAPTER ONE

CREATING BRAZILIANS

My mother is Japanese, my father is Taiwanese, and my wife is Korean – I am the best Brazilian of all.
William Woo, a politician from São Paulo, in an
interview with the author in 2001.

INTRODUCTION

Figure 1.1. "Migratory Streams," 1974 stamp celebrating immigration to Brazil.

The faces tell the official story. Entitled "Migratory Streams," the stamp insists that Brazilian identity is synonymous with the nation's immigrants. The background map, with its lines representing human movement from Europe, Asia, the Middle East, and the Americas, places Brazil at the center of the world.

Immigration is so important to Brazilian national identity that
even those not born abroad are often defined as "immigrants." In the
mid-1940s, when foreign entry was at its lowest in a century because of
the closing of sea lanes during World War II, Dr. Cleto Seabra Veloso
of the Federal Department of Children reflected that newborn babies
were "our best immigrant[s]. Let's not forget this profound truth and
let's support those who will make the future Brazil bigger, stronger,
and more respected."[1] Thirty years later, a new superhighway linking Brazil's Atlantic coast with the city of São Paulo was named the
Immigrant's Highway (Rodovia dos Imigrantes). Its path makes drivers
into immigrants metaphorically as they repeat the journey of the millions of Europeans, Asians, and Middle Easterners who arrived in the
nineteenth and twentieth centuries.

A number of countries in the Americas, from Canada to Argentina,
describe themselves as "nations of immigrants" just as Brazil's secretary
of the Ministry of Justice did in 2011.[2] In the United States, the myth
of the "promised land" suggests that foreigners better themselves upon
arrival because the nation is intrinsically great. In Brazil, however, the
relationship between immigration and national identity is different.
Many intellectuals, politicians, and cultural and economic leaders saw
(and see) immigrants as improving an imperfect nation that has been
tainted by the history of Portuguese colonialism and African slavery. As
a result, immigrants were often hailed as saviors because they modified
and improved Brazil, not because they were improved by Brazil. Yet as
we will see, "improvement" took place in the most Brazilian of ways,
through absorption and mixture, as well as with the use of increasingly
flexible racial and ethnic categories.

Most Brazilians understand immigrants and immigration in an equally
elastic way, challenging those who suggest that the exclusive definition
of an immigrant is "an individual who moves by choice from one nation
to another." In Brazil, individuals represent themselves and are labeled
as immigrants in situational ways. Brazilians often treat "immigrant"
as a status that is ancestral or inherited, one that can remain even

[1] Dr. Cleto Seabra Veloso, "Construindo gerações," *Boletim Trimensal do
Departamento Nacional da Criança*, 4: 19 (December 1944), 41. My thanks to
Cari Williams Maes for pointing this out to me.
[2] Paulo Abrão, National Secretary of Justice, quoted in "Brasil vira meca para mão
de obra imigrante: Regularização de estrangeiros salta de 961 mil em 2010 para
1,466 milhão até junho," *O Estado de S. Paulo*, 19 November 2011.

among those born in the country. Those of immigrant descent rarely use hyphenated categories (such as Japanese-Brazilian or Italian-Brazilian), instead focusing on the birthplace of their ancestors, calling themselves (and being called) Japanese or Italian. An advertisement for the Bandeirantes Television Network's 1981 hit nighttime soap opera (333 episodes over fourteen months) "The Immigrants" makes the point in a different way: "*Portuguese, Japanese, Spanish, Italians, Arabs – Don't Miss the Most Brazilian Soap Opera on Television.*"[3]

Immigrants and immigration, as these examples suggest, include both the settlement of foreigners and the belief that their descendants continue to improve national identity. The *idea* of immigration thus helped Brazil's elites (made up of landowners, politicians, intellectuals, and industrialists) to see a future that was different and better than their present one. Not surprisingly, immigrants and their descendants generally agreed with the elites. More telling, nonelites often took the same position, even when they had no direct contact with immigrants or their descendants. When Brazilians claim, as they often do, that they live in "the country of the future," they are suggesting that the country's national identity is changing for the better. Immigration was one of the main components in the improvement, and thus the finite experience of movement did not end with the arrival of foreigners. Immigration was and is about creating a future, superior Brazil.

In 2003, Luiz Inácio Lula da Silva, a migrant from the Northeast to São Paulo whose career ranged from metallurgical worker to labor leader to politician, was elected president. While his personal story was unusual in a country where politics has traditionally been elitist, nondemocratic, and often repressive, his ideas about immigration as a source of strength and national improvement followed traditional patterns. President Lula and his allies insisted that Brazil was a multicultural country and that the slogan "Brazil – Everyone's Country" was not only about economic class. The visual representations for the motto often included photographs of Brazilians from many different ethnic backgrounds.

Celebrations of the immigrant past were notable during Lula's presidency, with the state investing significant funds, as it did for the 2008 centenary of the first Japanese arrivals. Much of the language that government institutions produced for the event insisted that Brazilians of Japanese descent were permanent immigrants, that there was little

[3] *Jornal do Imigrante* (São Paulo), 4: 422 (September 1981), 2.

difference in the high status of their great-grandparents born in Japan and their own Brazilian citizenship. The rise to prominence of another politician at the end of the Lula presidency reinforced the idea that immigrants and their descendants had created a "better Brazil." Petar Stefanov Rusev fled political persecution in Bulgaria, arrived in Brazil in the 1930s, and became a successful businessperson. In 2011 his daughter, Dilma Rousseff, became president.

A walk down any main street in Brazil, whether in a huge metropolis or small town, emphasizes the importance of immigration to national identity. A common Brazilian bar food is kibe (a torpedo-shaped fried croquette made of bulgur and chopped meat), even though most consumers are not descendants of the hundreds of thousands of Middle Eastern immigrants who arrived in the nineteenth and twentieth centuries. Since the 1960s, many young middle-class Brazilians have been obsessed with manga (a type of Japanese cartoon magazine), while older Brazilians eat sushi and practice "new Japanese religions" in significant numbers. Most are not of Japanese descent, but they live in the country with the largest population of Japanese immigrants and descendants in the world. The huge Brazilian home appliance manufacturer BRASTEMP advertises its products with such lines as "An Arab married to a Japanese – what could be more Brazilian." Orthodox Jewish ritual events are often promoted to the public by serving sushi. In Brazil's largest city, São Paulo, a common saying holds that a typical paulistano (resident of the city) is a "Japanese who speaks Portuguese with an Italian accent while eating an esfiha" (a pizza-like dish topped with meat and vegetables common in the Middle East).

A Hemispheric Perspective

Nowadays, Latin America often appears as a region of emigrants. The press and politicians in the United States frequently suggest that "Latin American" problems like crime and poverty are related to the movement of peoples north across the Rio Grande, whether by foot or plane. This contemporary image, however, is a new one. Europeans arrived in Latin America in large numbers from the sixteenth century until the middle of the nineteenth century. Millions of African slaves were forcibly settled, often together with smaller numbers of free colonists.

By the early nineteenth century, the descendants of those who had settled, whether slave or free, were forming all sorts of new and changing "Latin American" identities. Their aspirations led to the creation of new nations. The new national elites, be they Argentine or Brazilian or Honduran, often disdained the local indigenous, African, and mixed-descent inhabitants who made up the majority. Many in the dominant classes wanted to remake their national populations and they looked to Europe. By the mid-nineteenth century, both North and South America had become destinations for emigrants with the United States, Canada, Argentina, and Brazil receiving the largest numbers. Yet the absolute numbers of entries are not the only important statistics. In countries with small indigenous populations, like Argentina and Uruguay, the impact of immigrants on population growth was significantly higher than in the United States. Foreign newcomers, both slaves and free immigrants, were also demographically crucial to the growth of Brazil, Cuba, and Chile. Even in Peru and Mexico, where the numbers of immigrants were relatively small in comparison with the large populations of indigenous peoples, immigration weighed heavily on the minds of policymakers and the public.

Between about 1870 and 1930, roughly four million immigrants settled in Argentina, two to three million in Brazil, perhaps one million in Cuba, and 400,000 in Uruguay. In North America, Canada received more than 1.3 million newcomers, while the United States settled more than twenty million. Although most immigrants to the Americas came from Europe, significant numbers arrived from the Middle East and Asia. These numbers challenge contemporary academic and popular stereotypes of Latin America as populated almost exclusively by indigenous people, those of African descent, and people of mixed backgrounds.[4] The multiple origins remind us that newcomers from Asia, the Middle East, and Europe (and more recently in Brazil, from places like Bolivia, Argentina, Portuguese-speaking Africa, and Nigeria) played crucial roles in national identity formation. The presence and the attitudes of enslaved and free people were of equal importance in the creation of national identity among Latin America's other multicultural nations.

Throughout Latin America, immigrants were and are part of the discussion of national identity. In the Andes and Mesoamerica, national identity discourses often hail an Incan or Aztec past while dismissing it in practice. In Peru, Mexico, and Brazil, some immigrant leaders from Japan, China, Lebanon, and Poland claimed that Indians were in fact

[4] Peter Wade, *Race and Ethnicity in Latin America*, 2d ed. (London: Pluto Press, 2010).

a lost tribe and thus that their new immigrant group was in fact native. Peru's former president (1990–2000) Alberto Fujimori, for example, dressed as both an Inca and a samurai as part of the political marketing of his Japanese descent.

Claiming to have an indigenous past was not in conflict with taking advantage of state policies that were often designed to keep indigenous people at the lower rungs of the political, social, and economic hierarchy. For many immigrants, this boost meant that by the mid-twentieth century, those who were described, or described themselves, as descendants of Middle Eastern, Asian, and European immigrants came to play important roles in all sectors of these societies. Politicians of Arab descent are common in Argentina, Bolivia, and Ecuador. In those countries, as in Brazil, the large majority of Middle Eastern immigrants and their descendants are Christian. Some of Mexico's most powerful tycoons are the children of German and Lebanese immigrants. Many Honduran economic elites are of Christian Palestinian background.

In the Caribbean and Portuguese America, where the largest numbers of colonial-era residents were African slaves and their children, free immigrants played an equally important role. In those regions, foreigners became part of a discussion about blackness and whiteness that continues to dominate both popular and elite discourses. The Southern Cone countries of Chile, Uruguay, and Argentina also were populated with African slaves and indigenous people, but independence leaders conveniently forgot them as they proposed the settlement of immigrants in "unpopulated" territory.

How does Brazilian immigration compare with that of other countries in the Americas? In many ways Brazil is unique. Its size is bigger than that of the continental United States. It now has the fifth largest population in the world, which is by far the largest in Latin America. Unlike the more populous countries of China, India, and Indonesia, however, most of the population of Brazil originated as migrants, arriving either involuntarily as slaves from Africa or voluntarily as free immigrants. Yet Brazil is important not only for its size. Its three-hundred-year status as a colony of Portugal (from 1500 to 1822) inhabited mostly by African slaves gives unique inflections to everything from language to food.

In Brazil, many in the elite believed in the mythical greatness of the Amazon's indigenous people. While this echoes aspects of Mexican and Peruvian national ideals of a "cosmic race" of mixed indigenous and European pasts, Brazil's innovation was the addition of Africa. Yet in spite of the Brazilian "myth of the three races" (where Africans, Indians, and Europeans supposedly melded together to form a single and unique Brazilian "race"), much of the discussion of immigration was based on the Southern Cone model of newcomers populating virgin lands. Elites often saw immigrants (who in turn saw themselves) as replacing the local population with something better. Newcomers helped to form another myth of Brazilian nationhood, that of a "country of the future" where whiteness would eclipse blackness.

Brazil, however, also reminds us of many other American republics. In both the United States and Argentina, Central European immigrants arrived in the early years of the nineteenth century and were followed by large numbers of Southern Europeans, especially Italians. Brazil, like Peru, Canada, Cuba, and the United States, had numerous decades of intense Asian immigration. In the Southern Cone and in Central America, large numbers of Middle Easterners arrived in the late nineteenth and early twentieth centuries.

Brazil is also similar to other countries in the Americas where immigrants entered within a context of slavery, although abolition in Brazil came only in 1888. Yet immigrants were not slaves, even if they were often treated poorly. Many immigrants separated themselves, often aggressively, from slaves or free people of African descent. This separation was ongoing and dynamic: While some immigrants "became white" by distancing themselves from blacks and indigenous people, others moved in the opposite direction, either by marrying a person of color or not fulfilling certain cultural, social, and occupational expectations. Those who did not conform to the whiteness mandate through self-segregation often lost the advantages of being an "immigrant." The new ethnic identities that emerged among the descendants of immigrants in the Americas must thus be understood in relation to broader attitudes about creating racial, social, and political separation from those of African descent.[5]

THE SEEDS OF MASS IMMIGRATION

In the seventeenth and early eighteenth centuries, the Portuguese crown coerced less-than-desired populations to settle Brazil's frontiers

[5] Eric L. Goldstein, *The Price of Whiteness: Jews, Race, and American Identity* (Princeton, NJ: Princeton University Press, 2007); David R. Roediger, *Working Toward Whiteness: How America's Immigrants Became White: The Strange Journey from Ellis Island to the Suburbs* (New York: Basic Books, 2006).

with the Spanish colonies that would become Argentina, Paraguay, and Uruguay. As a result, Brazil's inhabitants included some indigenous peoples, many Portuguese settlers and their descendants, and even more slaves toiling in the plantation economy. Political leaders, confronting a vast territory and believing that the population ought to be less "black" and more "white," increasingly looked to immigrants from Europe. Those they wanted – industrious, enterprising, light-skinned people who could nevertheless thrive in Brazil's unfamiliar climate – were not easy to attract. The people they were more likely to get – refugees, political and religious exiles, those in jails, and the poor – were correspondingly less welcome.

In the mid-1700s, however, new ideas began to emerge. The Portuguese prince regent, Dom João V, centralized "colonization" policy throughout a far-flung empire that stretched from South America to South Asia. His goal was to convince non-Portuguese to settle in Brazil, and in 1748, just two years before his death, he employed an agent to bring thousands of Azoreans from those crowded Atlantic islands to Brazil's southernmost territories and to Pará at the mouth of the Amazon River in Brazil's North.[6] These plans had only modest success but set the stage for future state-sponsored settlement plans.

When Napoleon and his French Army invaded Portugal in 1807, the Braganças, the royal family now headed by Dom João VI, fled across the Atlantic. As they stepped off the ships in Rio de Janeiro's Guanabara Bay on January 28, 1808, the center of the Portuguese Empire shifted to Brazil, now a de facto independent nation. Members of the royal court were struck by the vast differences between elite European and Brazilian society. They wondered whether encouraging European immigration would help to recreate the world that they had left behind. Dom João's first step was to open up Brazil's economy and culture. He decreed that non-Portuguese ships could now dock at Brazilian ports, and non-Portuguese subjects received the right to own land. For many Portuguese leaders in exile, Brazil was on the road to nationhood. Once the independence genie popped out of the lamp it would never return.

Independence was fed by Enlightenment ideas. Abolitionist literature from England encouraged members of the Brazilian elite to speculate about ending slavery as a step toward nationhood. Portuguese Prime Minister in Exile (1817–1821) Tomás António de Vila-Nova worried

[6]   Karl Heinrich Oberacker, *A Contribuição Teuta à Formação da Nação Brasileira*, 2d ed. (Rio de Janeiro: Editora Presença, 1968), 207.

about the oppressive labor system in ways that would have been considered heretical a decade earlier. To the minister, slavery made Brazil "intrinsically weak" by preventing the growth of "a people" with a "national spirit." When the royal court had been in Portugal, all foreigners had been "categorically suspected of subversive activity."[7] With the move to Rio de Janeiro, non-Portuguese subjects were welcomed as residents and potential Brazilians.

New political and cultural ideas about foreigners as immigrants, rather than as spies, helped to reignite the discussion of slavery. For most elites, the system seemed necessary for short-run prosperity even if it, and slaves themselves, created barriers to national aspirations. At the same time, British pressure to end the slave trade was intense, albeit not wholly effective. Political and economic elites desiring to resolve the two positions looked north to the United States, which from afar seemed to be getting whiter, more European, and more productive. As Kirsten Schultz has noted, immigration "meant that in the new prosperous empire, at least in official visions of the political-economic future, whiteness and the ideal of utility as embodied in the small farmer could challenge successfully the ideal of linguistic, historic, and cultural unity and religious homogeneity of a heroic Portuguese nationhood that both exiles and residents evoked in explaining the transfer of the court."[8]

Many in the Portuguese court realized that the people they most wanted as immigrants were least likely to want to come. The sluggish response to Brazil's early-nineteenth-century desire for European immigrants forced political and business leaders to reevaluate their approaches. One idea was to target potential immigrants in France, England, and the United States by promoting Brazil as a neo-European country filled with empty land, where white immigrants would gain instant status in a slave society. However, the booming economies and political systems of all three countries meant that French, English, and Americans were not inclined to emigrate. Elites thus began taking other approaches. One was to use word of mouth, especially by inviting scientists who might return to Europe with positive impressions and create an aura of possibility for potential emigrants. Travelers, however, were rarely convinced. Their reports emphasized Brazil's Africanness,

7 Kirsten Schultz, *Tropical Versailles: Empire, Monarchy, and the Portuguese Royal Court in Rio de Janeiro, 1808–1821* (New York: Routledge, 2001), 111.
8 Ibid., pp. 111, 210.

the elite's sense of privilege, and the poverty of those few immigrants in the country. Other tactics were needed.

THE CREATION OF A MULTIETHNIC BRAZIL

As Brazil moved from a colony of Portugal (1500–1822) to independent empire (1822–1889) and then republic (1889–present), a number of processes led to the creation of a pluralistic society with a racial hierarchy that placed whiteness at the top and blackness at the bottom. The fluidity of these terms and their meanings, however, meant that Brazil became a multicultural nation even as its citizens often imagined themselves and their country becoming whiter. Terms like *white*, *black*, *European*, *Indian*, and *Asian* (among others) were not fixed in the Brazilian context. As different people and groups flowed in and out of these ever-shifting categories, Brazilian national identity was often simultaneously rigid (whiteness was consistently prized) and flexible (the designation of whiteness was malleable).

Beginning with the arrival of Europeans in the early sixteenth century, Brazil was increasingly filled with migrants from throughout the Portuguese Empire and from Africa who came in contact with the indigenous populations. The newcomers were not immigrants in the classic sense; few arrived voluntarily and most were coerced. Portuguese subjects arrived as members of four distinct categories: The smallest numbers were those from religious orders or those in political leadership positions who chose to come to Brazil, often believing that they were engaged in a temporary service to the king. Most migrants, however, were either *degredados* ("degraded ones") or soldiers. Degredados were criminals sent to Brazil to populate frontier regions as a condition of their release. Soldiers, like degredados, were coerced to move within the empire and had no say in their postings. The fourth category, Portuguese women, arrived in low numbers, either accompanying their formerly imprisoned husbands or as orphans sent by religious orders to marry white men in the colony. The data for entry in the centuries after 1500 are incomplete, although it is estimated that about 700,000 Portuguese subjects were sent to Brazil between 1500 and 1760.[9]

When gold was found in Brazil in 1693, entries grew markedly. In the 1720s, when diamonds were discovered, the numbers exploded. About

9   Instituto Brasileiro de Geografia e Estatística, available at: http://www.ibge.gov. br/brasil500/index2.html.

one million Portuguese subjects settled in Brazil during the eighteenth century, many of them prospectors and artisans. António Gomes Freire de Andrada, governor of the southern Provinces (which included parts of today's Uruguay and Argentina) and later viceroy of Brazil, used the newcomers to fortify Brazil's frontiers against the Spanish. Starting in the 1730s, he founded a number of forts, *presídios* (a kind of early-stage fort), and military garrisons that were supposed to be the seeds of towns and cities on the borders. The forts and garrisons had soldiers; the presídios (which today means "prisons") were filled with young Portuguese men, most of them degregados who were also responsible for public works.

The centuries between the initial Portuguese arrival in 1500 and the declaration of the Brazilian Empire in 1822 witnessed another huge group of involuntary migrants to Brazil: African slaves. More than 4.8 million slaves, some forty-five percent of all the Africans who made up the Atlantic trade, were forced to settle in Brazil. About two-thirds of the Africans were men, and they labored in mining, on sugar plantations, and in urban areas. Women often worked directly in the homes of slave owners and their families.

Even though Portugal's prime minister, the Marquês de Pombal, abolished slavery in mainland Portugal in 1761, it continued in Brazil until 1888. Brazil's slaves, of course, resisted their bondage. Often they formed runaway communities, and over time, the owners freed many children and grandchildren of slaves. Africans and their descendants, both enslaved and free, always had contact with immigrants and thus are a crucial part of our story. Even so, this book does not focus on those who had no choice in the matter of their migration. Furthermore, many Portuguese and Africans came during the period when Brazil was just one of Portugal's numerous colonies and thus settled in a land without a clear sense of national identity.

WHITENING

When Brazil declared its independence from Portugal in 1822, immigration and national identity took on new meanings. Foreigners were expected to become citizens who would make the new country strong in everything from policy to culture. Yet many old attitudes remained, especially in the conflation of nationality and biology and the certainty that there was a hierarchy of race, with white Europeans at the pinnacle.

The linkage of blood and nation may have originated in the sixteenth century with the Inquisition, which sought to ensure the blood purity of Catholics. By the nineteenth century, human hierarchies were part of a larger Euro-American elite culture, and different institutions helped to naturalize and formalize racial difference. In the United States, segregation legally separated whites and blacks, and miscegenation was a subject of terror. In Argentina, miscegenation and racism meant that the visibility of those of African descent decreased markedly. By the twentieth century, many elite and middle-class Argentines had come to believe that blacks had disappeared and that the country was white and European, rather than multicultural.[10]

In Brazil, however, miscegenation had different consequences. Elites often tried to figure out who was white, who was black, who was neither, and who was both. Immigrants did the same, realizing that they had some influence on their own placement in the racial (and thus social and economic) hierarchy. Many nineteenth-century Brazilian elites, therefore, embraced a new political and cultural philosophy on race. *Whitening*, as they called it, meant that the population could be physically transformed from black to white through a combination of intermarriage and immigration policies. "Strong" white "blood" would overwhelm that of "weak" nonwhites, and the law would prevent the entry of "feeble" races. Immigrants often accepted and used these categories. Becoming "white" was as important to the newcomers as it was to the national elite.

Whitening was crucial to the formulation of Brazil's modern immigration policy. Almost two million European immigrants entered Brazil between 1820 or so and 1920, although many left as well. The newcomers were not evenly distributed across the nation. Indeed, immigrants were lured mainly to the central and southern sections of Brazil. This population concentration was one result of an enormous shift in the Brazilian economy, which had been strongest in the sugar-growing and gold areas of the North during the early colonial period and had moved toward the center of the country with the discovery of diamonds in the midcolonial period. Most immigrants arrived in the middle of the nineteenth century with the growth of the coffee economy in the South.

European newcomers arrived in a superior position to the ex-slaves, who for generations had been deprived of formal education and whose

[10] George Reid Andrews, *The Afro-Argentines of Buenos Aires, 1800–1900* (Madison: The University of Wisconsin Press, 1980).

work had been largely uncompensated. Brazil's highly racialized social and economic spheres were reinforced with the unreliable statistics that were a hallmark of nineteenth-century "scientific" states. The numbers showed that Afro-Brazilians had higher levels of illiteracy, malnutrition, and criminality than the population as a whole.[11] These kinds of statistics helped policymakers argue that whites were better than blacks.

Much of the late-nineteenth and early-twentieth-century ideas about race in Brazil stemmed from earlier European pseudoscience about race and human difference. For example, many in Brazil's educated classes accepted the craniometrical scale created by the German physician Johann Friedrich Blumenbach in 1776, providing a continuum of racial excellence with European whites at the top, Asians (whom he called Mongoloids) in the middle, and black Africans at the bottom.[12] In the nineteenth century, many Brazilian elites became enthralled with the ideas of Jean-Baptiste Lamarck, a French naturalist who theorized that traits and culture were acquired via local human and climatic environments. He proposed that a single "national race" was biologically possible, and this provided the scientific scaffold for the creation of Brazilian immigration policies where "miscegenation did not inevitably produce 'degenerates,' but could forge a healthy mixed population growing steadily whiter, both culturally and physically."[13]

Intellectuals and politicians often saw themselves as social chemists using Brazil as a "racial laboratory" for whiteness. The chemistry metaphor reminds us that elites viewed the population as a base to which human "reagents" could be added or subtracted. In other words, policymakers used eugenics to create a correlation between immigrant entry and racial change. An influential nineteenth-century book on colonization, originally written as a formal report to Brazil's minister of agriculture, is an excellent example. João Cardoso de Menezes e Souza's *Theses*

[11] Warren Dean, *Rio Claro: A Brazilian Plantation System, 1820–1920* (Stanford, CA: Stanford University Press, 1976), 173–174.
[12] Johann Friedrich Blumenbach, *On the Natural Varieties of Mankind: De Generis Humani Varietate Nativa* (New York: Bergman Publishers [1776] 1969), 273.
[13] Thomas E. Skidmore, *Black into White: Race and Nationality in Brazilian Thought.* (Durham, NC: Duke University Press, 1993), 65; see also Nancy Leys Stepan, *"The Hour of Eugenics": Race, Gender and Nation in Latin America* (Ithaca, NY: Cornell University Press, 1991).

on *Brazilian Colonization: Solutions to the Social Questions Related to This Difficult Problem* proposed that Brazil was a unique national "embryo" that had to be rejuvenated in order to extinguish the country's African heritage. Immigrants were the "seed" from which would spring the "powerful force of homogeneity and cohesion that will pull together and assimilate" the population at large.[14]

MASS MIGRATION

More than five million immigrants flowed into Brazil between 1872 and 1972, although the statistics on immigration are not always reliable since many returned to their homelands or left for other countries. For example, during the first decades of the twentieth century, any person arriving by ship without a first-class ticket was considered an "immigrant," even if he or she was a short-term visitor. Many foreigners migrated only temporarily, but the Brazilian government kept information about entry and often ignored exit. In one period for which we have both entry and exit information, from 1908 to 1936, the number of exits from Santos (Brazil's primary port of arrival) represents more than fifty percent of the total number of entries (1,221,282/667,080), according to the records of São Paulo's Office of Land, Colonization and Immigration.

The tables that follow show high numbers of European immigrants arriving in Brazil. Yet the "Japanese" column also stands out. How Japanese immigrants fit into the whitening paradigm is an important question in Brazil and one that we will explore in Chapter 6. The other surprising column in the tables is labeled "Others." Who was represented in this category in which Brazilian officials (and academics) often placed immigrants without distinguishing their places of origin? Many were Middle Easterners and Eastern Europeans whose national classifications often shifted (from Turk to Syrian to Lebanese – from German to Polish and then back) and who together made up a large part of Brazil's immigrant stream. As we will see in Chapter 5, there were moments when almost twenty percent of all Jews leaving Europe went to Brazil and other periods in which Christians from today's Syria and Lebanon made up very significant percentages of total entries.

---

[14] João Cardoso de Menezes e Souza, *Theses sobre Colonização do Brazil: Projecto de Solução às Questões Sociaes, Que se Prendem a Este Difficil Problema* (Rio de Janeiro: Typographia Nacional, 1875), 403, 426.

Table 1.1. *Immigration to Brazil, by Nationality*

	Nationality						
	Portuguese	Italians	Spanish	Germans	Japanese	Others	Total
1872–1879	55,027	45,467	3,392	14,325	–	58,126	176,337
1880–1889	104,690	277,124	30,066	18,901	–	17,841	448,622
1890–1899	219,353	690,365	164,293	17,084	–	107,232	1,198,327
1900–1909	195,586	221,394	113,232	13,848	861	77,486	622,407
1910–1919	318,481	138,168	181,651	25,902	27,432	123,819	815,453
1920–1929	301,915	106,835	81,931	75,801	58,284	221,881	846,647
1930–1939	102,743	22,170	12,746	27,497	99,222	63,390	327,768
1940–1949	45,604	15,819	4,702	6,807	2,828	38,325	114,085
1950–1959	241,579	91,931	94,693	16,643	33,593	104,629	583,068
1960–1969	74,129	12,414	28,397	5,659	25,092	51,896	197,587
1970–1972	3,073	804	949	1,050	695	9,017	15,588
1872–1972	1,662,180	1,622,491	716,052	223,517	248,007	873,642	5,345,889

Source: Maria Stella Ferreira Levy, "O Papel da Migração Internacional na Evolução da População Brasileira (1872 a 1972)," *Revista de Saúde Pública*, supplement, 8 (1974), 71–73.

These "Others" make Brazil's largest metropolis, São Paulo, one of the largest "Italian," "Japanese," and "Lebanese" cities in the world.

Attention to those in the Japanese and Others columns changes an often-told story about Brazil that focuses on Catholic immigrants from Italy, Portugal, and Spain. The hundreds of thousands of non-European entries often led to strong responses, usually spoken in very direct ways. Unvarnished racism against immigrants, and by immigrants, tell us much about Brazilian national identity. So do the stories of immigrants, be they the numerically dominant ones from Southern Europe or the many Asians, Arabs, and Jews who received disproportionate attention from the press, policymakers, and intellectuals. "Other" immigrants were as important to the creation of Brazilian national identity as Portuguese and Italians.

Tables 1.1 and 1.2 show significant shifts over time in countries of emigration. Eugenic-influenced policy in the nineteenth century supported the entry of German, Portuguese, Spanish, and Italian workers as *braços para a lavoura* (literally, "arms for agricultural labor"). Yet fears of social and labor activism and concerns about assimilation encouraged a look at non-European groups. Most important were immigrants from Japan, seen as modern, hardworking, and docile. These Brazilian ideas were reinforced by Japan's growing international power and industrial strength. Japanese intellectuals and politicians often promoted themselves as citizens of Asia's only "white" nation, and this

Table 1.2. *Immigration to Brazil, by Nationality as a Percentage of the Total*

	Nationality						
	Portuguese	Italians	Spanish	Germans	Japanese	Others	Total
1872–1879	31.2	25.8	1.9	8.1	–	33.0	100
1880–1889	23.3	61.8	6.7	4.2	–	4.0	100
1890–1899	18.3	57.6	13.7	1.4	–	8.9	100
1900–1909	31.4	35.6	18.2	2.2	0.1	12.5	100
1910–1919	39.1	16.9	22.3	3.2	3.4	15.1	100
1920–1929	35.7	12.6	9.7	8.9	6.9	26.2	100
1930–1939	30.9	6.7	3.8	8.3	29.8	20.5	100
1940–1949	40.0	13.9	4.1	6.0	2.5	33.6	100
1950–1959	41.4	15.8	16.2	2.9	5.8	17.9	100
1960–1969	37.5	6.3	14.4	2.9	12.7	26.3	100
1970–1972	19.7	5.2	6.1	6.7	4.5	57.8	100
1872–1972	**31.1**	**30.3**	**13.4**	**4.2**	**4.6**	**16.4**	**100**

Source: Maria Stella Ferreira Levy, "O Papel da Migração Internacional na Evolução da População Brasileira (1872 a 1972)," *Revista de Saúde Pública*, supplement, 8 (1974), 71–73.

appealed to many in Brazil's dominant classes. A Brazilian elite desire for white immigrants, regardless of their ostensible biological race, thus matched neatly with immigrant hopes to be included in the desirable category.

The changes we see in the nationality of immigrants should not, however, suggest that the concept of whitening became less important. Rather, what it meant to be white shifted markedly over the course of the twentieth century. Federal Deputy Acylino de Leão summed it up with clarity in 1935 when the Brazilian Chamber of Deputies voted to give subsidies to Japanese, but not to Portuguese immigrants: "[T]he Japanese colonists … are even whiter than the Portuguese [ones]," he proclaimed.[15]

VISIONS OF THE OTHER

Emigrants do not simply pick up and leave their countries of birth. Those considering migration usually evaluate the global market for labor, economy, and culture with the available information. Twenty-first-century ideas of nations are often created by visual images, music, and marketing. The nineteenth century was not so different, and when Dom João VI

[15] Speech of Acylino de Leão, September 18, 1935. República dos Estados Unidos do Brasil, *Annaes da Camara dos Deputados: Sessões de 16 a 24 de Setembro de 1935*, Vol. 17 (Rio de Janeiro: Off. Graphica D' "A Noite," 1935), 432.

sought to "promote and expand the civilization of the vast Kingdom of Brazil" with European settlements in 1818, international marketing was crucial.[16] Brazil sent immigration agents to Europe to promote the country, often with government-produced brochures in multiple languages (the cover of this book shows one example).

From the early nineteenth century through the mid-twentieth century, Brazilian supporters of immigration sought to populate parts of the country that they considered empty. While these areas often had indigenous populations, they were dismissed or ignored by policymakers who looked to Europe for newcomers. Brazil's most spectacular early attempt at selling itself to emigrants thus started in a small city in Switzerland and ended in the highlands of the Province of Rio de Janeiro. It included deceit, disease, and religious disputes, setting the stage for mass immigration to Brazil at the end of the century.

The colony of Nova Friburgo (New Freiburg) was named for a city in Switzerland. The location, in the state of Rio de Janeiro, was chosen by Brazilian politicians in large part because the climate seemed similar to what they envisioned that of Switzerland to be.[17] There, an economic downturn had led to unemployment and food shortages. As Swiss politicians began encouraging emigration to reduce population, Brazilian politicians saw an opportunity for white immigrants par excellence. Dom João VI and his advisors were ready to make a financial investment and political commitment. They believed that Swiss immigrants would step off the boat and transform an unpopulated area into a European town of white farmers and artisans.

The plan was to create a colony from scratch. Dom João would offer passage, land, housing, and logistical support to one hundred Catholic families, along with a free return to Switzerland if things did not go well. He hoped that most of the immigrants would become small landowners growing crops. He believed that some artisans and other professionals would settle and teach their trades. Nothing, however, worked as planned. Many colonists were Protestant who converted to Catholicism in order to migrate. A malaria epidemic struck the embarkation point in Europe, creating a human disaster. Of the 2,018 emigrants who left, only 1,631 arrived in Brazil, a mortality rate of close to twenty percent.

[16] Martin Nicoulin, *A Gênese de Nova Friburgo: Emigração e Colonização Suíça no Brasil (1817–1827)* (Nova Friburgo: Fundação Biblioteca Nacional, 1996).

[17] Magnus Mörner and Harold Sims, *Adventurers and Proletarians: The Story of Migrants in Latin America* (Pittsburgh, PA: University of Pittsburgh Press, 1985), 41.

Figure 1.2. *Vila de Nova Friburgo* (1820). Painting by Jean-Baptiste Debret.
Source: Courtesy of the Archives of the Centro de Documentação D. João VI –
Nova Friburgo, RJ.

The conditions in Nova Friburgo (depicted in Figure 1.2) were not
that much better than those on the ship. The newcomers were unpre-
pared for the tropics, and mortality rates continued to be high. Dom
João learned that many of the newcomers were Protestant rather than
the Catholics for which he had contracted. This discovery precipitated a
small crisis with the pope, who opposed having non-Catholic settlers in
the supposedly Catholic-exclusive Brazil. Yet Dom João decided to reject
the pope's criticism and open the doors. When he hired a Protestant
minister in 1819, most colonists reconverted to Protestantism.[18] The
decision to support Protestant entry was not based on a commitment to
religious freedom. Rather, Dom João and his allies believed that order
and progress (not, coincidentally, the slogan on the modern Brazilian
flag) would be implanted in Brazil via Northern European Protestants,
whom they saw as uniquely industrious and as indisputably white. The
inverse was applied to Catholics, seen by many at court as retrograde
and unmodern.

Nova Friburgo, in spite of the human, economic, and political invest-
ments, was a failure. The high mortality rates created demographic and
psychological problems for the settlers. They were untrained for the
climate, and farming was not successful. Many colonists returned to
Switzerland or remigrated within Brazil. Dom João quickly lost interest
in the Swiss colony but it did not disappear. Today, Nova Friburgo is
a city of 175,000 and the place where religious tolerance first became

---

[18] Martin Dreher, "Imigração e religião no Rio Grande do Sul do século XIX," in
Loraine Slomp Giron and Roberto Radünz, eds., *Imigração e Cultura* (Caxias do
Sul: EDUCS, 2007).

part of Brazil's immigration policy. Dom João's decision to defy the pope paved the way for streams of newcomers from across the globe in the late nineteenth century.

Who Will Do the Hard Work?

Dom João VI and many of his supporters dreamed of remaking Brazil in the image of Central Europe. Nova Friburgo, in spite of its failure, helped elites imagine Brazil as a magnet for immigrants who would transform the country racially, economically, and culturally. The experiment's failure made clear that centralized political involvement was needed to ensure that immigrants were recruited well, were treated with some measure of respect, and would become self-sufficient. Successful colonization needed concrete policies aimed at populating territory with "ideal" immigrants.

Settling Brazil with white European immigrants left two important questions unanswered: Who would do the hard work, and how could plantation labor continue without African slaves? One elite answer was that peasants in the northeastern parts of Brazil would become pliant, docile, and hardworking, in effect citizen-slaves.[19] Another solution involved giving temporary contracts to Chinese workers as a bridge between slave and free labor. Policymakers argued over whether and how Chinese laborers might fit into Brazilian society. Analysis of the cultural and physical traits of the "Mongolian type" in numerous nineteenth-century intellectual and political treatises were divided over the utility of Chinese labor. There were regular debates at the provincial and imperial levels as the Brazilian press hailed and mocked the possibilities.

The debates showed another side of the immigration coin – to some elites the failure of Nova Friburgo meant that Brazil had to try harder, but Chinese immigration, others feared, would be dangerous if it succeeded. While few Chinese immigrated to Brazil before the mid-twentieth century, Brazilian elites were familiar with China and its people. Portugal had been the first European maritime power to establish direct relations with the Chinese Empire in 1511. In the nineteenth century, Portugal was deeply invested in Asia, through its port/colonies in Goa and Macau. The relationship between the two empires was found even

---

[19] Stanley Blake, *The Vigorous Core of Our Nationality: Race and Regional Identity in Northeastern Brazil* (Pittsburgh, PA: University of Pittsburgh Press, 2011).

in language. The word *mandarin*, flowing from its etymological roots in the Portuguese word *mandar* ("to send or to order"), was introduced to describe members of the Chinese elite. The Chinese word for tea, *chá*, continues to have wide usage in Brazil.[20] Brazilian elites were not the only ones considering Chinese labor. Throughout the Americas, debates emerged about whether Chinese workers would enrich countries or harm national culture. These discussions were entangled with questions about slavery and abolition. Many intellectuals erroneously believed that Chinese workers would not remain in Brazil permanently because they had an unbreakable bond to their homeland. Impermanence and servility made Chinese slavelike but not slaves.

With the migration of the Portuguese court to Brazil in 1807, the foreign minister-in-exile in Rio de Janeiro, the Conde de Linhares, considered bringing two million Chinese to the country. His idea was to skirt the English suppression of the African slave trade and satisfy Dom João's desire to make tea a major export commodity. The plan was implemented in 1810 on a small scale: About 750 Chinese tea growers would eventually be employed on the imperial Botanical Garden in Rio de Janeiro. An economist and member of the high court of Salvador, Bahia, Judge João Rodrigues de Brito, encouraged the entry of Chinese laborers, noting that they were "not only hard workers but ... active, industrious and skilled in arts and agriculture."[21]

Chinese tea cultivation, like the Swiss Nova Friburgo colony, was a failure. Wilhelm L. von Eschwege, a German who spent eleven years in Brazil, beginning in 1810 as a colonel in the Royal Engineering Corps and Intendant General of Mines, pointed to the unhappiness of the Chinese workers, who were frustrated that "all the attempts to bring women were in vain."[22] John Luccock, a British merchant who spent a decade in Brazil beginning in 1808, put the onus on the Chinese workers in a different way. He claimed that they were overpaid and too "diligent ... too precise and [too] slow in their modes of culture," even though they had a "rapidity of comprehension which surpassed whatever I have observed of the

[20] Maria José Elias, "Introdução ao Estudo da Imigração Chinesa," in *Anais do Museu Paulista* 24 (São Paulo, 1970), 57–100, p. 60.
[21] João Rodrigues de Brito, *Cartas Econômico-Políticas sobre a Agricultura, e Commércio da Bahia* (Lisbon: Imprensa Nacional, 1821), 35.
[22] Wilhelm Ludwig von Eschwege, *Pluto Brasiliensis*, trans. Domício de Figueiredo Murta (Belo Horizonte: Ed. Itatiaia; São Paulo: Ed. da Universidade de São Paulo, 1979), II: 267.

kind in any other race."[23] Years later, in 1832, Charles Darwin visited the Royal Botanical Garden. He complained that the 164 acres of "insignificant little [tea] bush[es] ... scarcely possessed the proper tea flavor."[24]

Chinese workers were no doubt unhappy with their lives in Brazil. The director of the Botanical Gardens treated the workers harshly, suspecting that they had intentionally failed to reveal their most sophisticated tea-processing techniques. When a small group fled, the garden's director hunted them with horses and dogs. Those who escaped successfully settled in the city of Rio de Janeiro where they worked as peddlers and cooks. Those who remained complained regularly about their treatment; in 1819 they demanded that a worker who spoke Chinese and Portuguese be assigned as their official interpreter and be paid a special wage.[25] When the German traveler Johann Moritz Rugendas arrived on the royal estate in 1835, he found only three hundred Chinese still working.

Embedded in the elite disputes over Chinese labor were deep divisions about the relationship between immigration and Brazilian national identity. Those who favored immigration focused on increased economic production, while opponents feared social "pollution." On both sides were influential intellectuals, planters, and politicians, including Quintino Bocayuva (future head of Rio de Janeiro's powerful Republican Party), Senator Alfredo d'Escragnolle Taunay (later a leader of the Central Immigration Society), the progressive entrepreneur and industrialist Irineu Evangelista de Sousa (the Baron of Mauá), Liberal politician and president of the Province of Rio de Janeiro João Lins Vieira Cansanção de Sinimbú (later appointed prime minister), and the abolitionist politicians André Rebouças and Joaquim Nabuco, to name just a few. The "anti" group brought together fervent nationalist/racists who asserted that the Chinese were biologically degenerate, abolitionists who believed that Chinese laborers would form a neoslave class, and a few large landowners who were convinced that only Africans were biologically suited for backbreaking plantation work. The "pro" side included plantation owners who wanted to replace African slaves with a cheaper and more docile group, other planters who believed that Chinese workers

[23] John Luccock, *Notes on Rio de Janeiro and the Southern Parts of Brazil: Taken During a Residence of Ten Years in That Country from 1808 to 1818* (London: Samuel Leigh, in the Strand, 1820), 288.
[24] *Charles Darwin's Beagle Diary*, ed. Richard Darwin (Cambridge: Cambridge University Press, 1988), 67–68.
[25] Letter signed by fifty Chinese laborers on the Fazenda Real to Dom Pedro I, September 6, 1819. Manuscript Collection – General Collection, II 34.27.4, Biblioteca Nacional – Rio de Janeiro [hereafter BN-R].

were more biologically suited for agricultural laborer than Africans and thus would make Brazil more competitive in the world market, and abolitionists convinced that Chinese contract labor would be a step forward on the path to full wage labor. Neither side dominated, and as the nineteenth century progressed, the disputes over immigration continued.

CONCLUSION

The positions staked out in the Chinese immigration debate became more resonant as Napoleon's influence over Portugal ended in 1815. Yet there was little desire from the crown and its minions to return to the now-renewed metropolitan center in Lisbon. In what was certainly one of the most boring revolutions of all time, Brazilian independence was proclaimed in 1822. The eldest son and heir to Dom João VI of Portugal was now Emperor Pedro I of Brazil. He and his son, who would become Emperor Pedro II, both found their new nation's racial and ethnic composition problematic. To them, and to many others in the burgeoning Brazilian elite, slaves, indigenous people, free people of color, and *mestiços* (mixed-race people, often called *pardos*) would never be modern citizens. African slaves, forced to migrate to Brazil in bondage, formed almost thirty percent of the population. The German explorer Alexander von Humbolt provided the chilling statistics with his 1825 population estimates: Brazil, by his reckoning, contained 1,960,000 blacks, 1,120,000 pardos and Indians, and only 920,000 whites.

The Pedros were emperors of an enormous territory. Its almost 3.3 million square miles had only four million people, making it appear largely unpopulated. Settling the border areas with immigrants, the rulers believed, would guarantee territorial stability from the encroachment of Argentina and Paraguay, countries with which Brazil had a bellicose relationship. Like his father, Pedro I also believed that small immigrant freeholding would help to transform the country culturally and economically by diminishing the impact of what appeared to be unproductive plantations. In his mind, and that of most political and economic leaders for the next 150 years, Brazil had to recreate itself as a European-like nation.

The first step was the opening of Brazil's ports. This brought large numbers of foreigners into coastal cities and to the rural areas linked to them. The newcomers settled for different reasons than expected and, as Roderick Barman has noted, "If some came to seek their fortunes, many from France and Italy were political radicals who had left their native land to escape retribution from the restored monarchies.

Interacting with their Brazilian counterparts at every level of urban society, from that of the small folk to that of the high functionaries, the foreign immigrants acted as both agents for new ideas and as suppliers of the latest literature, both cultural and political."[26]

Even though immigration and colonization were the higher priorities, imperial leaders made Roman Catholicism the state religion.[27] Many potential immigrants were Protestant, however. They were cautious about settling in a nation where the public practice of their religion was illegal. Yet the existence of an official religion did not mean that the empire demanded Catholicism as a condition of entry. Dom João had provided a Protestant priest to the Nova Friburgo colonists, and in 1824 the Imperial government began subsidizing the entry of Protestant Central European immigrants, mainly poor farmers and former soldiers fleeing the aftermath of the Napoleonic Wars. Although they had to worship in private, many Protestant farmers did settle in southern Brazil. Concern about immigrant religion in the imperial era revolved around a simple bipartite distinction between Catholic and non-Catholic Christians. The entry of Muslims, Buddhists, Hindus, Confucians, or Jews was rarely considered. To most members of the Brazilian elite, non-Catholic immigrants were Protestants, and prior to the 1880s they were largely correct.

As the nineteenth century progressed, immigration highlighted one area of broad elite consensus and two of dispute. The agreement was that Brazil had to modify its population racially from blacker to whiter, an idea sometimes expressed as a shift from African to European. The differences had to do with how whiteness would be defined and how immigrant labor should be integrated in the context of slavery. Plantation owners and their political allies feared that large numbers of small farms would create competition. They often believed that immigrants should replace slaves in name only. For many elites, whiteness was a way to paint Brazil's population a different color without changing the hierarchies of power. Many Liberals at court (and later in independent Brazil) took a different position. They saw plantations as a problem. Immigrants were to create independent farms and diminish the power of the large landowners. For those Liberals whiteness was linked to capitalism and progress. It was the tension between these different positions that re-created Brazil as a "nation of immigrants."

[26] Roderick Barman, *Brazil: The Forging of a Nation, 1798–1852* (Stanford, CA: Stanford University Press, 1988), 56.
[27] Constituição de 25 de Março de 1824, I-Art. 5.

CHAPTER TWO

FROM CENTRAL EUROPE AND ASIA

IMMIGRATION SCHEMES, 1822–1870

Figure 2.1. 1974 stamp celebrating the arrival of German immigrants.

ALEMÃO (German): "a very white and pink-cheeked (i.e. does not become dark in the sun) individual"
ALEMOA (German woman): "a very white and pink-cheeked woman, but without charm"
PORTUGUESE: "It is said of an imbecile; stupid; really stupid"
     From Felisbelo da Silva (Police Investigator), *Dicionário de Gíria* [Dictionary of slang] (São Paulo: Editora Prelúdio, 1974), 16, 92

THE NEW POLITICS OF EMPIRE

In 1821, Dom João VI departed for Portugal. Soon thereafter he demanded that Brazil return to its subservient position as a colony. Brazilian nationalists refused, with the support of an important ally,

João's son Pedro, who had remained in situ as regent. Princess Maria Leopoldina, the Austrian-born daughter of Hapsburg Emperor Franz II and Pedro's wife, encouraged her husband. "The fruit is ready, it's time to harvest," she supposedly said in urging Pedro to declare Brazil's independence from Portugal. Pedro's shout of "Independence or Death" on the banks of São Paulo's Ipiranga River as he removed the blue and white Portuguese shield from his uniform has become Brazil's foundational moment. Whether the September 7 "Cry of Ipiranga" ever took place is open to debate. There is no doubt, however, that on December 1, 1822, Emperor Pedro I of Brazil was crowned.

Pedro I saw himself as a modernizing head of state. He and his political allies believed that Brazil should have a popularly elected legislature led by an emperor with executive powers. Large landowners interested in maintaining the social and political hierarchy often opposed him. In the new empire, the immigration debate wound through intertwined discussions among the elite about whether Brazil should have a modern export economy, whether slavery should continue, and whether landholding should be primarily of small or large scale.

There were areas of agreement among Brazil's elites. One was related to security. Brazil's four million inhabitants were scattered over a huge territory, with most concentrated along the Atlantic coast. Less than thirty percent of the population was of European descent while more than thirty percent were African slaves. The newly consolidated Argentine Republic sought growth just as Brazil's own expansion was taking place. Violent clashes with indigenous communities in both countries were common, and as borders were established and pushed outwards, Brazil and Argentina often found themselves in conflict. For newly independent Brazil, forming a powerful army seemed a necessity.

Another area of elite agreement was that Brazil's economy should be export oriented. The new empire had no colonies to exploit but needed money. Taxation did not seem an option since most subjects were poor and elites were uninterested in taxing themselves. Export products, such as sugar, coffee, and cotton, all of which demanded intense human labor, seemed to have the most potential for the rapid generation of wealth. A booming export economy, Brazil's leaders believed, would create a modern nation, prepared to sit at the table as a world power. Traditional class and racial hierarchies, however, would remain unchanged.

The expanding agricultural economy in the provinces of Rio de Janeiro, São Paulo, and Minas Gerais demanded labor. Most workers were African slaves, about 1.1 million of whom arrived between 1822 and 1850. There was also an internal movement of slaves in Brazil, and as the economy boomed in the South, slaves were transported in that direction. As cities grew, the need for urban workers was met by former and current slaves and Portuguese immigrants. While the European newcomers seemed especially suited to Brazil – they were Catholic and speakers of the national language – elites were not enthusiastic. Rather, they wanted immigrants willing to settle in rural areas, to occupy Brazil's frontiers, and to create a smallholding agricultural economy following the Central European and North American models.

National desires for whiteness and economic change, however, were challenged by slavery. Liberal elites considered human bondage unmodern and slaves unmodernizable, and inefficient, workers. The British increased the pressure when they abolished the slave trade in 1808 and then slavery throughout its empire in 1834. The British insisted that all other countries follow their lead, using force to achieve their goals. Although Brazilian elites realized that abolition was going to take place sooner or later, most did not believe that freed slaves could be productive wage laborers.[1] Thus, slaves remained the most important part of the labor force in northern Brazil, where elites remained deeply committed to traditional hierarchies and where few immigrants would settle in the nineteenth or twentieth centuries. Indeed, the systematic interest in replacing slave labor, which began in the early nineteenth century in southern Brazil and became the norm later in that century in the center, never took hold in the North.

In spite of the different regional attitudes about slavery, many elites favored immigrants as a workforce. The Portuguese, however, were frequently deemed unacceptable. Most already in Brazil were young, male, and poor. Beginning in the late eighteenth century, they had settled in urban areas as clerks and salespeople, remitting their wages back to their families. They often married and fathered families with women of African descent. The negative reaction by the dominant classes was similar to that which would happen in the mid-nineteenth-century United States, when Irish-black sexual unions took place and helped to create an impression that the Irish immigrants were not white. Brazil's dominant classes (themselves usually of Portuguese descent) worried that new Portuguese immigrants would be unable to whiten the country

---

[1] Emília Viotti da Costa, *The Brazilian Empire: Myths and Histories* (Chicago: University of Chicago, 1985), xxv.

or to transform the rural economy. Even in the late twentieth century, many Brazilians linked national problems to colonization by Portugal rather than one of the other European powers.

On May 30, 1823, a long letter in favor of replacing slaves with immigrants appeared in the influential Rio de Janeiro newspaper *O Espelho* [The mirror]. The letter was mysteriously signed by "The Philanthropist." A century later, the historian Helio Vianna discovered that Pedro I had been the author. The emperor argued that immigration was a way to end slavery, to modernize, and to populate rural regions with people who would create a better Brazil. "Slavery is the cancer gnawing at Brazil and it must be eradicated," The Philanthropist wrote. The system was causing "incalculable harm" and was making Brazilians unproductive: "Each slave master starts to look down on others from the time he is young. He gets used to acting as he wishes, without regard for the law.... [He] becomes used to feeling superior to all men.... He does not tolerate being reprimanded and his heart gets in the habit of getting revenge and satisfying its passions, in telling others 'if you were my slave ... '"[2]

One of the strongest supporters of a new immigration policy was José Bonifácio de Andrada e Silva, a politician who supported independence, abolition, and public education for Brazil. He believed that European immigrants would be more productive than slaves and could hasten abolition without causing economic upheaval. Newcomers would, Andrada e Silva was certain, only want to settle in "unpopulated" areas (indigenous people did not apparently count as inhabitants), and thus would fill the southern frontier areas bordering the Río de la Plata likely to be targets of Argentina's policy of expansion. Argentine leaders thought along similar lines, and the military and political leader Juan Manuel de Rosas began subsidizing Spanish immigration to those same areas in 1829. Andrada e Silva, on the other hand, looked to Central Europe, not to Spain. He found allies in Empress Leopoldina and the many politicians and intellectuals who believed that immigration was a quick way to "civilize" the country via racial "whitening," which would wipe blackness out of the Brazilian gene pool.

In 1824, Brazil promulgated a new constitution that made clear the national commitment to immigration. While remaining a formally Roman Catholic state, people of all religions were now "permitted to

[2]   *O Espelho*, 30 May 1823, reprinted in Hélio Vianna, *D. Pedro I, Jornalista* (São Paulo: Melhoramentos, 1967), 79–84; p. 80.

exercise their worship privately in buildings specifically designated for that purpose but without the exterior markings of a house of worship." Another article in the new constitution gave citizenship to all those born in Brazil and automatically to women who married Brazilian men.[3] With the legislation in place, the hunt for immigrants began.

WHY GERMANS?

The failure of the Swiss colony of Nova Friburgo only whetted the desire for more white immigrants. Empress Leopoldina, herself Austrian, insisted that Central Europeans had inherent cultural qualities that would improve the new empire. These included exceptional abilities as farmers and a sense of national pride that would transform immigrants rapidly into devoted Brazilian subjects.[4] New plans targeted the desired German-speaking peoples who lived in numerous European principalities. One was to develop a Brazilian foreign legion with thousands of Central European soldiers.[5] Another was to enact a landholding system to take advantage of a "natural" German inclination toward small-scale farming. Each immigrant would receive a *picada*, a long, narrow plot of land, as a start-up. What was assumed to be the German characteristic of self-reliance and independence would then supposedly make the land agriculturally productive. Other promises included free travel, immediate naturalization, freedom of religion, animals and money for two years, and freedom from taxes for ten years.[6]

The picada system put immigrants into potential competition with slave-owning plantation owners. When the owners resisted Pedro's plans, he proposed a two-year grace period during which slavery would be replaced by a mixed free-and-slave-labor system, with European immigrants paid wages. This transition plan was never enacted. The Brazilian Empire ended its participation in the Atlantic Slave trade only in 1850 and took almost forty more years to abolish slavery.

3   Brazilian Constitution of 1824, Title I, Article 5, and Title II, Article 6.
4   Martin Dreher, *Igreja e Germanidade: Estudo Crítico da História de Igreja Evangélica de Confissão Luterana no Brasil,* 2d ed. (São Leopoldo: Editora Sinodal, 2003), 29.
5   Neill Macaulay, *Dom Pedro: The Struggle for Liberty in Brazil and Portugal, 1798–1834* (Durham, NC: Duke University Press, 1986), 178.
6   Jean Roche, *La Colonisation Allemande et le Rio Grande do Sul* (Paris: Institut des hautes études de l'Amérique latine, 1959), 77, 428.

Brazil's new immigration policies took advantage of a population explosion in Europe that had increased pressure on the land and made hunger a growing reality. Hundreds of thousands of Europeans now looked abroad for their futures. Refracted visions of Brazil and Germany meant that the meeting of the two national imaginations created an environment for both emigration and immigration. Hundreds of books about immigration to Brazil were published in German between 1825 and 1875, most with positive conclusions. Yet the push-and-pull factors also created another immigration phenomenon that is as common today as it was two hundred years ago: scams.

The most sophisticated of the early con artists to link Germany and Brazil were a physician named Cretzschmar and a soldier named Schäffer. Dr. Cretzschmar, from Frankfurt, liked to write letters about science and nature to Brazilian scholars. He also appears to have taken it upon himself to help land-hungry Germans move to Brazil. In the 1820s, he began to circulate the story that Brazil was offering free, tax-exempt land, with the provision that males provide military service. Although the Congress of Vienna (1814–1815) had prohibited the emigration of soldiers in an effort to prevent the creation of a future Napoleonic army, Cretzschmar ignored the strictures. As the self-appointed agent in charge of immigration, he took cash from potential illegal immigrants, although it appears that no one followed through and migrated to Brazil. So many complaints were received that the Frankfurt Senate fined Cretzschmar after "[e]migrants began to appear at Bremen and Hamburg, the ports of departure for most Central Europeans going to the Americas, demanding free passage to the free lands of Brazil."[7]

Major Johann Anton von Schäffer, an Austrian, was a rather more sophisticated swindler. He was a confidant of Empress Leopoldina, and in the early 1820s represented himself in Germany as a Brazilian immigration recruiting agent. Apparently, he even appointed Cretzschmar as Brazilian consul in Frankfurt just around the time that German authorities were forcing the good doctor to end his activities. What is certain is that Pedro I had asked Schäffer to find soldiers for the aforementioned Brazilian Foreign Legion and to recruit settlers in German-speaking Europe. Schäffer's particular genius was the triple dip – he apparently made a profit by charging the colonists, the city governments, and the Brazilian Empire for his services.

---

[7] Mack Walker, *Germany and the Emigration, 1816–1885* (Cambridge, MA: Harvard University Press, 1964), 39.

"Profits" aside, Schäffer's job was complicated by the fact that many European leaders did not permit emigration to Brazil since they considered Pedro I an illegitimate ruler, a son who had betrayed his own father. Neither Schäffer nor Central Europe's impoverished populations, however, were deterred. Fifty percent of the first group of emigrants from Germany to Brazil in 1823 came from a single region near the French border that had been victimized by war for years.[8] Soon thereafter, Schäffer negotiated a contract with the grand duke of Mecklenburg-Schwerin for a group of criminals to be freed in order to join the military in Brazil.[9] This group, and any actual soldiers that Schäffer found, were not officially permitted to emigrate as this was a violation of the Congress of Vienna. No matter. Schäffer simply dressed the soldiers as peasants and boarded them as members of settler families.

The first part of the voyage was from Bremen to Hamburg. There, each emigrant was quarantined in preparation for a trip to Amsterdam and then across the storm-ridden Atlantic aboard the *Argus*. Arriving in Rio de Janeiro in January 1824, the 284 immigrants (150 were soldiers and the rest real colonists) were received with much fanfare by the emperor and empress. The settlers were confessionally mixed, with Catholics, Protestants, and even one colonist self-identified as Jewish. Brazil's first Evangelical pastor was also on board. The newcomers were celebrated for renouncing their citizenship and becoming Brazilians. They probably did not realize that now they could not return to their homeland, no matter how bad the situation in Brazil.

Over the next six years, 5,350 German-speaking immigrants crossed the Atlantic bound for southern Brazil.[10] This number represents only a fraction of those recruited. Many potential immigrants fled after learning of Major Schäffer's brutal tactics for keeping emigrants on ships while still in German harbors. One ship had a mutiny en route to Brazil, leading the captain to execute eight people on the high seas. Two other passengers were beaten to death for trying to murder the captain.[11]

---

8   Marcos Tramontini, *A Organização Social dos Imigrantes: A Colônia de São Leopoldo na Fase Pioneira, 1824–1850* (São Leopoldo: Editora UNISINOS, 2000).
9   Martin Dreher, *Degredados de Mecklenburg-Schwerin e os Primórdios da Imigração Alemã no Brasil* (São Leopoldo: Editora Oikos, 2010).
10 Jean Roche, *La Colonisation Allemande et le Rio Grande do Sul* (Paris: Universite de Paris III: Travaux et mémoires de l'Inst. des hautes études de l'Amérique latine, 1959), 77.
11 Mack Walker, *Germany and the Emigration, 1816–1885* (Cambridge, MA: Harvard University Press, 1964), 39, 41.

Eventually, Major Schäffer's bad image led the Brazilian government to recuse itself from involvement with his activities.

Most of the newcomers did not stay in Brazil's capital city. Rather, they disembarked for Rio Grande do Sul, settling in an area just north of the provincial capital of Porto Alegre called São Leopoldo. These first immigrants suffered great hardships. They also were pioneers in helping to create an image of a future white and modern Brazil for elites, especially by settling on lands inhabited by populations of primarily indigenous and African descent. The song supposedly sung by Germans as they left Europe makes this point clear: "America, free land ... Europe only offers slavery." A similar idea can be found in Amalia Schoppe's 1828 novel for youngsters about German immigrants in Brazil.[12] The eldest brother in the story helps to pay for the family's passage by making a deal with the ship's captain to be sold as a slave in Brazil (see Figure 2.2). However, the novel ends heroically with the family free and Brazil providing possibilities for success that were unheard of in Germany at the time.

A more recent example of the heroic view of German immigrants comes from Josué Marques Guimarães's 1972 novel *A Ferro e Fogo, I: Tempo de Solidão* [At all costs: Times of solitude]. The novel, once required reading in public schools in the state of Rio Grande do Sul, is set in 1825. It presents German immigrants as hyperindependent farmers caught in the middle of the Brazilian-Argentine conflicts. Like the authors of many historical novels, Marques Guimarães insists to readers that the text is more "reality" than fiction, and thus creates an idea of a past that never existed for the immigrants without revealing the complex political factors surrounding their settlement. The following quotation from the book jacket sums up the plot:

> The German immigrants lived their misery and disenchantment, their conquests, their moments of tenderness and yearnings, their work from dawn to dusk, their quarrels and hates. [The book] tells of the despair of those who were suddenly tossed into distant lands. Spaniards and Indians, warlords and politicians, soldiers and prostitutes, forming the backdrop of those who arrived in Brazil attracted by fleeting promises and guarantees. Over time

---

[12] Amalia Schoppe, *Die Auswanderer nach Brasilien oder die Hütte am Gigitonhonha; Nebst noch Andern Moralischen und Unterhaltenden Erzählungen für die Geliebte Jugend von 10 bis 14 Jahren,* 2d ed. (Wesel: Bagel & Co., [1828] 1852).

Figure 2.2. Illustration of a German immigrant sold into slavery.
Source: Amalia Schoppe, *Die Auswanderer nach Brasilien oder die Hütte am Gigitonhonha*. Courtesy of the Ibero-Amerikanische Institute, Berlin.

they lived with suffering, deprivation, work and war. Yesterday's immigrants are today part of our nationality, mixing the races and clearly helping national development in politics, the arts, and sports. This was done at all costs.

   Without the dates and historical minutia of an annoying textbook, *At All Costs* is a fascinating, dense and agile novel that tells the true saga of the colonization of the state of Rio Grande do Sul.

Late-twentieth century novels notwithstanding, most early immigration schemes were not particularly successful. The empire was unable, financially and politically, to be the sole guarantor of passage and land. By 1830, the government had stopped funding settlers and demanded that emigrants prove self-sufficiency prior to receiving travel permits. Private schemes and public/private partnerships thus began to gain a foothold. An 1834 law devolved colonization policy to the provinces, but local governments were as poor as the national one. Local leaders quickly began to rely on private interests to settle the vast swaths of land unpopulated by those other than indigenous peoples.[13]

In 1831, Pedro I abdicated in favor of his then five-year-old son who, following a regency, was crowned Emperor Pedro II in 1841. Like his father, Pedro II was a modernizer. He freed his own slaves and encouraged coffee production. As sugar declined and coffee boomed, Brazil's economy shifted from the north to the south. Railroads, telegraph lines, and other official indicators of material progress grew rapidly. Even so, and in spite of official encouragement, few immigrants came to Brazil between 1820 and 1875. The 330,000 who did arrive paled in comparison to some nine million who entered the United States, the clear winner in the international competition for immigrants.[14] Brazil's image in Europe was that of a disease-infested jungle with little economic opportunity. This impression was accentuated by racist fears among potential Brazilian immigrants, who worried about settling in a country with large numbers of slaves. To make matter worse, those who did immigrate did not seem to be particularly successful. As this information circulated in Europe, Brazil often seemed a poor option compared to the United States and Argentina. Only Portuguese arrived in large numbers, representing more than forty-five percent of the total, and often settling in cities rather than on the frontiers.

The numbers worried Brazilian politicians, who passed new laws designed to guarantee immigrant success. In 1848, about 275 square miles in each province were reserved for immigrants to have the opportunity to own land. Yet the laws did not prevent more schemes from materializing. Brazilian agents in Germany, following the innovations of Major Schäffer, arranged for "jail-birds, from the prisons of Potsdam

---

[13] Giralda Seyferth, A Colonização Alemã no Vale do Itajaí-Mirim; um Estudo de Desenvolvimento Econômico (Porto Alegre: Editora Movimento, 1974), 30–32.

[14] Report of the Immigration Commission, Statistical Review of Immigration, 1820–1910 (Washington, DC: Government Printing Office, 1911), 4.

[to be] dispatched instead of agricultural laborers."[15] With the prisoners came soldiers to fight in the 1851 Platine War between Argentina and Brazil, the latter allied with Uruguay and two breakaway Argentine provinces. The conflict took place in Uruguay, on the Río de la Plata, and in the northeast of Argentina known as the Platine region. The Brazilian emperor brought 1,800 German mercenaries to the fight, hoping that they would remain as members of the Foreign Legion. Two-thirds, however, fled and disappeared into the small German settlements that dotted Rio Grande do Sul. One of the deserters was Karl von Koseritz. This young and relatively educated soldier naturalized as a Brazilian in 1864, and his career would include politics and the editorship of the German-language Brazilian newspaper Deutsche Zeitung. Later in the century, von Koseritz founded the Sociedade Central de Imigração (Central Immigration Society) that, as we shall see, helped to stimulate Brazil's modern immigration policy.

Brazilian ideas about immigration began to change radically in the mid-nineteenth century. Emigration from Europe became more common as a result of wars, new means of transportation, and the sense that independent nations in the New World were not going to revert to colonial status. In 1850, the Queiroz Law abolished the slave trade, one response to intense British pressure following the entry of some 342,000 Africans in bondage between 1845 and 1850.[16] Abolition was on the horizon, and elites began to develop two new labor systems for Brazil: sharecropping and the establishment of small farms. Together, these new plans laid the groundwork for the millions of immigrants who would flow into Brazil starting in the latter decades of the 1800s.

PRIVATE COLONIZATION SOCIETIES

Even though large plantations were increasingly important to Brazil's economic growth in the mid-nineteenth century, many politicians focused on populating frontier areas with small farms. To foster this kind of settlement, they encouraged Private Colonization Societies

[15]   C. F. Van Delden Laërne, Brazil and Java. Report on Coffee-Culture in America, Asia and Africa, to H. E. the Minister of the Colonies (London: W. H. Allen & Co., 1885), 134.
[16]   Information available at: http://slavevoyages.org/tast/assessment/estimates.faces ?yearFrom=1501&yearTo=1866.

(PCS) to bring immigrants to Brazil and to help them purchase their own plots. Fundamental to the PCS system was the expectation that new arrivals would be successful in order to repay the costs of passage and loans with some interest. Immigrants were also expected to increase the value of the lots so that each PCS would make a profit when the land was sold to the farmer. The PCS even received subsidies from provincial governments to make up the difference in ticket prices from Germany to Brazil, which were significantly more expensive than those to the United States.

The colony of Blumenau, in the state of Santa Catarina in southern Brazil, was formed by a typical Private Colonization Society. Hermann Blumenau believed that his colony, founded in 1850, would be successful only if immigrants represented a range of professions, from physicians to farmers. Literary scholar Ana-Isabel Aliaga-Buchenau writes of a German-Brazilian novelist whose parents settled in Blumenau around 1880, and painted this heroic portrait of the man and colony: "A single man had had the strength and courage, to found a German colony, far from his homeland in an unknown country. He had bought land, had recruited young, strong people from home, they had cleared the virgin forest, and built houses, they had made sure the colony had a church and a school. And while they suffered many setbacks, he was never discouraged."[17]

Blumenau's approach worked well. His recruitment plans meant that in addition to agriculture, the colony became known for small industry. Two of the settlers were brothers from a family of artisans in Saxony, in northern Germany. The 43-year-old Hermann Hering emigrated in 1878, followed two years later by his younger brother Bruno. Hermann was a particularly skilled businessman who in 1879 acquired a circular loom, a rarity in Brazil at the time. The following year he and Bruno opened a cotton-textile plant in the colony, and during the next century the company would expand to more than thirty thousand workers, as the Hering brand became the Hanes or Fruit of the Loom of Brazil.

In his letters, Hermann Hering expressed the joint dream of immigrants and Brazilian elites: "Every immigrant, if he is not sick or a beggar, will rise to middle level social status in the German sense within

[17] Ana-Isabel Aliaga-Buchenau, "German Immigrants in Blumenau, Brazil: National Identity in Gertrud Gross-Hering's Novels," *The Latin Americanist*, 50: 2 (March 2007), 5–22; p. 9.

three or four years."[18] In an October 1883 letter to a cousin in Germany, Hermann was even more expansive:

We are sorry we did not bring our mother: She would have to deal with the transatlantic trip across the immense ocean and initially pass through many difficult times. But now we live in the pure air where the windows are open all day and the days are warm. Our life is among people like us – there are no counts and barons, beggars and vagabonds in our colony. Our mother would have a more agreeable life than in stuffy and narrow Brüdergasse where it is never summer.[19]

While the Herings are the most famous family to emerge from Blumenau, other colonists also found success, especially as they realized that "Germanness" had commercial possibilities in Brazil. Today, Blumenau is a city of 300,000 and an important Brazilian commercial and tourist destination. The city promotes its Europeanness (according to the 2000 census, almost ninety-five percent of the residents describe themselves as "white") by everything from the architecture of the homes to the food served in restaurants to the celebrations of the German past (see Figure 2.3). One result is that the current word used to describe those from Rio Grande do Sul, *gaúcho*, creates an entirely different image in Brazil than does the same word in Argentina, where a man on horseback comes to mind. In Brazil, gaúchos often represent Germanness and whiteness. It is a common nickname for those with blond hair, along with the even more direct *alemão* ("German").

The Germanness of southern Brazilians also played a role in the success of the Hering Corporation. The company logo is two herrings (a fish commonly eaten in Northern Europe). Consumers thus link Hering products to high quality and modern technology from Germany. This recognition means that Hering products promote their Brazilianness through Europeanness. Even so, many consumers would describe the company as "gaúcho," imbuing its products with German cultural characteristics.

---

[18]   Luiz Felipe Alencastro and Maria Luiza Renaux, "Caras e modos dos migrantes e imigrantes," in Fernando Novais, ed., *História da Vida Privada no Brasil*, Vol. II: *Império: A Corte e a Modernidade Nacional* (São Paulo: Companhia de Letras, 1997), 292–335; pp. 319–320.

[19]   Maria Luiza Renaux Hering, *Colonização e Indústria no Vale do Itajaí: O Modelo Catarinense de Desenvolvimento* (Blumenau: Editora da FURB, 1987), 92.

Blumenau _____ Santa Catarina - Brasil

Figure 2.3. A contemporary postcard promoting the city of Blumenau.

São Lourenço do Sul, a town in the state of Rio Grande do Sul, was also formed as a Private Colonization Society. The colony was in a region of fertile land and rolling hills first populated in the eighteenth century by Azorean soldiers who had fought the Spanish and received the land from the Portuguese crown. From 1800 to 1850, the area slowly grew as a population center. In 1850, a local landowner donated land for the establishment of a formal town. In 1857, Jakob Rheingantz, a Prussian agent, established the colony with fourteen hundred families from Pomerania, a German-speaking region of the Baltic that was claimed by both Poland and Germany. Rheingantz's PCS gave each settler a subsidy (from the empire but paid to Rheingantz instead) calculated as the price of passage.[20] In other words, colonists could choose to pay for their tickets and arrive with no funds, or borrow the money for the ticket and invest their savings in the success of their efforts after arrival. Most chose the latter approach and the colony thrived. Today, the city has a population of forty-five thousand and promotes tourism via the "Pomeranian Trail," where visitors are taught about the difference between São Lourenço do Sul and other German-Brazilian tourist cities like Blumenau.

[20] Arthur Blasio Rambo, *Cem Anos de Germanidade no Rio Grande do Sul, 1824–1924* (São Leopoldo: Editora Unisinos, 1999), 92.

Of course there were failures as well. Most spectacular were those launched by Hugo Grüber, the editor of a German-language newspaper in Rio de Janeiro and later a founder of the Central Immigration Society. His first plan, to bring five thousand Volga Germans (ethnic Germans from the south of Russia) to Brazil in 1869, was rejected by imperial officials who "had already learned by experience that the great majority of immigrants, more especially from Eastern Europe, are not well fitted for agricultural labor. And besides, they had already been obliged to send five or six hundred turbulent Polish colonists back to Europe."[21] Grüber was not deterred and persuaded some of that group to go to the state of Paraná, where "they received such wretched lands, that most of them left the country again, and went to Europe, North America, or the Argentine Republic."[22] Another Grüber plan, to bring thirty thousand people from Hungary, never even got off the ground.

Many German settlements succeeded, although the total numbers of immigrants were small. In general, the colonies were in remote locales and unconnected to other populations except by river. These realities were not always clear to newcomers, even if they had contact with those who had already settled. Immigrants, for example, would send postcards home (a common practice among Central Europeans) with city images, the only ones available, though they lived in rural areas. In one case, a German immigrant sent an entire set of postcards, with a portion of a letter on each, to a relative in Berlin. The photographs were primarily of urban scenes, including modern buildings and clean plazas. Only one, of a native peasant with his arm around a donkey and labeled "a patient couple," was mockingly representative of life in rural Brazil.[23]

German immigrants were relatively isolated linguistically and culturally, often traveling between colonies on boats. One ramification of the minimal contact with Brazilian natives was the development of a language called Riograndenser Hunsrückisch, a form of Old German modified by contact with Portuguese. Today, the language continues to be spoken occasionally and similar constructions that combine a preimmigration language with Portuguese are found among Italian, Yiddish,

[21] Laërne, *Brazil and Java*, p. 129.
[22] Ibid., p. 133.
[23] Kartenbrief aus Porto Alegre nach Berlin, in Fotos Gaelzer-Neto, VIII. Auswanderung nach Brasilien, Ibero-American Institute–Stiftung Preussischer Kulturbesitz, Berlin.

and Japanese speakers in Brazil. Use of Riograndenser Hunsrückisch declined after new laws demanded that only Portuguese be spoken following Brazil's entry into World War II on the Allied side in 1942. In the 1980s, there were even some attempts by judges to remove the Brazilian citizenship of Riograndenser Hunsrückisch monolinguals. Most recently, however, immigrant ethnic descent has become a more acceptable part of multicultural Brazil. One result has been a small boom in younger people learning and preserving the Brazilianized German of their ancestors.

PARCERIA – SHARECROPPING

If colonies of smallholders challenged plantations, *parceria*, or "sharecropping," buttressed them. The system was created by *fazendeiros* (plantation owners – based on the Portuguese word *fazenda* or "plantation") in south-central Brazil. They wanted to increase their labor supply as the numbers of slaves decreased following the passage of the 1871 Rio Branco Law, which made all newborn children free, even if their parents were in bondage. The plantations produced export goods with slave labor, and planters saw independent immigrant colonies as competition. Sharecropping, on the other hand, used immigrants to replicate slave labor in many ways.

Without the promise of land and independence, planters found themselves struggling to convince immigrants to settle on fazendas, especially because wages were higher in the United States and Argentina. Sharecropping was developed to compensate for salary-related differences. In theory, the planters would pay for the transatlantic crossing and delivery of workers in exchange for work and the chance for the immigrants to sell part of their production for profit. As the historian Thomas Holloway explains:

> The planters paid the costs of the immigrant families from Europe to São Paulo and advanced sufficient funds to sustain the new arrivals until they could harvest food on their own plots of plantation land. The worker was expected to reimburse the planter in full for the expenses, with an interest charge on the unpaid balance. Each immigrant was assigned a certain block of trees to cultivate, and he had no choice but to turn over the crop to the landowner after harvest. The worker was to receive half the net profit from the eventual sale of the coffee from the trees under his

care [and] the landowner was to receive half the production of these plots in excess of the subsistence needs of the worker.[24]

Plantations using immigrant sharecroppers were located throughout southern Brazil. In the mid-nineteenth century, a number of coffee plantations in the mountains around Rio de Janeiro were using the system, first with Portuguese immigrants. By 1855, however, many plantations in Rio de Janeiro State had German immigrant labor. As was the case elsewhere in Brazil, the experiences of these immigrants were mixed. Some fled, often to German colonies in southern Brazil where they could avoid sharecropping altogether. In the colony of Independência, on the other hand, many immigrants were able to work off their debts. An article published by the weekly *Allgemeine Auswanderungs-Zeitung* [General emigration newspaper] in 1860 noted that of the 330 immigrants, only ten had fled and that the rest "in spite of the initial difficulties ... were in a position to prosper."[25]

Most plantations were located in coffee-rich São Paulo State, and it was there that the majority of immigrants settled. By the mid-1800s, the state had sixty plantations with sharecroppers, and the experiences of immigrants showed that the theory of the parceria system was often divorced from the reality. The plantations owned by Senator Nicolau Vergueiro are a case in point. Immigrants to Vergueiro's lands had to sign a form of indenture contract before leaving Europe, and upon arrival they were closely controlled. Vergueiro and other fazendeiros believed that immigrants had a "a lack of ambition, of social experience, of elegance, of body posture, of a sense of opportunity and progress, of boldness, of perceptiveness, of wisdom. In fact, 'colono' means disgusting behavior."[26] By calling the sharecroppers "colonos," planters meant something different than did the owners of Private Colonization Societies. In southern Brazil, colonos were hardworking and independent immigrants on the road to land ownership. For most fazendeiros, however, the word *colono* meant nonslave servitude.

---

[24] Thomas Holloway, *Immigrants on the Land: Coffee and Society in São Paulo, 1886–1934* (Chapel Hill: University of North Carolina Press, 1980), 71.

[25] *Allgemeine Auswanderungs-Zeitung*, 24 February 1860, cited in Débora Bendocchi Alves, "Cartas de imigrantes como fonte para o historiador: Rio de Janeiro – Turíngia (1852–1853)," *Revista Brasileira de História*, 23: 45 (July 2003), 155–184; p. 166.

[26] Sérgio Alves Teixeira, *Os Recados das Festas: Representações e Poder no Brasil* (Rio de Janeiro: Funarte, 1988), 54.

Words, of course, often change meanings, and Vergueiro's definition did not last. In 1934, the federal government began to celebrate "Colono Day," insisting that European immigrants were creators of a modernized wage-labor Brazil.

Whether called sharecroppers or colonos, most laborers on São Paulo's plantations were in precarious circumstances from the minute they agreed to immigrate. They were billed for the cost of transport from the port of Santos to the plantation (as much as fifty percent of the cost of the transatlantic voyage) and were given a relatively high interest loan (at six percent a year) for the basic tools and seeds needed for agricultural success. Many plantation owners used questionable weights and measures to skim part of the parceiro's production. Immigrants were charged for virtually ever service they needed. On the Vergueiro plantation, the retainer of a German-speaking doctor was charged to the immigrants, as were the costs of the local teacher. All goods (even pencils and paper for school) had to be bought at inflated prices at the plantation store. The situation was so bad that some immigrants would flee the plantations without collecting for months of work, but also without paying off their debts.

Debts were arranged in family units so that everyone (including children) became responsible. As historian Warren Dean notes, "[I]f the husband died, the widow and the children would be obliged to serve out the contract, as would the orphans if both parents died."[27] Not surprisingly, immigrants often felt hopelessness and anger. The Swiss traveler Johann Jakob von Tschudi visited Brazil between 1857 and 1859 and was appointed Swiss ambassador the following year. He reported that many immigrants were depressed and lethargic. Even so, he placed much of the blame for failure in Brazil on the colonists, just as the planters did.[28] (See Document 2.1: Report of Johann Jakob von Tschudi, 1866, in the chapter Appendix.)

The result of the unfair treatment was that immigrants and landowners disputed everything, from contract language to pay. One area of contention surrounded the interpretation of the standard contractual clause that planters would "furnish" transportation from the Brazilian port of Santos to the colony. Fazendeiros insisted that furnish meant "arrange," rather than "pay for." Colonists understood "furnish" as "pay

[27] Warren Dean, *Rio Claro* (Stanford, CA: Stanford University Press, 1976), 91.
[28] Johann Jakob von Tschudi, *Viagem às Províncias do Rio de Janeiro e São Paulo* (São Paulo: Martins Livraria Editora [1866] 1953), 146–147.

the costs of" and rarely learned the truth until after they had arrived at the colony.

Abusive economic structures were matched on the social side. Plantation owners saw themselves as the local law enforcement and judicial system. Grumbling was often categorized as "political" and thus a cause for repression. Some complaining colonists were expelled for being "socialists." Debt peonage, bankruptcy, and social restrictions created immense tensions on the plantations. Immigrant revolts were frequent and many fled, as had slaves before them. In 1856, a revolt took place when a group of immigrant parceiros on Senator Vergueiro's lands were pushed too far.

The "Uprising of 1856" began on a small scale when various worker grievances on Vergueiro's Ibicaba plantation were dismissed out of hand by the senator. The protests expanded when a Portuguese immigrant was fired after demanding that the price per kilo of coffee beans paid to him by the plantation actually be the market price. The tension increased even more at a birthday party for Senator Vergueiro. Workers had been invited to the event to show local authorities, also in attendance, that labor relations on the fazenda were calm. The workers, however, refused to attend the party, showing exactly the contrary. In response, Vergueiro fired still more people.

One of the leaders of the protests was Thomas Davatz. Born in 1815 in the small Swiss village of Fanas, Davatz was a teacher and local political leader. In 1845, he and a group from Fanas had signed a standard sharecropping contract with the Vergueiro Company to emigrate to Brazil, where they were placed on the Ibicaba Fazenda. Davatz, who emigrated with his wife and children, had been commissioned by the Swiss cantonal authorities in his homeland to report on conditions in Brazil. While Davatz had initially received preferential treatment from the planter and his managers, he was not fooled. His draft report was highly critical of conditions, and when it fell into the owner's hands, members of the Vergueiro family threatened to murder the immigrant.

Because of his semiofficial status, Davatz often stepped forward to try to help with worker grievances. The immigrants involved in the Uprising of 1856 had drawn up a list of demands, and Davatz was enlisted to bring the document personally to Senator Vergueiro in his mansion. At the meeting, the argument became heated. Fluent Portuguese speakers who accompanied Davatz to the meeting (other languages spoken were French and German) believed that they heard

Vergueiro ordering Davatz to be killed. As the news spread, armed workers marched on the mansion. Threats were made. Davatz urged calm, but it was only the intervention of Brazilian and Swiss authorities that kept the peace.

While violence was kept to a minimum, the Uprising of 1856 frightened landowners, workers, and both governments. The Brazilian government sent an investigator to the Ibicaba plantation in January 1857. He was followed by the Swiss consul in Rio de Janeiro, who made a three-week onsite visit. Most of the immigrant complaints were confirmed, although according to the officials, there was little that could be done because the workers had forfeited most of their rights in the signed contracts. Still, one of Vergueiro's sons was dismissed as a manager and Davatz had his debts excused and his passage back to Switzerland paid for by consular authorities. The Swiss consul, however, understood the truth: His report noted that the planters simply wanted to replace black slaves with white ones. Davatz's memoirs followed along the same lines: "Disobedience of any regulation or order of the plantation director, no matter how arbitrary, is fined. The most modest complaint leads to a fine.... In [one] colony the plantation owner ... tried to prevent a father from visiting his daughter who lived in another location. In another case one of the plantation bosses threatened to kill a lady if she tried to get advice from me on family matters."[29] (See Document 2.2: Report of Thomas Davatz, 1850, in the chapter Appendix.)

News of the difficult conditions in Brazil spread throughout Europe and the Americas. European visitors emphasized the poor treatment of immigrants in their travelogues. Robert Avé-Lallemant (July 25, 1812–October 10, 1884) was a German physician and explorer who moved to Brazil in the mid-1830s, eventually heading a sanatorium in Rio de Janeiro. He spent two years in the late 1850s exploring Brazil on an expedition funded in part by Emperor Dom Pedro. Avé-Lallemant's comments on the lives of immigrants were shocking to European readers. In the north of Brazil, where few immigrants settled because of a stagnant economy and deeply rooted landholding patterns, he met a group of colonists, and, he wrote: "In that sordid home I found sixty people. More than half were sick. Most had been tricked by German traders in human flesh. Now they found themselves crazed in their

[29] Thomas Davatz, *Memórias de um Colono no Brasil* (São Paulo: Martins/Edusp, 1972), 45.

bodies and souls, with a terrible future and, according to their contract, the need to survive for a year."[30] Brazil's image as a hell on earth had a major effect. In 1859, the Prussian government adopted the Heydt Edict, which prohibited active recruitment of immigrants. Advertising and subsidies for passages were barred as well. In 1871, following German unification, the ban was applied to the entire country and only in 1896 was it lifted entirely. The British government took a similar approach. It publicized its warnings about Brazil in early 1875 and then again a year later: "Emigrants should also remember, that in going to Brazil, they go to a country where the language, the laws, the religion, and the habits of the people, will be strange to them; and although it is promised that a church and schools shall be hereafter provided, neither at present exists."[31] (See Document 2.3: Caution to Emigrants, Government Emigration Board, United Kingdom, in the chapter Appendix.)

With the German and British governments prohibiting emigration to Brazil, new migrant streams from very poor areas of Europe began. Most notable was the expansion of Polish immigration, primarily to the province (and then later state) of Paraná. Between about 1860 and 1940 some 150,000 Poles settled in Brazil, although as we will see in Chapter 4, the religious character of the migratory stream changed from Catholic to Jewish after 1920. Today, Polishness is an important component of official Paraná state identity. After Pope John Paul II visited the capital city of Curitiba in 1980, an official Memorial to Polish Immigration was built, complete with log houses, wagons, and images of the Black Madonna of Czestochowa (Poland's national icon).

IMMIGRATION OF U.S. CONFEDERATES

Brazil's elites wanted Central European immigrants. They also wanted those from the United States who, they believed, would be white, modern, and forward thinking. Yet attracting Americans proved difficult. Following the end of the Civil War (1861–1865), however, an opportunity arose. Dom Pedro II offered land and subsidies to defeated Southerners in the hope that they would bring whiteness, political and

[30] Robert Avé-Lallemant, *Viagem pelo Norte do Brasil no Ano de 1859* (Rio de Janeiro: Instituto Nacional do Livro, Ministério da Educação e Cultura, 1961), 179.
[31] Government Emigration Board, "BRAZIL – Caution to Emigrants," June 19, 1875, in Laërne, *Brazil and Java*, pp. 135–136.

cultural conservatism, and modern cotton production to Brazil. A significant number of Southerners accepted the offer, eager to continue life in a country where racial hierarchies were more clearly defined than those emerging in the United States during Reconstruction. Information on the numbers of Southerners who settled in Brazil are not exact, but records suggest that about twenty thousand arrived between 1865 to 1885. North Americans spread throughout the country, with the largest concentration in the colony of Americana (São Paulo State), whose founders included an Alabama state senator. Today, Americana is a city of more than two hundred thousand. In the mid-twentieth century, the city briefly incorporated the Confederate flag into its own banner, although outrage from abroad led to a change. Many of the Confederates sent letters back to their families in the United States, often trying to convince them to migrate to Brazil. One of them was Naval Master W. Frank Shippey, who had commanded a number of Confederate naval vessels in 1864 and early 1865. When the Civil War ended in April 1865, Shippey migrated to Brazil where he reestablished himself as a plantation owner. In one letter he wrote: "The hearts of all true Confederates, in this, the exile's home, have been gladdened by the news of the success of your efforts in behalf of our people, and we earnestly pray to God that you may be spared to return to us, accompanied by many of our true Southern friends, in order that we, their predecessors, may be able to welcome to our new South, those who shall determine to leave the scenes of their childhood and once happy homes, to, emigrate to the hospitable shores of Brazil."[32] (See Document 2.4: Letter from a Southern U.S. immigrant to Brazil, in the chapter Appendix.)

The descendants of the immigrants from the United States produced a Brazilian ethnicity known today as *Confederado*. Many practice Baptism, a relative rarity in Brazil. Americana, whose current population is less than ten percent Confederado, hosts an annual "Confederate" festival that celebrates a past that has erased the issue of slavery from its institutional memory. Linguists from the United States study "Confederado English" to get a sense of the language and how it was spoken in the nineteenth century. Today, being a Confederado is

---

[32] Ballard S. Dunn, *Brazil, the Home for Southerners: or, A Practical Account of What the Author, and Others, Who Visited That Country, for the Same Objects, Saw and Did While in That Empire* (New York: G. B. Richardson etc. 1866), 70–72.

a charming part of multiethnic Brazil. Yet that migration reminds us of the intense hierarchies that were so much a part of all immigrant experiences in the country.

BRAZIL BECOMES A PARIAH

The same images of racial distinction and slaveholding embraced by Confederates were rejected by much of the world in the mid-nineteenth century. Germany restricted emigration to Brazil, and England expressed its fury at the continuation of slavery. The parceria system seemed to cause more revolts than production and was a liability from the perspective of both the immigrants and planters.

The 1870s were a watershed for immigration. In 1871, the Rio Branco Law (also known as the Law of the Free Womb) legislated the freedom of all newborn children of slaves. While it would take almost two more decades to realize full abolition, slavery was ending. During the 1870s, new technologies changed the cost structure of agriculture, and especially coffee planting. The machinery for processing decreased the number of workers needed while improving product consistency. Railroads increased the amounts of picked coffee that came to market. New ideas about labor organization led planters to consider whether better treatment of slaves might lead to higher productivity. In São Paulo State, coffee production doubled during the decade.

Domestic and international pressure led plantation owners and politicians to contemplate what had gone wrong under their earlier immigration policies. Central Europeans had not transformed Brazil racially or economically. Soon, a surprising panacea for the labor problem was reintroduced: Chinese labor. Both those opposed and those in favor of slavery were interested. The Chinese would be free yet servile; they were experienced in agriculture. Many elites continued to believe that an obsessive Chinese desire to be buried in their homeland meant that they would never remain in Brazil.

Interest in Chinese immigration had begun before the empire was declared (see Chapter 1). Brazilian merchants and planters were impressed by the mid-nineteenth-century expansion of the United States, Peru, and Cuba on the backs of Chinese workers. This interest was matched by the realization that slavery was waning. Britain, the world's dominant naval power, had begun to patrol against slave ships in the Atlantic in 1834, and in 1845 enacted the Aberdeen Act that allowed the British navy to treat slave vessels as pirate ships.[33] In late 1854, the Brazilian Imperial Government ordered its legation in London to bring six thousand Chinese laborers as a debate was raging over the issue. The players, and their positions, had not changed much over the decades. Those who favored Chinese immigrants focused on an increase in economic production, whereas opponents feared social "pollution."

The most significant attack on Chinese immigration came in 1855 from Luiz Peixoto de Lacerda Werneck, a coffee planter whose frequent editorials in the Rio de Janeiro newspaper *Jornal do Comércio* summed up the connections between immigration and national identity. Werneck argued that Protestant Germans were "moral, peaceful and hard-working," while Chinese were "animal-men" whose "character ... is seen by all travelers in unfavorable and terrible colors.... [T]heir vile egoism, their pride, their barbarous insensitivity fed by the practice of child abandonment and decapitation ... are the general vices of China." Chinese culture, claimed Werneck, would "degenerate" Brazil's population, which had already suffered "the deformity of the indigenous and the African."[34]

Powerful anti-slavery, pro-immigration (and pro-Chinese) voices responded. Federal Deputy Aureliano Candido Tavares Bastos (1839–1875), an abolitionist, led the way. He linked the end of slavery with the development of free labor, spontaneous immigration, and a modern Brazilian nation. Since "racial mixture in all peoples will create a new population ... vigorous, intelligent and able," Tavares Bastos wrote, he wondered if Brazil's population, which already had "the imagination of the African and the reflection of the white," should include Chinese as well.[35] Pointing to economic growth in the United States and the English Caribbean, he insisted that the Chinese, as a result of their

---

[33] José Pedro Xavier Pinheiro, *Importação de Trabalhadores Chins: Memória Apresentada ao Ministério da Agricultura, Comércio e Obras Públicas e Imprensa por sua Ordem* (Rio de Janeiro: Typ. de João Ignacio da Silva, 1869), 35, 49.

[34] The editorials were collected and published in a book as Luiz Peixoto de Lacerda Werneck, *Idéias Sobre Colonização Precedidas de uma Succinta Exposição dos Princípios Geraes que Regem a População* (Rio de Janeiro: Eduardo e Henrique Laemmert, 1855). These editorials can be found on pages 14, 28, 78, and 98.

[35] Aureliano Candido Tavares Bastos, *O Valle do Amazonas: A Livre Navegação do Amazonas, Estatistica, Producções, Commercio, Questões Fiscaes do Valle do Amazonas*, 2d ed., Serie Brasiliana #106 (São Paulo: Comp. Editora Nacional, 1937), 364.

"sobriety, perseverance and aptitude for commerce," were an interme-
diate step between unintelligent and depraved (though imaginative)
African labor and European immigrants who were too smart to go to
Brazil's hinterlands.[36]

It is not surprising that the discussion of Chinese immigration
reemerged in the years following the passage of the Law of the Free
Womb. In 1878, soon-to-be Prime Minister João Lins Vieira Cansanção
de Sinimbú (at the time president of the Imperial Council and minister
of agriculture, commerce and public works) convoked a conference of
large landowners with representation exclusively from southern provinces. Northern landowners held their own conference the same year
and debated immigration as well. Yet the concerns were very different
in each region. As Northerners deliberated about how to attract immigrants, the southern landowners used their discussion as an elite refer-
endum on Chinese labor. In his opening speech, Sinimbú argued that
European immigrants were more interested in being landowners than
salaried workers and that the success of English, French, and Spanish
colonies was based on Chinese labor. In spite of their "notorious inferior-
ity ... [the Chinese] are content with a small salary that could not satisfy
even the most basic necessities of the European." Sinimbú looked abroad
to justify his position on Chinese immigration: Even the United States
was filled with Chinese workers in spite of North Americans being "so
jealous about the purity of their Saxonic blood."[37]

Sinimbú's powerful position did not lead to a quick consensus.[38] One
representative feared that Brazil was "injecting into its veins a poor and
degenerate blood, toxic and noxious to the great laws of race mixing,"
and he portrayed a weak country teetering on the edge of a collapse of
national identity.[39] João José Carneiro da Silva, a representative from
Rio de Janeiro Province, disagreed. He posited that if "the white race
produced so many mulattos of distinction, why can't we do the same
for the Chinese, a race incontestably superior to the African?"[40] The

---

[36]   A. C. (Aureliano Candido) Tavares Bastos, "Memória sobre immigração," in *Os
Males do Presente e as Esperanças do Futuro (Estudos Brasileiros)*, Serie Brasiliana
#151 (São Paulo: Comp. Editora Nacional, 1939), 55–127; p. 104.

[37]   Speech of Minister Sinimbú, July 8, 1878, Congresso Agrícola, *Collecção de
Documentos* (Rio de Janeiro: Typ. Nacional, 1878), 128–129.

[38]   Pedro D. G. Paes Leme, "A nossa lavoura," October 17, 1877, republished in
Diário Oficial – Império do Brazil – Rio de Janeiro (Rio de Janeiro: Typ Nacional,
1878), Anno 17: 165, July 11, 1878, 6.

[39]   Congresso Agrícola, *Colecção de Documentos*, 38–39.

[40]   Congresso Agrícola, *Colecção de Documentos*, 65.

differences meant that Sinimbú was only able to convince planters to approve a weak resolution that encouraged the "acquisition of workers of other peoples from races or civilizations inferior to ours," including free Africans and "well chosen coolies and not those who live on the water or packed in large slums."[41]

The debates continued, and in 1882 the Companhia de Comércio e Imigração Chineza (CCIC – Chinese Commerce and Immigration Company) was founded to bring twenty-one thousand workers to Brazil. The following year the Chinese government sent two representatives for an in-country visit. Tong King-sing was a wealthy Cantonese entrepreneur who oversaw a shipping company owned by one of China's most powerful warlords. His executive assistant, G. C. Butler, was an American living in China. The two caused a public stir when they met reporters at São Paulo's Grand Hotel wearing traditional Chinese clothing and complimenting Brazil and its people in English. Tong was certainly the first Chinese person that the reporters, and most planters, had ever met. An article in the *Correio Paulistano* noted that he "conserves, in spite of his European affinities, his national costume, the silk tunic, the little gold buttons, the shoes with fleece soles and the black beret with a red top, insignia of the educated class."[42] Executive Secretary Butler, an African American, also confounded observers by being "intelligent" and having "all the refinement of Parisian elegance."[43] Karl von Koseritz, by then the editor of the *Deutsche Zeitung* and an ardent opponent of Chinese immigration, dismissed Tong as a seller of "Mongolian meat" but was impressed by the "Negro from California, resplendent with diamonds."[44]

Tong and Butler were horrified by Brazilian attitudes toward race. An audience with Dom Pedro II left Tong convinced that anti-Chinese sentiment was the norm among elites.[45] When the emperor informed Tong that travel and housing subventions for Chinese workers would come from planters rather than the central government, an outraged Tong

---

[41] "Proposta de Resolução," Article I, Congresso Agrícola, *Collecção de Documentos*, 83.

[42] *Correio Paulistano*, 19 October 1883, p. 2.

[43] Henrique C.R. Lisboa, *Os Chins do Tetartos* (Rio de Janeiro: Typographia da Empreza Democratica Editora, 1894), 11.

[44] Carl von Koseritz, *Imagens do Brasil*, trans. Afonso Arinos de Melo Franco (Belo Horizonte: Ed. Itatiaia, 1980), 221–223.

[45] *Gazeta de Campinas* article, "VIAJANTE CHIM," reprinted in *Correio Paulistano*, 26 October 1883, p. 1; *Jornal do Agricultor* article reprinted in *Correio Paulistano*, 30 October 1883, p. 1.

reportedly told Dom Pedro that "this scheme must fall through; I will be no party to bringing Chinamen here except as free immigrants."[46] Dom Pedro had similar feelings, exclaiming after the meeting that "I am sure that the ethnic influence of these peoples will aggravate even further the heterogeneous aspects of our people."[47]

Following the meeting, Tong and Butler cut their visit short and left for London. Some planters blamed Dom Pedro, while others blamed the Sinophobic press and politicians. The British government had played a behind-the-scenes role, pressuring Tong not to sign contracts with members of Brazil's slavocracy. Tong and Butler appear to have been genuinely outraged by the palpable bigotry they encountered. In a letter to the Companhia de Comércio e Imigração Chineza, Tong wrote of his "astonishment at the prejudice entertained by your government and by the enlightened classes of your nation against Chinese labor."[48] The CCIC subsequently went bankrupt. The plans to bring Chinese were over.

THE MUCKERS

As the debates over Chinese entry raged in São Paulo, a different type of immigrant story was taking place in Rio Grande do Sul. This time the homeland was Prussia, where a Pietist religious group emerged in the late eighteenth century that came to be known as the Muckers (the German word *Mucker* was initially used to mock Pietists as hypocrites and bigots but later was taken up by some Pietests to describe themselves). The movement was popularized by Johann Wilhelm Ebel (1784–1861), but when a powerful former initiate accused him of sexual improprieties, the resulting public outcry led to persecution of the Muckers. Many went underground or left Prussia. Two of them, Libório

[46] Tong King-sing, quoted in letter of Charles H. Allen (secretary of the British Anti-Slavery Society) to the Earl Granville, principal secretary of state for foreign affairs, December 6, 1883, reprinted in full in Laërne, *Brazil and Java*, 149–153.

[47] Fidelis Reis and João de Faria, *O Problema Immigratorio e Seus Aspectos Ethnicos: Na Camara e Fóra de Camara* (Rio de Janeiro: Typ. Revista dos Tribunaes, 1924), 130.

[48] Tong King-sing (Rio de Janeiro) to the Society for the Promotion of Commerce and Immigration from China, October 28, 1883; Letter of G. C. Butler to Mr. Chapman (Rio de Janeiro), March 8, 1883, "Missão especial ao Celeste Império China, 1893–1894 – Barão do Ladario," Manuscript Collection–Coleção Afro-Asiatica, 20, 2, 5, BN-R.

Mentz and Ernestina Magdalene Lips, immigrated to the German colony of São Leopoldo in southern Brazil. Mentz built the first Protestant church in the colony in 1826, but he also appears to have maintained some of the Mucker philosophy.

Fast-forward to the 1870s when São Leopoldo was still a remote rural community. Medical care was in the hands of local healers, and Mentz's granddaughter, Jacobina, was one of them. Jacobina cared for patients with Bible readings and homemade medicines, and she often seemed to be possessed by spirits. Some scholars interpret Jacobina's actions as a form of epilepsy, but many people in the colony believed that she had miraculous powers. In 1873, Jacobina and her husband, João Maurer, founded a religious sect with hundreds of followers (the estimates of the exact number vary widely), who treated her as the reincarnation of Jesus Christ.

Jacobina's followers split from the local church and school and soon came to be called Muckers by those following more conventional religious norms. Jacobina's most public opponent was Karl von Koseritz. He used his position as the editor of the *Deutsche Zeitung* in Porto Alegre, capital of the state of Rio Grande do Sul, to attack the group as antimodern and as detrimental to the image of Germans in Brazil. When local police harassed and arrested the movement's leaders, von Koseritz wrote delight-filled editorials and gave positive speeches. After one particularly violent exchange with officials, João Maurer went to Rio de Janeiro to deliver a complaint personally to the emperor.

On May 24, 1874, Jacobina called a mass meeting to announce the end of the world. According to the police, she also ordered the assassination of sixteen families who had left her movement. The first killing took place in June. Burning of homes followed, leading to the deaths of adults and children. A police battalion was dispatched to the colony to control the situation. They did so by attacking the Mucker compound, but Jacobina's escape only served to further convince followers of her divinity. In early August 1874, the police were given a tip that led to Jacobina Mentz's hideout. She was killed along with the majority of her followers.

Jacobina's death is not the end of the story. Twenty years later, three murders were attributed to a renewed Muckers movement led by Aurélia Maurer, Jacobina's daughter. In 1895, a crowd of German immigrants murdered five self-professed Muckers. The continued agitation played heavily on the minds of members of the Brazilian elite. The Muckers seemed to represent the opposite of the order that Germans immigrants were expected to bring to Brazil. The conflicts ended eventually but the memories did not. Two late-twentieth-century feature films were made about Jacobina. Both have given contemporary audiences the impression that religious conflict, sexual promiscuity, and violence were typical of the German immigrant experience in Brazil. The more interesting of the two films, from the perspective of Brazilian immigration history, is Fábio Barreto's 2002 *A Paixão de Jacobina* [Jacobina's passion]. The movie reinvents the Jacobina story by giving her a love interest very different from her real husband, the German-Brazilian João Maurer. In the film, Jacobina is the paragon of white female Brazilianness who loves, and lusts for, a Brazilian army officer of Portuguese descent. The director's first choice to portray Jacobina was none other than the super-model Gisele Bündchen, whose whiteness, German-sounding name, and marriage to National Football League star Tom Brady have contributed greatly to Brazil's image abroad.

In Brazil, many people continue to "remember" the Muckers. When a series of homicides took place in 1993 near São Leopoldo, Rio Grande do Sul's newspaper of record, *Zero Hora*, headlined one story with "Violence Is Resurrected in the Land of the Mucker."[49] Fifteen years later, two Evangelical pastors brought together descendants of the warring Mucker and anti-Mucker families for a peace ceremony.[50] The past and the present of immigration and national identity had merged yet again in Brazil.

CONCLUSION

For many of Brazil's elite, Germans appeared to be ideal immigrants. They seemed indisputably white. They were farmers. They had a reputation for hard work. They seemed willing to settle in areas that would help fortify the Brazilian state against Argentina. Yet the vision of perfection was not matched by reality. Germans, like all immigrants, brought with them aspects of their culture that did not fit easily with the Brazilian elite demands for conformity. They were not willing to be

---

[49] João Biehl, "The Mucker War: A History of Violence and Silence," in Mary-Jo DelVecchio Good, Sandra T. Hyde, Sarah Pinto, and Byron Good, eds., *Postcolonial Disorders* (Berkeley: University of California Press, 2008), 279–308; p. 280.

[50] *Zero Hora*, "Abraço sela a paz entre descendentes dos Mucker e anti-Mucker em Sapiranga." 24 May 2009.

poorly treated and had the means to report back to Europe on false-hoods about the immigrant experience in Brazil.

Immigration seemed to stall at midcentury just as slavery's end grew nearer. Desperate elites began to consider the impact of migrants in new ways. By the 1880s, Southern Europeans, Asians, Middle Easterners and non-Christians would begin arriving in large numbers. With them would come significant changes in Brazilian national identity as the path to creating a "nation of immigrants" extended into an uncertain future. By the end of the nineteenth century, the immigration question in Brazil would reach a fever pitch.

APPENDIX

Document 2.1. *Report of Johann Jakob von Tschudi, 1866*

Despite the adverse situation, many settlers were able to get out of debt and each year some families freed themselves from their contracts. If they were able to make early payments, very few would not have become independent financially, except for some vagrants or those families who were victims of misfortune. It would be unjust to attribute the failure of this type of colonization solely to harmful contracts and to plantation owners. I believe that the fault is mostly with the settlers themselves. The emigration agents, who were paid on commission, tried to get the largest number of families or individuals possible, without investigating if they were the right people for the work for which they were destined. The press, the publication of flyers, and the seductive talk of certain subagents, convinced emigrants by painting a bright picture of a brilliant future in South America. Once they arrived at their destinations, the settlers realized the deception and became dejected. The immigrants started to work without enthusiasm, relying on the help of others instead of on their own strength. In this way they gradually drowned in debt. Many of the immigrants were undesirable elements and vagrants.... Would it be reasonable to expect that these kinds of individuals would be reborn in an alien land where they could easily get credit without worrying about the debt they would contract? It is necessary to have contact with such people, to have spoken to them or heard their allegations; it is necessary to know about their background, to see the results they would obtain as settlers to be able to evaluate fairly the degree of culpability they had in their own misery.

Source: Johann Jakob von Tschudi, *Viagem às Províncias do Rio de Janeiro e São Paulo* (São Paulo: Livraria Martins Editora, [1866] 1953), 146–147.

Document 2.2. *Report of Thomas Davatz, 1850*

[In many colonies] disobedience of any regulation or command from the boss, even if arbitrary, results in fines. A simple complaint from a settler about the injustices practiced against him by the owner may result in a penalty for the complainer. In one colony, as a result of these arbitrary regulations, immigrants were forced to clean up a road. When they refused, they were fined two thousand reis by the authorities. This amount quickly became twelve or fifteen thousand reis because the settlers did not have the money to pay the sum immediately....

In this same colony, the fazendeiro demanded that the settlers, both Catholics and Protestants, contribute an annual sum to the construction of a church in a city located three and a half hours away, even though this church was not used by Protestants for their baptisms. In another colony, it is said that the following event happened: Some settlers who had their own coffee trees and fields also tried to do some work in the farms that belonged to neighbors so as to make extra money. This reasonable plan, however, was prevented by the fazendeiro. In the same colony the plantation owner also tried to prevent a father from visiting his daughter who lived in another location. In another case one of the plantation bosses threatened to kill a lady if she tried to get advice from me on family matters.

Source: Thomas Davatz, *Memórias de um Colono no Brasil* (São Paulo: Martins/Edusp, 1972), 45.

Document 2.3. *Caution to Emigrants: Government Emigration Board, United Kingdom, 1876*

Government Emigration Board,
Downing Street, 19th June, 1876.
BRAZIL.

Her Majesty's Government having been informed that another scheme is in progress for promoting emigration from the United Kingdom to Brazil, the Emigration Commissioners have been directed by the Secretary of State to remind intending emigrants of the unhappy results that have attended previous schemes of emigration to that country. In 1872 and 1873 several parties of emigrants, amounting in the whole to about a thousand souls, emigrated from the United Kingdom to Brazil under promises of being provided with land on favourable terms, and of assistance in its cultivation until they could support themselves, and in the expectation that they would be able to get their first crop at the end of six months. These promises and expectations were not fulfilled. The emigrants did not obtain their land, sickness broke out among them, many died, and those who were able to do so made their way down to the capital in the hope of obtaining assistance from Her Majesty's minister there. Since then some of the widows and children of the men who died have been sent home, some of the emigrants have been removed to other settlements, and Her Majesty's minister is still engaged in endeavouring to obtain from the Government of Brazil assistance for those that remain. The accounts which these emigrants give of their present situation show that they have suffered great hardships and privations, and have been far from improving their condition by emigration to Brazil.

The settlement which it is now proposed to form appears from the prospectus put out by the promoters to be situated on the high lands where the climate is healthy and the soil fertile. But, on the other hand, it is remote from any market at which the settlers could sell their surplus produce, or procure the supplies they might require; the nearest town of any size, Curitiba, the capital of the province, being at the distance of 62 miles. A tramway will, it is said, be constructed between the settlement and Curitiba, but such works are unavoidably slow in construction in a country where labour is scarce and expensive. The distance of the port being 114 miles, and the voyage from thence to Rio de Janeiro by steamboat 40 hours more, the alleged market to be found at Rio for all produce may be put out of account.

Emigrants should also remember, that in going to Brazil, they go to a country where the language, the laws, the religion, and the habits of the people, will be strange to them; and although it is promised that a church and schools shall be hereafter provided, neither at present exists. It is very important that before making up their minds to emigrate to Brazil, emigrants should well consider these facts, and should understand that if they decide, notwithstanding this caution, to do so, they must accept the responsibility of the result.

By order of the Board, Government Emigration Board, Richard B. Cooper. Downing Street, S. W. 10th February, 1875.

Source: Government Emigration Board, "BRAZIL – Caution to Emigrants," June 19, 1875, in C. F. Van Delden Laërne, *Brazil and Java. Report on Coffee-Culture in America, Asia and Africa, to H. E. the Minister of the Colonies* (London: W. H. Allen & Co., 1885), 135–136.

Document 2.4. *Letter from a Southern U.S. immigrant to Brazil, 1866*

BARRA DE JUGUIÁ,
June 2, 1866.
REV. BALLARD S. DUNN, RIO DE JANEIRO:

DEAR SIR:

The hearts of all true Confederates, in this, the exile's home, have been gladdened by the news of the success of your efforts in behalf of our people, and we earnestly pray to God that you may be spared to return to us, accompanied by many of our true Southern friends, in order that we, their predecessors, may be able to welcome to our new South, those who shall determine to leave the scenes of their childhood and once happy homes, to, emigrate to the hospitable shores of Brazil.

Since the surrender of our armies, I have roamed in exile, over the fairest portions of the globe, but it has been reserved for me to find in Brazil that peace which we all, from sad experience, know so well how to appreciate. Here, the war worn soldier, the bereaved parent, the oppressed patriot, the homeless and despoiled, can find a refuge from the trials which beset them, and a home not haunted by the eternal remembrance of harrowing scenes of sorrow and of death.

This portion of Brazil, I firmly believe, to a greater extent than any other, offers inducements to emigrants, and in particular, to those of our unfortunate countrymen, whose feelings or interests render a longer stay in the Southern States, undesirable or impracticable, while the liberal policy of the government, the equity of its laws, the climate, soil, and vast resources of these hitherto unexplored lands, promises fair to reward the efforts of the settler with wealth and prosperity, while their social relations can be maintained without fear of intrusion or arrest.

We, the advance-guard of the legion of Confederates, who are hereafter to settle and cultivate the soil, watching, as we do, with painful solicitude, the condition of our friends in our late home, earnestly and fondly look for the consummation of your plans and efforts, and I believe that I express the sentiments of all the good and true, when I say that the prayers of the people are with you, and that the children and children's children of those who join our standard, under your auspices, will rise up to call you blessed.

Permit me to reiterate the professions of sincere regard which we all entertain for you, and of the confidence which we repose in your ability, and in the rectitude of your intentions, and wishing you a pleasant and prosperous voyage to the United States, and a safe and speedy return to Brazil.

I remain your friend and obedient servant,
W. FRANK SHIPPEY

Source: Ballard S. Dunn, *Brazil, the Home for Southerners: or, A Practical Account of What the Author, and Others, Who Visited That Country, for the Same Objects, Saw and Did While in That Empire* (New York: G. B. Richardson etc. 1866), 70–72.

CHAPTER THREE

Mass Migrations, 1880–1920

A New World Order

By the late 1800s the American republics could be divided into three categories – those rapidly filling with immigrants, those whose elites believed they could be filled with immigrants in spite of evidence to the contrary (i.e., few had settled), and those nations in which policy-makers had deemed immigration a failure. Brazil was in the first group. Imperial power had declined, and landowners, especially in the prosperous and politically powerful coffee-growing state of São Paulo, had tightened their grip on the political and economic system.

Brazil's size (larger than the continental United States) and its expanding economy meant that Europeans, North and South Americans, Asians, and Middle Easterners were increasingly willing, and sometimes eager, to accept the opportunity to resettle in Brazil. C. F. Van Delden Laërne, an employee of the Dutch Department of the Interior in Java who went to Brazil to report on coffee culture in 1884, spoke with many fazendeiros about immigration and found it

> remarkable what a universal and firm belief in a future immigration on a large scale exists among the born Brazilians, the sons of the land. To their minds it seems enough that they should will that immigration, in order to cause the stream of emigrants from all ends of the earth, flow into Brazil. This belief is assuredly not founded on past experience; for the history of colonization there points to a very different conclusion.
>
> In my opinion that faith is not based on any such grounds, but exclusively on the strikingly pronounced complacency with which the Brazilians regard their native land. I shall not say that

they think it perfect in all respects; – far from that; – many – far too many of the higher classes I am told – sound the praises of their native land from the great cities of the Old World. But the praises and enthusiasm continue to be lavished on the immense treasures buried there in the lap of earth; on the incomparable beauty and unparalleled fertility of the land. [It has become] a favorite catch-word to speak habitually of the rich, the favored Brazil, of the blessed land, of the blessed daughter of the Gospel![1]

A significant challenge to the nation's blind belief in divine favor was slavery. Most other countries in Europe and the Americas had abolished bondage, and increasing numbers of Brazilian elites saw the system as economically and culturally backward. Some were embarrassed by the association with Africa, which many Europeans saw as cursed with the scourge of slavery. Slaves themselves challenged their bondage by fleeing and revolting. As the nineteenth century neared its end, soldiers and police officers increasingly petitioned to be relieved of slave-catching duties, no longer seeing it as part of their job. Politicians agreed and in 1886 lashing was prohibited as a punishment for slaves. As the political commitment to slavery diminished, large landowners pressured the empire for policies and funding that would put labor on their plantations and fill the country with European workers. Foreigners would be better workers than slaves and ex-slaves, recreate Brazil in Europe's image, and transform the economy to wage labor, or so the fazendeiros mistakenly believed.

Abolition finally came in 1888. The following year the empire came to a peaceful end without resistance from Emperor Dom Pedro II. Lawmakers in the new republic created subsidies for immigrants that were far more attractive than the previous ones. In 1891, legislation guaranteeing public religious freedom was enacted in order to attract Protestant immigrants, whose whiteness, elites believed, would help to de-Africanize Brazil's population. At the same time, politicians banned immigrants from Africa and Asia, and diplomats (at embarkation points) and police (at Brazil's ports) were made responsible for enforcement of immigration rules.[2]

---

[1] C. F. Van Delden Laërne, *Brazil and Java: Report on Coffee-Culture in America, Asia and Africa, to H. E. the Minister of the Colonies* (London: W. H. Allen & Co., 1885), 125.

[2] Decree Law 528, June 28, 1890, Art. 1.

The new policies paved the way for more than 2.6 million immigrants to enter Brazil between 1890 and 1919. Yet the new streams reflected more than political changes in situ. At play were global forces like population growth and technology.[3] High-tech steamships replaced wind-powered vehicles, and the arduous three-month voyage to Brazil that early-nineteenth-century immigrants from Europe had suffered took only two weeks by the early twentieth century. Shorter time shipboard and advances in medicine made high death rates a thing of the past on transatlantic and transpacific voyages. Prices fell as speed increased, the cost of passage from Italy to Brazil dropping as much as fifty percent between 1880 and 1920. Quicker trips at lower prices led to other results. Goods that had been hard to export (like coffee) became engines for economic growth. The dual processes of industrialization and urban development created both a push in Europe, where a population increase was not fully absorbed, and a pull in the Americas, where the economy was expanding. Emigration from Italy, Spain, and Portugal to the Americas boomed. Similar patterns in Eastern Europe, Asia, and the Middle East led to increasing outflows of people.

A BETTER AMERICA

Potential emigrants thought about more than local poverty and overpopulation in making decisions about possible new homelands. The economic and social possibilities in different countries helped them to understand how to invest in their futures. The most desirable location was the United States, and about twenty million immigrants with the ability to pay their own passages and settle independently went there between 1880 and 1910. Argentina was next on the list with 3.5 million entries, but many, especially from Italy, were in fact temporary workers. Canada received 3.1 million immigrants, only about half of whom remained permanently. Fourth on the list was Brazil, with 2.6 million entries, although the numbers who stayed permanently were far fewer.

Why did so many choose the United States? The resolution of internal strife with the end of the U.S. Civil War in 1865 led to an economic boom, spurred by liberal policies on land acquisition. The country effectively promoted itself as geographically similar to Europe, and the relatively short trip from Europe to the United States when

---

[3]   Jose C. Moya, *Cousins and Strangers: Spanish Immigrants in Buenos Aires, 1850–1930* (Berkeley: University of California Press, 1998).

compared to Brazil or Argentina was attractive. Yet the United States was an expensive, and often impossible, choice for those with too little money to invest in their own passage and initial settlement. Thus, about twenty percent of all transatlantic European immigrants went to Latin America. Even higher percentages arrived from the Middle East and Asia. In some periods, the numbers flowing south were huge. In the two decades after 1875, for example, almost seventy percent of Italian emigrants went to Latin America. In all periods, the majority of Portuguese and Spanish emigrants went to South, not North, America. By World War II, about eleven million immigrants had relocated to Latin America.

Brazilian elites were keenly aware of the competition for immigrants in the Americas. The image problem created by unscrupulous recruiters and landowners during the empire meant that the country needed to be rebranded now that it was a republic. Brazil's marketing no longer focused on a "New Europe" but on a "Better America." Pavilions at international expositions promoted Brazil's soil fertility and temperate climate as similar to that in the United States and Argentina. The French-language booklet created for the 1889 Paris Exhibition was explicit: "Brazil came to Paris ... to solidify its ties to Europe and to open up new markets for its raw materials. But most of all, [Brazil] came to Paris to inspire confidence in those who might be ready to choose it as their new homeland so that they bring to Brazil their labor and their capital."[4]

The initial attempts at image remaking were not particularly effective. Using expositions in France, Germany, the United States, and England, countries that sent few emigrants in the late 1800s, was a mistake. Potential immigrants were smarter than Brazilian elites imagined. They had access to information that the propaganda tried to hide, especially about diseases like yellow fever (eliminated in Rio de Janeiro only in the early twentieth century and still later in other regions of Brazil). Even those desperate to leave Europe often rejected Brazil because of its disease-ridden image. One example came in the late nineteenth century when the German Central Committee for Russian Jews sent Oswald Boxer, a Viennese journalist and friend of the Zionist leader Theodore Herzl, to investigate possibilities for the resettlement of impoverished

---

4   Frederico José de Santa-Anna Nery, Le Brésil en 1889: Avec une Carte de l'empire en Chromolithographie, des Tableaux Statistiques, des Graphiques et des Cartes (Paris: Syndicat franco-brésilien, 1889), xi.

and violently oppressed Russian Jews as farmers in Brazil. Boxer's enthusiastic report following his visit to São Paulo in May 1891 was dismissed
when he died of yellow fever a few months later in Rio de Janeiro.[5]
The lack of immigrants worried large landowners, who demanded
new approaches for "selling" Brazil. Consortiums subsidized with public
funds set up storefronts, not unlike those used today to recruit soldiers
for the U.S. Armed Forces, in European port cities. Recruitment centers were placed next to shipping company offices, ready and eager to
sell passages to Brazil and elsewhere. Immigrants were offered passages
and work contracts, and pamphlets used hard sells and half-truths, such
as the following:

> In America – Land in Brazil for Italians. Ships leave every week from
> the port of Genoa. Come build your dreams with the family. A country
> of opportunity. Tropical climate and abundance. Mineral wealth. In
> Brazil you will be able to have your castle. The government will give
> land and tools to all.[6]

Brazil's main competitor for immigrants was Argentina. The 1853 proc-
lamation by the influential political theorist and diplomat Juan Batista
Alberdi that "to govern is to populate" reflected the Argentine oligarchy's support of European mass immigration. This cultural and political orientation led Argentina to constitutionally guarantee freedom of
worship in 1853, and in 1884 new civil laws limited the influence of the
Catholic Church in many areas of private life. In 1888, the government
began to subsidize passage. Argentina's booming agricultural export sector kept wages high and the cost of passages low: In 1900 an agricultural
worker in Argentina could pay back the cost of passage with just two
weeks' work.[7] Not surprisingly, by the early twentieth century, almost
half the population of Buenos Aires was foreign born.
This was not the case in Brazil. There, elites often treated immigrants more as servile laborers than as agents of development, and
wages were significantly lower than in Argentina. Furthermore, immigrants were often unskilled at the kinds of agricultural work expected of

---

[5]   Nachman Falbel, "Oswaldo Boxer e o projeto de colonização de judeus no
Brasil," *Jornal do Imigrante*, 10 (December 1987/January 1988), 18.
[6]   The cover image can be found at *http://www.bentogoncalves.rs.gov.
br/005/00502001.asp?ttCD_CHAVE=32588*.
[7]   Magnus Mörner and Harold Sims, *Adventurers and Proletarians: The Story
of Migrants in Latin America* (Pittsburgh, PA: University of Pittsburgh Press,
1985), 41.

them. As the historian Emília Viotti da Costa has pointed out, "On the Fazenda São Lourenço, in Rio Claro [São Paulo State], one immigrant family could care for only 420 square feet of land and this did not even cover the costs of the interest on the loan they took [to come to Brazil]. Slaves, on the other hand, on average cared for three thousand square feet of land.[8]

The comparison with Argentina shows the complexity of attracting immigrants to Brazil. Incentives other than wages were thus necessary. One approach favored by landowners in rich areas was to turn immigration into a government enterprise. States with powerful economies could thus create better incentives to attract foreign labor. Funding new colonies near older Central European ones in southern Brazil was another approach. Such changes led to results. Starting in the late 1880s, Italian entry exploded as immigrants settled on new colonies in Rio Grande do Sul, Paraná, and Santa Catarina or as subsidized rural laborers in São Paulo, Rio de Janeiro, and Minas Gerais. Hundreds of thousands of Portuguese also arrived, following already established patterns of urban settlement and commerce. Spaniards started to come in significant numbers (though always less than in Spanish America), replicating aspects of both Italian and Portuguese settlement.

Brazil's foreign-born population in 1890 was 750,000, about 5.2 percent of the total. This was a small number when compared to those in the United States (9.2 million/14.7 percent), Argentina (1 million/25.4 percent) or Canada (643,000/13.3 percent). Yet immigrant concentration in Brazil's most economically and politically powerful states meant that the impact was far larger than the absolute numbers. Nowhere was this more apparent than in São Paulo, where a booming coffee economy led the state's population to grow almost twice as fast as that of Brazil as a whole. The majority of all Brazil's immigrants settled in São Paulo. By the twentieth and twenty-first centuries, they and their descendants would occupy the Brazilian national imagination much as immigrants in Rio Grande do Sul and Santa Catarina had earlier.

ACTION AND REACTION

Brazilian society changed in profound ways during the second half of the nineteenth century. Economic expansion was led by coffee. The pace of

[8] Emília Viotti da Costa, *Da Senzala à Colônia* (São Paulo: Editora UNESP, 1998), 127–128.

urbanization was rapid and the rural labor force was transformed from slave to free. Many Afro-Brazilians migrated into cities and became part of the poor industrial, manual, and service workforce. As the percentage of the economy representing the professions, commerce, and administration grew (from about ten percent in 1920 to over thirty percent in 1980), Afro-Brazilians became even more marginalized.[9]

The cultural, economic, and social changes inspired new institutions. One of the most important was the Sociedade Central de Imigração (SCI, the Central Immigration Society). Three Central European immigrants to whom readers have already been introduced founded the organization in 1883. They included the journalist and federal deputy from Rio Grande do Sul Karl von Koseritz, Herman Blumenau (founder of the colony bearing his name in Santa Catarina), and colonizing failure and journalist Hugo Grüber. Their goal was to use immigrant colonies to promote Brazil's modernization. Their enemy was the landed oligarchy who, they believed, would never treat labor in a manner that would create a tractable workforce.

That von Koseritz, Blumenau, and Grüber would become leaders in creating a national immigration policy is not surprising. Typical of nineteenth-century immigrants throughout the Americas, their commitment to their new homeland was intense. They were certain that the future was in the New World and that Brazil's future was with European newcomers. They agreed with many in the native-born elite that those of African and mixed descent prevented the country from achieving a position of world leadership. The three German immigrants had promoted these positions earlier in the century in southern Brazil and were sure that national application was appropriate. C. F. Van Delden Laërne, so critical of the large landowners' attitude toward immigration, was enthusiastic about the colonization approach of the SCI. After a visit to the German colony of Dom Pedro II in Rio Grande do Sul, he wrote:

> The colonists ... for the most part, have lost their nationality and, with a few exceptions, speak Portuguese.... General experience goes to prove that, even should all the immigrants retain their nationality and their pride in it, this is assuredly not the case with children born and bred in Brazil. These are, and remain, in the first place Brazilians.

[9] George Reid Andrews, *Blacks and Whites in São Paulo, Brazil, 1888–1988* (Madison: University of Wisconsin Press, 1991), 235.

Figure 3.1. A farm in a colony of Germans and German-Brazilians in Rio Grande do Sul, circa 1900.
Source: Gaelzer-Neto Photographic Collection, IV Rio Grande do Sul. Used with the permission of the Ibero-Amerikanisches Institut Preussischer Kulturbesitz (Berlin).

[In] the province of Rio Grande do Sul, where the German element is at present most numerously represented, the descendants of the Germanic immigrants speak of themselves with a certain pride as Deutschlanders ... [yet] it is not so much that they dote on Germany and the social conditions there as that they count their extraction higher than that of the Brazilians of the colonial period. Of all immigrants the Germans are those that lose their nationality first.[10]

(See Figure 3.1, which shows a farm in Rio Grande do Sul.)

Von Koseritz, Blumenau, and Grüber were national thinkers. They, like a number of their Brazilian supporters, insisted that abolition would create a labor crisis and suggested that smallholdings would inevitably replace plantations. Civil marriage and ease of naturalization, they argued, would create spontaneous emigration from Europe. The letter

[10] Laërne, *Brazil and Java*, pp. 128, 133.

that they sent to announce the first meeting of the SCI even suggested how to market the values of immigration to the Brazilian public. (See Document 3.1: Invitation letter for the creation of the Sociedade Central de Imigração, in the chapter Appendix.)

Von Koseritz despised the fazendeiros. In his 1885 memoir, he described the SCI as "declaring war on the latifundia." He attacked the plans for Chinese contract labor discussed in Chapter 2 as creating a "yellow" slave caste.[11] Whether or not von Koseritz held his tongue at the first public meeting of the SCI on September 14, 1883, is not known. What is certain is that the invited politicians, businesspeople, and journalists responded enthusiastically. This was what the three founders wanted. Now they could turn the SCI over to a Brazilian-born leadership, based among the traditional (albeit modernizing) elite. Von Koseritz and Grüber returned to their newspaper work and Blumenau to Germany.

By the end of 1883, the SCI was on firm footing and was publishing its own newspaper, A Imigração [Immigration]. Members included immigrant merchants from Portugal and England, a Swiss writer, a geologist from the United States, and a German teacher. Among the Brazilian born were the abolitionist André Rebouças and the modernizing technocrat Senator Alfredo d'Escragnolle Taunay. At its height, the SCI had about four hundred members who represented a new stream of political engagement. The society developed an articulate critique of the planter class and the traditional ways in which Brazilian society functioned.

The SCI linked labor and Europeanization through its support of "whitening." While members did not agree on exactly who was white, they did agree to despise Brazil as it was racially constituted. Members argued that the landowning elite was oppressive and that the broader population of African and mixed descent (the 1872 census showed the population at about sixty percent nonwhite) was retrograde. For supporters of the SCI, mass immigration was about repopulating Brazil.

The implications of this position were broad. The SCI favored ethnically cohesive immigrant núcleos, the biological word (as in the nucleus of an egg) they chose to describe colonies. Retention of premigratory culture among immigrants would improve Brazil. The SCI wanted small farmers to break the monopoly of large plantations and create a modern

---

[11]   Karl von Koseritz, *Imagens do Brasil* (São Paulo: Livraria Martins Editora, 1972), 204–205. The original *Bilder aus Brasilien* was published in 1885, with the first Brazilian edition appearing only sixty years later.

wage system. There were only two flaws in the proposal: Immigrants seemed more interested in their own well-being than in being cogs in a transformative national plan, and fazendeiros were unwilling to break up their plantations.

Another important feature of the SCI was its racism. A *Immigração* regularly attacked plans for Chinese immigration as bringing a "weak bastard race, filled with hedonistic vices, without a doubt inferior to the ethnic elements we have."[12] The SCI even sent a delegation to Europe to discourage Chinese diplomats from considering Brazil as an emigration site. The SCI also sought to deport the tens of thousands of Middle Easterners (from today's Syria and Lebanon) who had quietly settled in Brazil since the mid-nineteenth century and to make sure no others entered.

Many of the SCI's proposals became state or federal policies by the close of the nineteenth century. The immigrant recruiting process was professionalized, and racism was codified through the prohibition of entry by Asians and Africans.[13] The openness to immigrants who did not speak Portuguese or practice Catholicism was sanctioned in the rejection of official religion and language. Yet the SCI failed to diminish the power of the planters, who continued to resist better treatment of laborers in return for higher production. These planters counterpunched by forming the Sociedade Promotora de Imigração (SPI, the Immigration Promotion Society) in 1886. The SPI was opposed to state-sponsored immigration. Rather, they wanted private companies to handle recruitment and placement.

The SPI's members were wealthy and politically powerful. They had different class and ethnic roots than those of the SCI, with its immigrant founders, middle-class outlook, and view of Rio Grande do Sul and Santa Catarina as models. The SPI, to the contrary, was founded by Martinho Prado Júnior, a member of a prominent slaveholding and landowning family in São Paulo. One of Martinho's brothers, Antônio Prado, was a politician and railroad owner. Another brother, Eduardo, was a monarchist, journalist, and author. They and their colleagues in the SPI were not eager for open market capitalism, but instead wanted to continue using the state to support their own interests. Yet they were similar to SCI members in one way: They believed in racial hierarchies with whiteness at the top.

---

[12]   A *Immigração – Órgão da Sociedade Central de Immigração* 1: 3 (April, 1884), 9.
[13]   Decree Law 528, June 28, 1890, Art. 1.

The Sociedade Promotora de Imigração was a family affair. Martinho was the president and in charge of propaganda. He bribed foreign newspapers for favorable articles about Brazil. He also produced a glossy booklet funded by a grant from the imperial Ministry of Agriculture headed by his brother Antônio. The third brother, Eduardo, was hired to write much of the booklet of which eighty thousand copies were printed in Portuguese, German, and Italian.[14] Distributed at the 1889 Paris Exposition, the colorful propaganda materials hearkened back to an earlier time of selling false impressions that immigrants might mistakenly believe were contractually solid. The text was often comparative, suggesting that Brazil was superior to the United States or Argentina as a location for resettlement. A fold-out map cleverly presented Brazil as an enormous Atlantic world country, and São Paulo State as filled with "unpopulated land." (See Figure 3.2 for a similar map distributed in Italy.)

The SPI saw itself not simply as a promoter of immigration. In 1887, it became the de facto immigration ministry of the state of São Paulo. Soon thereafter, Martinho Prado Júnior visited northern Italy to examine emigration conditions. While there he set up a branch office in Genoa that promoted Brazil, processed subsidy requests, and screened potential workers. From just mid-1886 to mid-1888, the numbers of immigrants contracted through the SPI grew almost ten times (from less than 6,000 to more than 60,000) even as the expenditure per immigrant dropped. Of the 60,749 immigrants brought under the 1888 contract, more than 44,000 were Italian, with about 10,000 Portuguese, 3,700 Central Europeans (listed as German and Austrian), and 2,800 Spaniards. (See Table 3.1 for totals and percentages from 1882 to 1929.) After the Brazilian republic was established in 1889, the SPI continued to work closely with the São Paulo Department of Agriculture, Commerce and Public Work, but the organization was no longer needed by the end of the century.

FAZENDO AMÉRICA – MAKING AMERICA

In 1891, national expenditures on immigration doubled to more than eleven percent of the total budget. In São Paulo, the portions of the

---

[14] *A Provincia de São Paulo no Brazil: Emigrante, Lede Este Folheto antes de Partir* (São Paulo, 1886), 17.

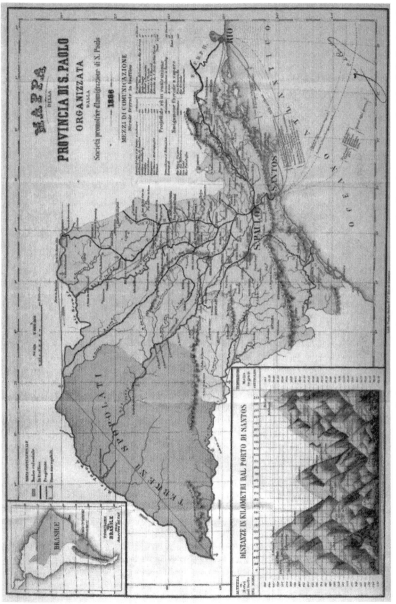

Figure 3.2. Map produced by the Sociedade Promotora de Imigração in 1886 for distribution in Italy. The left third of the map is labeled "unpopulated land."

Table 3.1. *Total Immigration to Brazil and Percentage to São Paulo, 1882–1929*

	Immigration to Brazil	Immigration to São Paulo (%)
1882–1884	87,178	14
1885–1889	319,541	53
1890–1894	600,735	70
1895–1899	597,592	69
1900–1904	249,042	52
1905–1909	373,365	54
1910–1914	667,778	58
1915–1919	147,675	56
1920–1924	373,126	53
1925–1929	473,521	61
Total	**3,889,553**	

Source: Thomas W. Merrick and Douglas H. Graham, *Population and Economic Development in Brazil: 1800 to the Present* (Baltimore: Johns Hopkins University Press, 1979), Table V-2, p. 95.

budget directed toward immigration were consistently higher than in other states, reaching over ten percent in seven of the years between 1892 and 1910 and over five percent in thirteen other years.[15] The expenditures correlate directly to the costs of subsidies and, thus, to the numbers of immigrants entering the state. Between 1890 and 1930, more than two million immigrants entered São Paulo, about half with passages paid for by the state government. Between 1872 and 1972, fifty-seven percent of the 5.35 million newcomers to Brazil would settle in that one state.

Subsidies were ostensibly for healthy, European, rural workers. In many cases, however, the immigrants misrepresented their agricultural experience. All were supposed to come with families, since Brazilian landowners feared a replication of the temporary migration patterns that marked the back-and-forth of Italian migration to Argentina. Yet immigrants learned to work the system in order to garner the subsidies that helped to pay for their transportation and settlement. For example, "families" were often composed of adults who were not formally married. Sometimes they had met each other just before signing up for subsidies. Furthermore, as Table 3.2 shows, the stated desire for families was rarely achieved.

---

[15] Statistics from Gloria La Cava, *Italians in Brazil: The Post-World War II Experience* (New York: Peter Lang, 1999), Tables 1 and 2, pp. 18–19.

Table 3.2. *Demographic Characteristics of Selected Immigrants Arriving at the Port of Santos, 1908–1936*

	Italians	Portuguese	Spanish	Japanese	Total of All Immigrants
Total population	202,749	275,257	209,282	176,775	1,222,282
# of families	28,374	35,044	33,955	31,412	175,928
% single	42	53	18	5	37
AGE					
% over 12	78	81	68	70	77
% 7–12	8	7	12	11	8
% under 12	14	12	20	19	15
MARRIAGE STATUS					
% married	42	43	37	42	39
% single	55	55	60	56	58
% widowed	3	2	3	2	2
ILLITERACY(%)	32	52	65	10	34
FARMERS (%)	50	48	79	99	59

Source: São Paulo, Secretaria da Agricultura, Indústria e Comércio, Directoria de Terras, Colonização e Immigração, *Boletim,* 1: 1 (October, 1937), appendix; Table "Movimento Immigratorio pelo porto de Santos, 1908–1936" and Table A-16, p. 69.

ARRIVAL

In the late nineteenth century, the transatlantic voyage from Europe to Brazil lasted around thirty days, although the time shortened as the twentieth century progressed. Immigrants arrived primarily at three ports: Salvador (in the northeastern state of Bahia), Rio de Janeiro, and Santos (in the state of São Paulo). The smallest numbers of immigrants arrived in Salvador, but significant numbers were processed at the Ilha das Flores Hospedaria dos Imigrantes (Immigrant Hostel and Reception Center) that was constructed in 1883 to move workers to coffee plantations in Rio de Janeiro State.

The overwhelming numbers of immigrants arrived in Santos, destined for the booming coffee plantations in São Paulo State. As each ship filled with immigrants steamed into the port, officials would telegraph the information to the Hospedaria dos Imigrantes located in the city of São Paulo fifty miles away. The newcomers disembarked and boarded a train that wound its way from the coast through the mountains, stopping at the British-built Luz (light) train station in central São Paulo. As the train chugged through the city to the Hospedaria's own platform, immigrants would have been impressed

Figure 3.3. European immigrants in the refectory of the Hospedaria dos Imigrantes, São Paulo (circa 1900).
Source: Gaelzer-Neto Photographic Collection, VII – Auswanderung nach Brasilien. Used with the permission of the Ibero-Amerikanisches Institut Preussischer Kulturbesitz (Berlin).

by the efficiency of the system. To most, the arrival seemed to augur good things.

The positive impression continued as they left the train. Most new arrivals went first to the Hospedaria's dining hall (see Figure 3.3). Traditional Brazilian peasant food was served, and the heaping portions of rice and beans, potatoes, vegetables, and coffee must have impressed those coming from precarious situations in Europe. Ill newcomers were sent to the medical sector of the Hospedaria, and others received checkups and vaccinations. Everything seemed clean and modern, and immigrants recalled being impressed by the privacy of the bathing and bathroom facilities. Written materials were distributed to newcomers in six languages, although many were not literate enough to read the information. This detail was critical. An inability to understand the contracts they had signed, and which allowed their subsidies to be paid, had serious implications. Many people erroneously believed that rural conditions were similar to those at the Hospedaria, and as historian Michael Hall notes, the first generation

Figure 3.4. European immigrants in the courtyard of the Hospedaria dos Imigrantes, São Paulo (circa 1900).
Source: Gaelzer-Neto Photographic Collection, VII – Auswanderung nach Brasilien. Used with the permission of the Ibero-Amerikanisches Institut Preussischer Kulturbesitz (Berlin).

of immigrants tell "an almost unrelieved tale of exploitation and bitter disappointment."[16] (See Document 3.2: Letter from an Italian immigrant, in the chapter Appendix.)

The Hospedaria, in its construction and organization, is an indicator of how Brazilian elites imagined immigrants and immigration. Built in 1887 to replace a rundown welcome center, the building had classic Roman and Greek architecture, which suggested Brazil's new status as a country that attracted the immigrant masses (see Figure 3.4). Its architect was Antônio Martins Haussler, a German-Brazilian whose whiteness, Europeanness, and modernity seemed unquestionable. The location in Brás, a neighborhood outside the city center, gave an impetus to the factories that moved into the area.

This Hospedaria was built for efficiency and speed. It could sleep about one thousand people at a time but often processed two or three times that number each day. When the esteemed historian Warren Dean visited the building in 1963, he was reminded of how the architecture masked the difficulties that so many immigrants faced:

> The Hospedaria dos Imigrantes is Brazil's Ellis Island [yet] unlike the grim old institution in New York Bay, the Hostel has not been closed down for lack of clients. Now it receives an even larger swarm of

[16] Michael M. Hall, "The Origins of Mass Immigration to Brazil, 1817–1914" (unpublished Ph.D. diss., Columbia University, 1969), 116.

people, peasants from the Brazilian Northeast who come to São Paulo to find work on the cotton or sugar plantations or to harvest coffee or oranges.

A high fence of iron pickets, broken by a wide gateway, then a broad courtyard, and one faces the Hostel itself. A stupendous façade, three stories high and two hundred yards wide, plastered and painted with São Paulo's ubiquitous cream-colored white wash, and relieved only by rows of great windows. The Hostel is a surprise among the shabby working class tenements that share its streets.

One passes through an arched vestibule whose walls bear maps showing where São Paulo's immigrants have come from – Italy, Portugal, Spain, Japan and lately from [the Brazilian states of] Minas, Bahia and the Northeast. Passing through the archway one finds a large square of buildings; along their unplastered brick walls runs spindly wooden porticoes. In the midst of the square are two more buildings – a small hospital and a newer looking commissary. About the courtyard, leaning against the porticoes, sitting on the porches or simply standing or squatting on the cobbles, are hundreds of ragged people, men, women and children. The whole scene, the aged brickwork, the peeling paint, even the sunshine, a cold winter morning sun, is an instantaneous revelation of utter despair.[17]

When I visited the Hospedaria, most recently in 2009, I saw a location whose function had changed radically. Today, the factories in the Brás neighborhood seem tiny. Korean and Bolivian immigrants are more prominent than European ones, and foreign immigrants and Brazilian migrants have not passed through the location in years. The buildings, so modern in the late nineteenth century, had been renovated (in 2011 the facility was being renovated yet again) as charming reminders of another era. In 1998 the Hospedaria was renamed the Memorial do Imigrante (Immigrant Memorial), and a museum inside seeks to create a positive memory of the immigrant experience. The exhibitions focus on economic success stories and how immigrants helped to create contemporary Brazil's national identity.

The museum includes a research center, which it boasts has a record for every immigrant who passed through the building's doors between 1888 and 1978. The space is often filled with people examining passenger

---

[17] Warren Dean, "Visit to the Hospedaria," unpublished manuscript of May 13, 1963, quoted in La Cava, *Italians in Brazil*, Table 7, p. 59.

manifests for the boats on which their ancestors arrived. Many use the information as a first step in applying for second passports based on their parents' or grandparents' birthplace. Visitors can take a one-kilometer steam train ride to memorialize the experience of immigrants arriving at the Hospedaria from the port of Santos. Multiculturalism is presented as a positive nineteenth-century value, and the government's catch-phrase "Everyone's São Paulo" is the major trope.

NEW TENSIONS

Between 1882 and 1978, when the Hospedaria received its final "guest," some three million immigrants, representing more than sixty national-ities (recall the large "Others" column in Tables 1.1 and 1.2 of Chapter 1), were processed. Portuguese, Spanish, Italian, and Japanese repre-sented the largest numbers of immigrants, but eight other national groups came in such large numbers that they were taken out of the Others category and given their own (see Table 3.3).

With mass immigration also came discontent among those unwilling to endure terrible treatment on plantations and in factories. European immigrants increasingly insisted on their own whiteness, assuming a new form of race consciousness in Brazil. Fearing that fazendeiros would link them with slaves and slavery, immigrants actively separated them-selves from the Afro-Brazilians who worked and lived with them in the countryside. Many refused to marry Afro-Brazilians as one way of reinforcing the color line. Immigrants often treated Afro-Brazilians aggressively, and the police records are filled with cases of violence. In the stereotypes at the time, Italian immigrants and Afro-Brazilians were associated with crime, and an academic study of a region with high numbers of immigrants found Italians, Portuguese, and Afro-Brazilians to be overrepresented in accusations of violence, both against persons and property. Even so, the types of ethnic criminal gangs associated with immigration to the United States were rarely found in Brazil, where elites saw gangs as competition and refused to protect them. The police usually sided with local elites, not law-breaking immigrants.[18]

Newcomers also turned to political agitation in order to better their lives. Few immigrants, however, had had much contact with organized

[18]   Karl Monsma, Oswaldo Truzzi, and Silvano da Conceição, "Solidariedade étnica, poder local e banditismo: uma quadrilha calabresa no oeste paulista, 1895–1898," *Revista Brasileira de Ciências Sociais*, 18: 53 (October, 2003), 71–96.

Table 3.3. *Migratory Movement at the Port of Santos, 1908–1936*

Nationalities	Entry	Exit	Families	Alone	Married	Single	Widows
Portuguese	275,257	160,920	35,044	147,020	117,704	151,412	6,141
Spanish	209,282	107,179	33,955	38,434	77,557	126,141	5,584
Italian	202,749	176,991	28,374	85,802	84,616	112,174	5,959
Japanese	176,775	12,615	31,412	8,974	74,730	99,161	2,884
Brazilian	125,826	95,845	11,525	79,809	40,385	82,926	2,515
German	43,989	34,816	6,718	19,687	17,925	25,206	858
Turk	26,321	12,364	3,054	16,543	8,587	17,452	282
Romanian	23,756	7,126	4,033	2,066	8,797	14,502	457
Yugoslavian	21,209	5,134	3,719	1,363	8,221	12,660	328
Lithuanian	20,918	3,373	3,147	4,965	7,350	13,111	457
Syrian	17,275	7,587	2,583	8,390	6,423	10,483	369
Polish	15,220	6,612	2,356	6,601	6,072	8,917	231
Austrian	15,041	7,180	2,325	5,059	5,724	9,050	267
Other	47,664	29,338	6,683	21,644	17,893	28,702	1,069
Total	**1,221,282**	**667,080**	**174,928**	**446,357**	**481,984**	**711,897**	**27,401**

Available at: http://www.memorialdoimigrante.org.br/portalmi/templates/historico/e5.htm.

labor prior to stepping off the boat. Formal and informal rules in Brazil threatened workers considering labor activism with the loss of a job, imprisonment, or expulsion. Most avoided movements, and activists found cohesion difficult to create. Immigrants from different countries, regions, and towns of origin often distrusted one another. The Italians who dominated the labor market were often contemptuous of other immigrants, especially those from Portugal and Spain. Some labor unions in Brazil used only the Italian language in assemblies and publications, functionally excluding large numbers of workers. Native-born Brazilians often treated newcomers as job stealers. New laws were passed to prevent labor leaders from entering the country. The legislation did not work perfectly; one study of São Paulo and Rio de Janeiro revealed that between 1890 and 1920, more than 65 percent of high-ranking activists were born in Europe, with most, not surprisingly, of Italian, Spanish, and Portuguese descent.[19]

By the early twentieth century, the elite desire for immigrants was matched by their fears of the same. Sílvio Romero, a literary critic,

[19]   Sheldon Maram, "The Immigrant and the Brazilian Labor Movement," in Dauril Alden and Warren Dean, eds., *Essays Concerning the Socioeconomic History of Brazil and Portuguese India* (Gainesville: University Presses of Florida, 1977), 178–210; pp. 183–184.

lawyer, and politician, embodied both positions. In the late nineteenth century, he had supported immigration for its whitening potential. By the early twentieth century, however, his position had changed. Now he emphasized the need for a strong central state that repressed immigrant identity. Romero initially believed, for example, that German immigrants would absorb the best parts of Brazilian culture and transfer their "natural loyalty" to Brazil.[20] Yet the Germans who settled in Rio Grande do Sul terrified him, especially as Germany's international power grew in the years leading up to World War I.

Romero attacked German immigrants (and those of German descent) in two widely circulated books, the more famous of which had the provocative title *Germanism in the South of Brazil: Its Dangers and its Conspiratorial Ways*. In these works, Romero argued that unintegrated immigrants would ally with Germany, making Brazil a target for potential domination:

The Germans in Brazil are, socially, completely distinct and independent of Brazilians. They have a different language, a different religion, different customs, different habits, different traditions, different hopes, different work habits, different ideas.

They are imprisoned here only by territorial bonds but not by effective political bonds since they do not take part in our lives in this regard.

They are like islands, or an oasis in the middle of what we call our Brazilian desert.[21]

Some Germans living in the Americas did support the German army's entry into Belgium, France, and Russia during World War I. The United States even interned more than two thousand German residents during that period. Yet Romero's position was not simply about enemies. He believed, like so many elites before him, that German immigrants (as an idea) would improve the national identity of Brazil. Real German immigrants, on the other hand, were a "peril."

---

[20] Thomas Skidmore, *Black into White: Race and Nationality in Brazilian Thought* (Durham, NC: Duke University Press, 1993), 56. Professor Skidmore generously helped me think through much of the material on Romero that is, as noted, often contradictory.

[21] Sílvio Romero, *A América Latina* (Porto: Livraria Chardon, 1906), 315; the original title of *Germanism in the South of Brazil* is *O Allemanismo no Sul do Brasil: Seus Perigos e os Meios de os Conjurar* (Rio de Janeiro: Ribeiro, 1906).

The tensions expressed by Romero about Germans reflected broader cross-class worries about immigrants among native Brazilians. A 1907 anti-Portuguese article in the São Paulo newspaper of the anarcho-syndicalists (a branch of anarchism), A *Terra Livre* [The free land] – ironically founded by an immigrant from Portugal – complained that "It is quite ridiculous the role the Portuguese ... are now playing here. These poor 'Maneis' [a play on the common Portuguese name Manuel] ... run to the police headquarters, in order to become puppets ready to assassinate strikers, when those who produce everything and enjoy nothing demand one more piece of bread." When a port workers' union in Rio de Janeiro elected Portuguese immigrants to the union's leadership in 1908, native workers largely of African descent rioted. The result was one dead, three wounded, and a union membership that dropped from four thousand to two hundred in one year.[22] A decade later, a large majority of the fifteen hundred workers who were arrested during Rio de Janeiro's huge 1920 general strike were foreign born.

Tensions between immigrants and Brazilians, and rich and poor, were also apparent in the countryside. One of the most famous cases involved a young Italian named Angelo Longaretti. He had immigrated with his family in 1890 to work on the Nova America (New America) plantation in the Araraquara region, 150 miles northwest of the city of São Paulo. Diogo Salles, a local political boss and brother of Brazil's president Campos Salles, owned the plantation. According to the reports, Salles's son Raul had attempted to seduce each of Longaretti's three sisters, ages nineteen to fifteen. When the youngest refused, Raul and a henchman tried (and failed) to carry her away one night. Angelo, fearing for his sisters' safety, began to look for employment on a different plantation, but when word reached Raul, he had Angelo jailed. Immigrants on the plantation showed their solidarity with the young man by striking, which forced his release.

A few days later Diogo Salles and the Longaretti patriarch appear to have gotten into an argument and perhaps a fistfight. The now-free twenty-two-year-old Angelo, seeking to protect his father, unholstered his revolver and shot and killed the plantation owner. Then he fled the plantation and hid in the nearby forest. The Salles family believed

[22] A *Terra Livre* (São Paulo), February 5, 1907, p. 3, in Sheldon L. Maram, "Labor and the Left in Brazil, 1890–1921: A Movement Aborted," *Hispanic American Historical Review*, 57: 2 (May, 1977), 254–272; pp. 259–260.

that there would be a quick resolution after they ordered the police to hunt him down. Instead, the case became a cause célèbre. Other immigrants on the plantation refused to sell out Angelo to the police and so the Salles family sent in thugs to beat them. The small number of Italian immigrants who had become economically and socially successful in Brazil, often as middleman entrepreneurs in the coffee trade, were aghast. The open threats and the affront to Italian honor implied by the attempted seduction of the Longaretti sisters inspired the better-off immigrants to act. A group pooled funds to hire one of Brazil's most important lawyers to defend the young man. They also pushed the Italian government to intervene, and diplomats began to pressure the president of Brazil (i.e., Diogo Salles's brother) to resolve the case.

Angelo was tried in absentia by a Brazilian court and given a twelve-year sentence, outraging immigrants rich and poor, as well as Italian political leaders abroad and in Brazil. The socialist newspaper *Avanti!* editorialized: "[Longaretti] is not one more immigrant, he is *the* immigrant, the living and painful image, the personification of the miserable human meat whom they lured from far across the sea to substitute for the freed slaves. His story is the story of all immigrants, his vengeance and painful and fatal insurrection against a shameful system of exploitation."[23]

Intense public pressure led to a retrial. Immigrant workers testified against the owner, revealing that attacks on honor (i.e., sexual assault) were typical on Diogo Salles's plantations. In 1908, when Campos Salles was no longer president, a court pardoned the Italian immigrant. The new judgment seemed to suggest that Brazil's political system no longer supported the openly poor treatment of immigrants by fazendeiros. The court made clear that the pardon was an acknowledgment that if Angelo had not killed Diogo, Diogo would have had his henchmen kill Angelo. The Longaretti family subsequently returned to Italy where Angelo died in 1960, never having set foot in Brazil again.[24]

---

[23] *Avanti!*, 8–9 June 1901.
[24] Further discussions of the Longaretti case can be found in Jacob Penteado, *Belenzinho, 1910: Retrato de uma Época* (São Paulo: Carrenho Editorial/Narrativa Um, [1962] 2003), 32; Warren Dean, *Rio Claro: A Brazilian Plantation System, 1820–1920* (Stanford, CA: Stanford University Press, 1976), 181–183; Angelo Trento, *Do Outro Lado do Atlântico: Um Século de Imigração Italiana no Brasil* (São Paulo: Nobel, 1989), 113–114.

Table 3.4. *Distribution of the Foreign Population in Brazil, 1920 Census*

Country of Origin	% in São Paulo	Total Brazil	% of Foreigners in São Paulo	Total São Paulo
Japanese	87.3	27,976	2.9	24,435
Spanish	78.2	219,142	20.6	171,289
Italian	71.4	433,577	48.1	398,797
Portuguese	38.6	433,477	20.1	167,198
Total		1,565,961	91.7	829,851

Source: Brazil, Directoria Geral de Estatística, *Recenseamento do Brasil realizado em 1 de Setembro de 1920* (Rio de Janeiro: Typ. da Estatística, 1922–1930), IV: 1a. parte, pp. 313–317.

URBANIZATION

Mass immigration helped to change the physical way in which Brazil's population was dispersed: São Paulo would eclipse Rio de Janeiro's population and wealth during the twentieth century. In 1872, São Paulo had just 31,000 inhabitants, but by 1920, that number had swelled to almost 830,000 (see Table 3.4) and then doubled again by 1940. Rio de Janeiro's population jumped from 275,000 in 1872 to 1.15 million in 1920 and 1.7 million in 1940. Porto Alegre, the largest city in southern Brazil, grew from 44,000 in 1872 to 179,000 in 1920 and 270,000 in 1940. With the changes, politicians, intellectuals, and business leaders who lived in cities came to worry about the realities of increasingly crowded urban spaces. As cities grew, so did poor and working-class neighborhoods, often called *cortiços* ("beehives") or *cabeças de porco* ("pork heads," referring to rooming houses).

As more immigrants migrated to the cities, ethnic institutions began to play a larger role in Brazilian life. In 1911, eleven São Paulo newspapers were published in languages other than Portuguese, including four in Italian, four in Arabic, and others in French, Spanish, and German. By 1935, two of the eight largest daily newspapers in São Paulo were targeted toward immigrants and their descendants. The primarily Italian-language *Fanfulla* had a circulation of 35,000, while the primarily German-language *Deutsche Zeitung* boasted 20,000 readers.[25] The cinema was another cultural form enjoyed by immigrants in Brazil. Some movie houses were associated specifically with immigrant groups (for example, those showing Yiddish- or Japanese-language films), while

[25] Joseph Love, *São Paulo in the Brazilian Federation, 1889–1937* (Stanford, CA: Stanford University Press, 1980), 91.

others offered a diverse range of films from North America, Europe, and Brazil. The Cine Belém, inaugurated in 1910, was located in a working-class and largely immigrant neighborhood near São Paulo's Hospedaria dos Imigrantes. The entertainment often opened with immigrant circus performers and a live band playing Italian marches. Families brought meals and spent the entire day watching the events. Audiences enjoyed French, Italian, and American films, and they seemed equally enthusiastic about listening to polkas or popular Brazilian music. Jacob Penteado, who chronicled (and poked fun) at life in early twentieth century Brazil, noticed how much contact different immigrant groups had with one another in public spaces. He told the story of a beautiful Italian performer at the Cine Belém named Pimpinella. According to Penteado, "her charm and manner led a young Syrian businessman to do anything she asked," eventually leading him to bankruptcy and insanity.[26]

CONCLUSION

While most immigrant groups used the same formats (newspapers, cinemas, music, food, clubs) for cultural expression, ethnic culture differed, depending on nation of origin, size of the population, and how the generations born in Brazil engaged with broader society. The growth of urban, immigrant, public cultural spaces makes the word colônia ("colony") critical to the rest of our story. According to the historian Jürgen Buchenau, the word originated during the Italian Renaissance, when outsiders from one city (usually merchants) lived in specified areas of other cities. In this way, European merchant colonies could interact socially with local elites, especially in contrast to Jewish ghettos that were built to prevent such intermingling. In Latin America in the early nineteenth century, the term became widespread to describe immigrants whose "effort to preserve the home culture involved a sense of superiority over the host society, membership in a close-knit community, and a 'territorial consciousness.'"[27]

In Brazil, the late-nineteenth-century definition of colônia began to change when it became clear that the children of immigrants were ethnic Brazilians. The term thus came to mean "ethnic community." Part

---

[26] Jacob Penteado, "O Cinema Belém" in Belenzinho, 1910, pp. 171–176.
[27] Jürgen Buchenau, Tools of Progress: A German Merchant Family in Mexico City, 1865–Present (Albuquerque: University of New Mexico Press, 2004), 32–33.

of the new meaning was related to the aforementioned discussion of plantation workers as *colonos* who were different from slave labor. Yet the movement from individual colono to ethnic colônias had deeper implications. This can be seen in the revival of the story of Angelo Longaretto long after he left Brazil in 1908.

Celso Lungaretti is the grandchild of Italian immigrants and apparently a relative of Angelo. He came of age under the brutal military dictatorship that took power in a coup d'état in 1964. As a high schooler in 1967, he began to participate in Brazil's growing student resistance to the dictatorship, and in 1969 he joined a militant movement called the Vanguarda Popular Revolucionária (Popular Revolutionary Vanguard, or VPR). In 1970, after participating in a number of VPR armed actions, he decided to turn himself in to the authorities. For years, members of the Left accused him of telling the military about a secret VPR training camp and treated him as a traitor. In 2004, with the military no longer in power, Lungaretti began a campaign to rehabilitate himself. One tactic was to link himself to nineteenth-century Angelo Longaretto, whom he described in an article as a freedom fighter like himself.[28] It seems to have worked. Today, Celso Lungaretti is a cultural commentator who, many believe, never betrayed his colleagues to the military.

---

[28] Celso Lungaretti, "Mussolini vive. Dante morreu," Centro de Mídia Independente, available at: http://www.midiaindependente.org/pt/blue/2009/05/446746.shtml.

APPENDIX

Document 3.1. *Invitation letter for the creation of the Sociedade Central de Imigração, 1883*

Esteemed Sirs!

A labor crisis threatens our country in the near future. It is the undisguised truth that large plantations must be transformed into small property holdings. This will create more productivity and a feeling of well-being and tranquility on our fertile land. This is why all eyes are directed anxiously to immigration that has given the United States the colossal progress that brings the world's admiration. This is confirmed by the fact that Brazil's legislature, after giving equal citizenship rights to naturalized citizens and non-Catholics, is now looking to allow civil marriages and make naturalization simple, two essential conditions for the spontaneous creation of a migratory current to Brazil. But the legislative action is not enough. We need more marketing in Europe and in Brazil. This is what the Central Committee of Economic Geography, with the support of the Empire, has done for years. This marketing has led to good results and now is the time for similar propaganda from the Brazilian side so that foreigners know that Brazil will match their efforts.

It is in the recognition of these truths that the signatories below, who have worked for years in the German press in Brazil, have come to believe that the time is right. We must encourage those who have represented our cause in Germany, whence our first set-tlers came and to which the provinces of Rio Grande do Sul and Santa Catarina owe their progress. Those signing below, whose competency to take on this initiative lies solely in years of work in favor of German emigration to Brazil, are not so ambitious as to put forth any plan or any idea. They wish only to unite statesmen, journalists, and capitalists to focus on immigration and deliberate about the decisions that must be taken together. Those signing below invite you to be present on Sunday at 11 AM in the Liceu Imperial de Artes e Ofícios. Trusting in your patriotism and your interests in immigration, the below expect that you will favor the projected meeting with your wisdom and great intelligence.

God bless you.
Rio de Janeiro, October, 1883
Dr. Hermann Blumenau
C. von Koseritz
H.A. Grüber

Source: Karl von Koseritz, *Imagens do Brasil* (São Paulo: Livraria Martins Editora, 1972), 218–219.

Document 3.2. A letter from an Italian immigrant, 1889

Dear Professor,

On January 27th we left the Hospedaria dos Imigrantes, where my grandfather Sisto, a son of Antonio Barel and a daughter of Antonio Celotto died. The day before a revolution took place there: the immigrants were so fed up that they threw everything in the kitchen into the yard: soup, meat, bread, everything through the window. All the workers, cooks, and employees ran away.

The guards and the cavalry arrived to calm down the immigrants, telling them to be patient and that the next day the cook would be changed and the food would be better. No one was hurt and the food improved.

The Brazilian civilians in favor of the new Republic hoped for support from the immigrants at the Hospedaria dos Imigrantes. However no one spoke up so that the women and children would not be scared. The Italians from Napoli who reside in São Paulo, with businesses, restaurants, also wanted the Republic. They want to boss around everyone. They are brutes, liars, and without religion.

The Brazilians are good: most are black and everyone lives very well: they are happy people, without worries. At night they have parties … and they like dancing, singing, and being happy.

There are six families here on the fazenda, distributed in two houses. We are almost finished building four more houses. The boss, Giovanni de Toffole (he is not the owner, and must be an administrator) gives us everything we need. Together we make one big family. He pays us two "francs" each day.

Here everything is expensive, it costs a lot to live. This year the harvest is abundant. It is not like in Italy: we do not suffer drought and it rains all week. The land is fertile and does not need to be cultivated. The forests are dense, of an extraordinary size.

If you could see how marvelous the coffee plantings are! The beans that fall from the tree seem like hazelnuts.

All the plantations are lined up, with roads between them that allow cars to pass. There are oranges, lemons, and other fruits. There is tobacco to smoke.

We have all sorts of comforts: infinite wood, an abundance of water, a small windmill that goes through the land: good water, nice bosses.

In America the roads are terrible. You can't imagine! Fourteen enormous bulls are needed to pull a two-wheel cart, weighing one thousand pounds. If there were any will it would cost little to fix the road. The train tracks are narrow and go through the forests. The trains move like the wind: they run faster than those from Italy. I left São Paulo at six in the morning and arrived in São José do Rio Pardo at four in the afternoon, a distance that I compare to Conegliano to Genoa.

Many immigrants regret that they are so far away from their native land. Many with three children ended up with none. The desperate mothers damned "Merica" and tried to return to Italy. Some others did not have luck with their families, and became desolate. Many died of broken hearts. It is necessary to think seriously before undertaking this long journey, because one can easily be ruined. I do not recommend emigration to those not called by relatives.

Here there is little religiosity. We are far away from the city's church, like from Feletto to Conegliano. Two or three of us go to parties when the weather allows. If it rains, no one goes.

Your friend,
Giuseppe Manzoni

Giuseppe Manzoni was a colono on a fazenda near the town of São José do Rio Pardo (state of São Paulo). About half the population of 24,000 in the area came from Italy. He sent this letter to his former teacher in the city of Feletto, in the Treviso province of Italy, on March 11, 1889, as Brazil was in the midst of the political agitation that would lead to a republic in November 1889. The original text can be found in Emilio Franzina, *Merica! Merica!: Emigrazione e Colonizzazione nelle Lettere dei Contadini Veneti in America Latina 1876–1902* (Milan: Feltrinelli economica, 1979), 174–175.

CHAPTER FOUR

THE CREATION OF EURO-BRAZILIAN

IDENTITIES

GALEGO: " Foreigner, gringo"

> From Felisbelo da Silva (Police Investigator), *Dicionário de Gíria*
> [Dictionary of slang] (São Paulo: Editora Prelúdio, 1974), 62

One of the great stories of the invention of national identities comes in the form of a conversation that probably never took place. "We made Italy, now we have to make Italians," said (or is said to have said) Massimo D'Azeglio, an aristocratic statesman and novelist, to Giuseppe Garibaldi, another statesman whose military exploits ranged from Italy to Uruguay to Brazil. Yet "Italian," like other emerging national identities in the nineteenth and twentieth centuries, was not just generated at home; it was also formed abroad. Immigrants to the Americas did not simply arrive labeled as Italian, Spanish, Portuguese, Japanese, Syrian, or Korean. They became actors who imbued these words with new meanings. In Brazil, like elsewhere, new national identities sat alongside region, class, religion, and gender as characteristics by which people defined themselves.

Creating new identities was only one of the experiences of immigrants to Brazil. Another was social and cultural discrimination, and this led many to try to separate themselves from the Afro-Brazilians with whom they shared labor, residential, and social spheres. European immigrants feared being placed in a nonwhite racial category and often treated Afro-Brazilians disrespectfully, an attitude that blacks rejected. Immigrant relations with natives meant that whiteness, even when it was not the major component of national identity in their birthplace, became salient in Brazil. The constant tension among immigrants, their bosses, and nonwhite natives melded with identities inspired by the Old World.

Southern European immigration was the result of two linked processes. One was poverty and population pressures. The other was the
end of slavery in Brazil and the desire of landowners and politicians
there to use poorly paid European workers as part of their national whitening project. Southern Europeans challenged nineteenth- and early-
twentieth-century Brazilian national identity in very different ways
than did the unexpected immigrants whom we will meet in Chapter
5, such as Arabs and Jews. While European immigrants worked hard
to reinforce a color line by which they were "white," being "desirable"
also had its downsides. This chapter thus focuses on the experiences of
Brazil's three largest "colonies" – from Italy, Portugal, and Spain – in
order to illustrate different aspects of the broad immigrant experience.

RURAL SETTLEMENT AND POLITICAL ACTIVISM: ITALIAN IMMIGRATION

Italians made up more than thirty percent of all immigrant entries to
Brazil between 1872 and 1972. By 1920, more than thirty-five percent
of all foreign residents in Brazil were from Italy. While the majority
of Italians settled in São Paulo State, significant populations could be
found in Paraná, Santa Catarina, and Rio Grande do Sul in the South.
The state of Espírito Santo today claims sixty percent of its population
as descended from Italians, the highest in Brazil. Italian newcomers had
a wide range of experiences that historians have learned about in various sources, from letters to articles in the extensive Italian-Brazilian
press. We also know a great deal about official reactions since Italy's
government, eager to guarantee the flow to Brazil, often sent diplomats
to plantations to report on, and influence, the treatment and behavior
of immigrants. Brazilian landowners and politicians focused on encouraging production and repressing agitation.

These numbers had an enormous cultural impact. Popular myth
has it that the Italian word ciao ("hello" and "good-bye") has become
the Brazilian tchau ("good-bye"). The city of São Paulo claims fifteen
hundred Italian restaurants, from simple cantinas to elegant tratto-
rias. Residents of the city are said to consume one million pizzas daily,
and the annual Pizza Day (when many restaurants sell pizzas for half
price) is linked to the celebration of the state's failed constitutional
revolution against the federal government in 1932. The historian Glen
Goodman reports that in Rio Grande do Sul, German-Brazilian restaurants explain dishes such as knödel (dumplings) by referring to them

as "like gnocchi" (an Italian potato dumpling). Long lines outside of Italy's six consulates are each filled with Brazilians seeking Italian passports (based on heritage) that could confer European Union citizenship, with all the consequent labor and cultural benefits associated with it.

As with all immigrant stories, this one starts abroad. Between 1875 and the beginning of World War I, people flowed out of Italy in waves. Most were from agricultural areas and they suffered intensely because of international competition and an impoverishing government monetary policy. Land distribution made the situation even worse: *Latifundia* ("large plots") were characterized by absentee owners, poor technology, and low productivity, while *minifundia* were simply too small to provide a living for even one family. One widespread response was emigration.

About 8.8 million Italians settled in just three countries, the United States (5 million), Argentina (2.4 million) and Brazil (1.4 million). Many moved back and forth across the ocean on a regular basis. Some felt dissatisfied with whatever country they called "home."[1] For others, the transitions represented an attempt to take advantage of seasonal labor opportunities. Nowhere was this more apparent than in Argentina. There, half the gross Italian immigration was of temporary migrants who worked the Southern Hemisphere harvest season. Nicknamed *golondrinas* ("swallows"), they recrossed the Atlantic to work the Northern Hemisphere harvest in Europe.

Italian immigration to the Americas had two distinct moments. From 1876 to 1900, immigrants from the north of Italy, especially the Veneto region in the midst of an agricultural crisis, went in large numbers to Brazil and Argentina. The earlier arrivals became small landowners throughout Brazil, while those who entered after 1880 largely worked as colonos on the expanding coffee plantations in São Paulo. From 1901 until World War I, migrants tended to be from southern Italy, moving in overwhelming numbers to the United States where they found employment as unskilled laborers and industrial workers (see totals in Table 4.1).

The class differences in the emigrating populations to Brazil, Argentina, and the United States are represented starkly in remittances,

---

[1] Samuel L. Baily and Franco Ramella, *One Family, Two Worlds: An Italian Family's Correspondence Across the Atlantic, 1901–1922* (New Brunswick, NJ: Rutgers University Press, 1988).

Table 4.1. *Permanent Italian Settlement in the Americas (entries minus exits)*

Dates	Origin	Brazil	Argentina	USA
1876–1900	North	561,756	519,034	99,023
1876–1900	South	252,632	282,328	673,769
1901–1913	North	137,961	445,780	678,361
1901–1913	South	255,201	505,190	2,486,590
Subtotal	North	699,717	964,814	777,384
Subtotal	South	507,833	787,518	3,160,359
Total		**1,207,550**	**1,752,332**	**3,937,743**

Source: Jorge Balán, *International Migration in the Southern Cone* (Buenos Aires: Centro de Estudios de Estado y Sociedad, 1985), 97.

the monies that foreign residents sent back to their families. Remittances are important for understanding the lives of immigrants for a number of reasons. First, generating savings for remittances was (and is) often a primary goal of those who believe that they will return home. As immigrants come to see their futures in the new homeland, however, remittances often decline. Second, remittances are linked to global and national economic factors like the value of currencies in different countries. In this regard, remittances represent investment decisions based on what savings earned in one place can purchase in another. Finally, remittances are cultural because some people or groups prioritize savings more than others.

Scholars have obtained a great deal of information about remittances from the records of Italians. We know, for example, that the funds sent from Brazil to Italy were very small in comparison with those that came from the United States. We also know that between 1884 and 1899, the value of money orders cashed in Italy from Argentina was higher than from Brazil. Yet from 1900 to 1914 there was a reversal, and in some years the values from Brazil were seventy percent higher than those from its southern neighbor.[2] How do we explain these differences? One interpretation is that the modest amounts initially sent from Brazil reflect lower savings because of low wages. A different interpretation is that lower remittances show higher immigrant investment in Brazil. This is in contrast to Argentina and the United States where higher

[2] Warren Dean, *Remittances of Italian Immigrants: From Brazil, Argentina, Uruguay and U.S.A., 1884–1914* (New York: New York University, Ibero-American Language and Area Center, 1974), 4–8; Table 2, p. 5.

Figure 4.1. The photograph is entitled "Harvest – Italian Colonos." The immigrants are picking coffee on the Núcleo Colonial Monção, in the center-west part of São Paulo State (circa 1910).

Source: Gaelzer-Neto Photographic Collection, VI São Paulo – Landw. Produkte, Fazendas. Used with the permission of the Ibero-Amerikanisches Institut Preussischer Kulturbesitz (Berlin).

wages may have led Italian immigrants to believe that they could return to Italy wealthier.

By the start of World War I, more than 1.2 million Italians had settled in Brazil. The majority were from the poorest strata of Italian society and had their passages subsidized by the state of São Paulo, which focused its budgetary resources on using immigration to support the coffee economy (see Figure 4.1). Italian experiences on plantations highlight the continuing difference between what potential immigrants were told and what they found upon arrival. As we have seen repeatedly, official sources often provided misinformation about wages, about treatment, and about the opportunity for land ownership. While much of the information came from Brazilian sources, shipping companies also had a vested interest in encouraging migration because they made significant profits on every passenger. The president of the Sociedade Central de Imigração, Alfredo Taunay, complained that immigrants regularly arrived with tickets stamped by agents in Europe that said "Ogni colono avra diritto a sei mesi di vitto e d'allogio gratis!" ("Every colonist is entitled to six months free board and lodging!").[3]

Even those immigrants not fooled by unscrupulous agents were shocked by conditions on the plantations. (See Document 4.1: Report of an Italian consular official following a visit to an Italian immigrant settlement in Bahia in 1907, in the chapter Appendix.) Traditional aspects of premigratory sociability in Italy, such as markets and festivals, were rare on plantations and often left immigrants feeling dislocated. This sense was exacerbated by the low numbers of religious and educational institutions available to rural workers. Colonos often lived in former *senzalas*, the slave quarters vacated with abolition, or in small, poorly constructed houses with dirt floors. Michael Hall has proposed that while immigrants may have been eating better in Brazil than they did in Italy (i.e., had a higher caloric intake), general health conditions were poor.[4] The situation was worsened by a lack of physicians (one per five thousand inhabitants at best). Even when medical help was available, it was so costly that families often had to choose between seeing a doctor and preserving their entire savings. Alcoholism and mental illness were noticeable among plantation workers, and since most colonos were Italian, a stereotype of instability developed that plagued the descendants of immigrants.

Tension and stereotypes of self and "the other" made violence a regular aspect of day-to-day life. Sometimes immigrants targeted landowners and their representatives, and vice versa. Violence, however, was more common in the relations between immigrants and natives. (See Document 4.2: Police report on a violent encounter between a Brazilian mason and Italian peddler, 1895, in the chapter Appendix.) The sociologist Karl Monsma tells of a 1906 religious festival in the town of São Carlos, in an area of São Paulo State with many immigrants from Italy, Spain, and Portugal. One day, Gaspar Sabino, an Italian immigrant, bumped into Heitor Rodrigues da Silva, a Brazilian described in police reports as "mulatto," at a local church. Gaspar became angry when Heitor tried to help him regain his balance, saying, "I am not drunk or crazy [so you do not need] to

---

3   C. F. Van Delden Laërne, *Brazil and Java. Report on Coffee-Culture in America, Asia and Africa, to H. E. the Minister of the Colonies* (London, W. H. Allen & Co., 1885), 137.

4   Michael M. Hall, "The Origins of Mass Immigration to Brazil, 1817–1914" (unpublished Ph.D. diss., Columbia University, 1969), 135–136.

hold me up." The argument continued with verbal insults and ended with Heitor stabbing Gaspar in the back.[5]

Social control was the norm, and plantation workers often received punishments similar to those meted out to slaves. Sleeping hours were tightly controlled by a bell known as the *silenzio*, and plantation owners punished those who did not comply. "Forward thinking" fazendeiros used monetary fines, while more traditional ones beat those whose lights remained on after the bell had rung. Those who were ill and missed work had their pay docked *and* were charged a fine as well. Planters also used company stores where poor-quality goods were sold at absurdly high prices. Although most contracts allowed immigrants to grow vegetables and raise livestock on their own time, the surplus could only be sold to the plantation, usually for well below market value. Debt burdens were made worse because planters refused to pay wages on time: A 1902 estimate from the Italian government suggested that sixty percent of owners were behind on payments.[6] The owners blamed coffee prices, but good times did not lead to on-time pay, and salaries long owed rarely appeared.

The consistent abuses of European colonos highlight the disjuncture between policies meant to encourage the immigration of free and independent wage labor and the continued preference of plantation owners for subservient labor. While Italians were not slaves, contemporary commentators often made such comparisons. São Paulo's Italian consul reported in 1893 that the "distinguished appearance" of fazendeiros could not hide "[an] old slave owner [and] feudal seigneur, aware of being the absolute master of his lands, and with his will the only norm of conduct."[7]

Italians, like all other immigrants and slaves before them, resisted poor treatment. If slaves had in large part created the conditions for their own freedom through revolt, immigrants did the same, although redressing injustice was difficult. Physical and financial abuse by plantation owners often had no consequences. Immigrants seeking to respond through legal means discovered that representation had high costs. Yet

[5] Karl Monsma, "Symbolic Conflicts, Deadly Consequences: Fights between Italians and Blacks in Western São Paulo, 1888–1914," *Journal of Social History* 39: 4 (Summer 2006), 1123–1152; pp. 1123–1124.

[6] Hall, *The Origins of Mass Immigration to Brazil*, p. 132.

[7] A. L. Rozwadowski, Italian consul in São Paulo, Italy, Ministero degli Affari Ester, *Emigrazione e Colonie; Rapporti di Agenti Diplomatici e Consolari*, 1893, p. 166, quoted in Hall, *The Origins of Mass Immigration to Brazil*, p. 123.

the poor conditions did not go unnoticed. In 1902, Italy's director general for emigration issued the "Prinetti Decree" that suspended vessels from bringing subsidized workers to Brazil.[8] Workers also took matters into their own hands. Many fled the plantations for urban areas where families were more protected from physical abuse, children had access to education, and cultural and religious institutions were more available. Rapid social ascension was more likely in cities, and remittances provide important evidence: Far more remittances (in absolute terms) were sent home by Italian immigrants in the city of Rio de Janeiro than by those working on São Paulo's plantations, in spite of the smaller size of Rio's Italian population.[9]

Although the overwhelming majority of Italian immigrants worked as laborers on plantations, there were other models in Brazil. In 1870, the first Italian colonies in Rio Grande do Sul were set up using the Private Colonization Society model discussed in Chapter 3. Within less than a decade, ten thousand newcomers had settled in what would become the towns of Garibaldi (named for the Italian statesman), Bento Gonçalves, and Caxias do Sul. By the end of the century, about eighty thousand more Italian immigrants would join them. Unlike the Germans who had settled in the state earlier, Italian immigrants, virtually all Catholic, were able to practice their faith openly. Like Germans, Italian colonos took aspects of their own culture and reformulated and commercialized them in Brazil. The best-known Italian example is wine. While grapes had been grown in the region prior to 1870 – Jesuit missions taught Guarani indigenous people to grow grapes in the seventeenth century and German immigrants had been making wine since their arrival – it was Italian immigrants who began to commercialize the product.

Most immigrants, be they plantation contract workers or independent farmers, were poor and needed to invest their labor on the land for subsistence. This was not, however, always the case. Some Italian immigrants arrived with minimal funds to invest, and there is a direct correlation between rapid economic success and *not* being an agricultural worker. In Brazil's emerging new middle class, immigrants and their descendants were highly overrepresented, often by those groups who were not linked to the land, notably Arabs and Jews. Many successful

[8] Zuleika Alvim, *Brava Gente! Os Italianos em São Paulo, 1870–1920* (São Paulo: Brasiliense, 1986), 53.

[9] Dean, *Remittances of Italian Immigrants*, Table 5, p. 9.

immigrants created mobile rural department stores via peddling, and this often led to shop and then factory ownership, as we will discuss in more detail in Chapter 5.

By 1920, the majority of industry in the state of São Paulo was owned by immigrants or their descendants. This hid the fact that most immigrants did not experience economic and social ascension. Observers correctly blamed fazendeiros, and one Italian observer noted in 1922 that a typical landowner was

> lacking any business sense and always late on paying salaries because he does not have money, and when he has it he wastes it, he loves traveling and city life, to make merry, champagne, and above all women.... [H]e is ingratiating and brutal, diffident and hospitable, a squanderer and greedy, a knight and a Jesuit, his psychology is the result of so many different bloods and contact with so many races that it sways between the virgin forests and Paris.[10]

Italian immigrants who were able to leave plantation work often became successful. In São Paulo, some immigrants were able to become small merchants, either because they arrived with money or were among the very few lucky ones to save enough to move off the plantation at the end of their contract. Other immigrants became small landowners, and a 1905 estimate suggested that Italians owned fourteen percent of the land in São Paulo State. Some even became industrialists. The most famous was Francesco Matarazzo, a young entrepreneur who came to Brazil in 1881 after hearing that fortunes could be made there. He arrived with enough money to set up a small store, and by 1910 he was a factory owner (now called Francisco) whose reach expanded during World War I to include everything from textiles to oil.[11]

A different example can be found in the case of Giuseppe Giácomo and Luigia Carolina Zanrosso Eberle. They arrived in 1884 with their four children, settling in the region of Rio Grande do Sul that would become Caxias do Sul. Giuseppe bought a small metallurgical shop just two years after arriving, but because he wanted to remain a farmer, put it in the hands of his thirty-two-year-old wife, known by her nickname

[10] Filippo Peviani, *L'Attuale Problema Italo-Brasiliano* (1922), quoted in David Aliano, "Brazil through Italian Eyes: The Debate over Emigration to São Paulo during the 1920s," *Altreitalie: Rivista Internazionale di Studi sulle Migrazioni Italiane nel Mondo* (July–December, 2005), 87–107; p. 93.

[11] Matarazzo's rise to prominence is chronicled in Warren Dean, *The Industrialization of São Paulo* (Austin: University of Texas Press, 1969).

Gigia Bandera. She was an entrepreneurial success, growing the product line into copper implements and small machines that were not easily available in Brazil. Between 1886 and 1896 she had six more children, and eventually turned the business over to her oldest, who expanded into areas like kerosene lamps and cutlery. By the mid-1920s, the company, now called Abramo Eberle & Company, was producing small weapons (like knives) for the Brazilian armed forces, and in the 1930s it began making electric engines. In the mid-1980s, another immigrant-created industry, the Zivi-Hercules group (founded by a German-Jewish immigrant to Brazil as a stainless steel cutlery producer), bought Eberle & Company, creating what is today the Mundial Corporation.[12]

As Italians and other immigrants experienced some social mobility and moved into cities in the first decades of the twentieth century, new aspects to our story appear. One of the most important involves the press. The history of *Fanfulla*, an Italian-Brazilian newspaper founded in 1894, is telling. The newspaper began as a small four-page broadsheet. In 1910, its daily printing was 15,000 copies, second only to *O Estado de S. Paulo* with 20,000. By 1915, when the Italian-descended population of the city of São Paulo was around 150,000 people (about thirty-five percent of the population), *Fanfulla* had twelve pages and a circulation of 35,000, making it the second-largest newspaper in São Paulo State. *Fanfulla*'s circulation remained generally consistent, even as it published more of its articles in Portuguese, its presses falling silent only in the mid-1960s.

Fanfulla's approach to news speaks to numerous aspects of the immigrant experience. As with most ethnic newspapers in the Americas, its language changed over time, from Italian to a mixture of Italian with Brazilian words, to Portuguese. From its inception, advertisements were in Portuguese and Italian. This suggests that non-Italian Brazilians saw immigrants as part of a national market using the dominant language. This phenomenon took place not only because Italian and Portuguese are both Romance languages and are somewhat mutually intelligible. The same was true for Brazil's presses in the Japanese, Yiddish, and Arabic languages. Advertisements helped immigrants retain aspects of their premigratory culture by promoting "Italian" products and introduced national foods, clothing, and entertainment that helped

---

[12] Valentim Angelo Lazzarotto, *Pobres Construtores de Riqueza: Absorção da Mão-de-obra e Expansão Industrial na Metalúrgica Abramo Eberle, 1905–1970* (Caxias do Sul: Editora da Universidade de Caxias do Sul, 1981).

them become "Brazilian." Products like sewing machines, icemakers, and record players were part of a broader global desire for modernity. Advertisements for high-quality liquor and vacations spoke to economic and social ascension. *Fanfulla*'s advertisements largely sold the immigrant dream of fancy goods and leisure time. The editorial content, however, aimed at reality. Articles focused on plantation life and labor movements. Many reports spoke (though using different words) to ideas of diaspora and transnationalism. Italian life in Argentina and the prices of passages back to Europe were regular themes.

It is ironic that the same ethnic newspapers that taught immigrants to behave as Brazilians (for better and worse) became a focus of the expanding anti-immigrant sentiment in Brazil after World War I. Some in the dominant classes argued that Italian immigrants were transporting fascism to Brazil, a position mirrored in the mainstream press. In late 1928, a group of law students destroyed the fascist-leaning immigrant newspaper *Il Piccolo*. *Fanfulla*, while not having a fascist orientation, was also threatened. As the unrest spread, a thousand police were put on the streets of São Paulo and the cavalry entered the law school. Eventually, two hundred people were arrested. While fascism scared some in Brazil's dominant classes, it was often a mask for a growing xenophobia linked to immigrant arrival. An editorial in the Brazilian newspaper *Diário Nacional* summed up some of the attitudes:

This exultation of the sentiment of Italianism is taken to the extreme, to the point of leading to deplorable irritations between Italians and Brazilians serving as a base to a probable and fatal conflict whose consequences cannot be predicted.... It is in that conflict between Italians and Brazilians that we see an extreme danger in the fascist activity in Brazil.[13]

One key aspect of general immigrant life was competition between groups. A majority of immigrants believed that they represented a group superior to others, and interethnic relations often had a very hard edge. Expressions of Italian-Brazilian identity, like all the Euro-Brazilian identities that began emerging in the late nineteenth century, frequently denigrated Afro-Brazilians. *Fanfulla* often presented Italian immigrants as a step up from "typical" Brazilians and created new racial, ethnic, and

---

[13] Editorial from the *Diário Nacional*, quoted in Mauricio Font, *Coffee, Contention, and Change: In the Making of Modern Brazil* (New York: Blackwell, 1990), 211.

national categories. The literary scholar May Bletz points to a July 1923 *Fanfulla* article describing victims of a clash with laborers that categorized them as "Brazilian," "Italian-Brazilian," or "black."[14] Italian-Brazilian newspapers also attacked Japanese immigrants in 1908 as a "Yellow Peril," mirroring sentiments widely expressed in other venues.

A particularly visible area of antagonism was sports. European immigrants had been informally playing soccer by organizing teams around their region of origin, but the official story is that the sport came to Brazil in 1894 via a student named Charles Miller who had lived much of his life in England. This made soccer an "elite" sport, and its foreignness gave it a certain cachet. As a European import, *futebol* was imagined by many Brazilians to be modern. By playing soccer, immigrants could both assert their "better" Brazilianness and create ethnic cohesion.

The most famous Italian soccer clubs were Cruzeiro in Belo Horizonte, Palestra Itália Futebol Clube in Curitiba, and Società Sportiva Palestra Italia (today called Palmeiras) in São Paulo. Other teams represented German and Portuguese immigrants. By the 1920s, teams with names like Vasco da Gama, based in Rio de Janeiro and named after the famous Portuguese explorer, and Portuguesa in São Paulo had formed. The teams linked the sport with various aspects of the new national identities emerging in Europe. The Italian consulate hoped that nationalism would motivate immigrants to send remittances back to Italy, and it helped to found Palestra Itália. The Portuguese Chamber of Commerce funded and became the headquarters of the Portuguesa Futebol Clube in order to increase its local political power. These patterns were matched in big cities and small towns throughout Brazil. Four of the twelve teams in the 1921 São Paulo championship had an immigrant base: Palestra Itália, Sírio (which existed decades before the modern Syrian republic was created), Portuguesa-Mackenzie, and Germânia.

In the City: Portuguese Immigration

Italians initially seemed ideal workers to landowners. The immigrants' unwillingness to accept poor treatment, however, made them less desirable. They created new forms of ethnic, social, and economic life that changed Brazilian national identity even while emphasizing whiteness and racial hierarchies. Yet if Italians teach us largely about

---

[14] May E. Bletz, *Immigration and Acculturation in Brazil and Argentina, 1890–1929* (New York: Palgrave Macmillan, 2010), 134.

Table 4.2. *Portuguese Immigration*

Dates	Brazil	Argentina (arrivals/net)	USA
1880–1889	104,690	1,811/1,151	15,186
1890–1899	219,253	1,653/653	25,868
1900–1909	195,586	7,633/3,709	65,154
1910–1919	318,481	17,570/9,622	82,849
1920–1929	301,915	23,406/14,628	44,829
1930–1939	102,743	10,310/3,660	3,518
1940–1949	45,604	4,230/2,061	6,765
1950–1959	241,579	12,033/8,096	13,928
Totals	**1,529,851**	**78,646/43,580**	**257,737**

Sources: Brazil totals from Maria Stella Ferreira Levy, "O papel da migração internacional na evolução da população brasileira (1872 a 1972)]," *Revista da Saúde Pública*, supplement, 8 (1974), 49–90; Table I pp. 73–74; available from Brazilian Institute for Geography and Statistics at: http://www.ibge.gov.br/ibgeteen/povoamento/portugueses.html. Argentina totals from Marcelo J. Borges, *Chains of Gold: Portuguese Migration to Argentina in Transatlantic Perspective* (Leiden: Brill, 2009), table 1.2, p. 10. U.S. totals from *Historical Statistics of the United States Millennial Edition Online*, available at: http://hsus.cambridge.org/HSUSWeb/table/continuedownload.do?id=Ad106–120&changeSeries=false&isTopmostOn=true.

immigrants on the land, the Portuguese who came to Brazil teach us about urban immigration. Because Portuguese often intermarried with Afro-Brazilians, their experiences also show the ways in which the relationship between immigration and whiteness changed over time.

Brazil's former colonial status and linguistic and cultural affinities encouraged Portuguese immigration. Between 1808 and 1930, about 1.11 million arrived, with twenty-five times more immigrants entering between 1884 and 1930 (1,070,351) than between 1808 and 1881 (42,741). These numbers were equally important for Portugal, a small country with a huge emigrant stream. From the mid-nineteenth century forward, more than eighty percent of its emigrants went to Brazil, with another fifteen percent to the United States and just two percent to Argentina (see Table 4.2).

Portuguese immigrants made up the largest number of foreigners until the early twentieth century in two Brazilian cities: Rio de Janeiro, the federal capital, and Santos, the major port of the state of São Paulo. In 1890, Rio de Janeiro's population of 522,651 included 106,461 Portuguese, an overwhelming majority of the city's 155,202 foreign-born residents.[15] Portuguese immigrants sent a great deal of money home

---

[15] Brazil, *Directoria Geral de Estatística*, 1895: xii, xxiii, xxvii.

inasmuch as their concentration in urban areas presented more via-ble opportunities for economic advancement than work as colonos on plantations. Furthermore, immigrants tended to be single males who were not supporting families in Brazil, freeing up more money for remit-tances. One study of Italian, Spanish, and Portuguese emigrants shows that only the latter maintained high levels of remittances, even when emigratory flows decreased.[16]

The "Portuguese of Brazil," as the immigrants often called themselves and were called, illustrate an important facet of general immigrant life: class divisions. On the one side were wealthy immigrant merchants and property owners who were linked to the political system and who cre-ated influential ethnic organizations. Some of these institutions, like the Real Gabinete Português (the Royal Portuguese Academy, founded in 1837) and the Benificência Portuguesa (Portuguese Beneficence Society, founded in 1840), claimed to speak for all Luso-Brazilians, often agitating in favor of certain policies or candidates (*Luso* as a pre-fix means "Portuguese," after the Roman province of Lusitania, which roughly corresponds to modern Portugal.) The majority of the immi-grants, however, were small shopkeepers, clerks, and factory workers. They understood the benefits of ethnic solidarity and thus often let wealthier Portuguese speak for them publicly, just as Italians had done in the Longaretti case discussed in Chapter 3.

The combination of prominence and proletarianism often made Portuguese immigrants a focus of negative attention. In the 1830s, anti-Portuguese riots broke out with some frequency. By midcentury, small shop owners were targeted by others in the lower working class as exploiters who were profiting from the rise in food prices linked to Brazil's growing focus on export agriculture. Portuguese merchants, of course, rejected these claims, often insisting that they were smarter and worked harder than the Brazilians who bought from them.[17]

Stereotypes of the Portuguese flowed between positive and negative in the public sphere. Immigrants often came from rural Portugal but settled in Brazil's cities, disappointing those seeking immigrant farmers. They were Europeans but they often married Afro-Brazilians. Indeed,

[16] Rui Pedro Esteves and David Khoudour-Castéras, "A Fantastic Rain of Gold: European Migrants' Remittances and Balance of Payments Adjustment during the Gold Standard Period," *Journal of Economic History* 69: 4 (December 2009), 951–985.

[17] Gladys Sabina Ribeiro, *Mata Galegos: Os Portugueses e Os Conflitos de Trabalho na República Velha*. (São Paulo: Brasiliense, 1989).

comments about Portuguese immigrants often relied on tropes linked to those of African descent. One widespread saying was that "For the Portuguese immigrant, the black man, and the donkey, three p's: bread (*pão*) to eat, clothes (*pano*) to wear, and a stick (*pau*) to work with."[18] The comparison of Portuguese immigrants with Afro-Brazilians led some politicians and intellectuals to see the newcomers as not really "white," as this 1870 newspaper editorial shows:

> Even if there is a difference in their physical appearance, it is often apparent that the African is superior to the Portuguese in the morality of their actions.... The African, even of the low level, works in our fields.... The Portuguese destroy our industry and annihilate our commerce. The Africans who came here frequently were the children of families of some status, because the barbarous custom of making prisoners of war into slaves continues [in Africa]. The Portuguese [who immigrate to Brazil] are police suspects, street criminals, gang bosses [and] counterfeiters; "galegos" ["foreigners"] who are just like what we call lazy blacks.[19]

By the late nineteenth century, Portuguese were often described by elites and masses as both white and nonwhite, as both Brazilian and foreign. Aluísio Azevedo's widely read 1890 novel O Cortiço [The slum] made this clear. The story takes place in the 1870s and tells of three Portuguese immigrants struggling to make it in a poor Rio de Janeiro neighborhood (the Portuguese word is cortiço). Much of the action takes place between immigrants and Brazilians of African descent, both slave and free.

Azevedo was an amateur ethnographer and thought of O Cortiço as true fiction.[20] João Carlos de Medeiros Pardal Mallet, a journalist and member of the Brazilian Academy of Letters, wrote about Azevedo's "fieldwork" disguised as a slum dweller: "The original notes for O Cortiço were collected in my company in 1884, in excursions to 'study habits'

---

[18] Antonio Cândido, *O Discurso e a Cidade* (São Paulo: Duas Cidades, 1993), 132–133.

[19] *O Povo*, 18 February 1849, quoted in Luiz Felipe Alencastro, and Maria Luiza Renaux, "Caras e modos dos migrantes e imigrantes," *História da vida privada no Brasil*, Vol. II: *Império: A Corte e a Modernidade Nacional*, ed. Fernando Novais (São Paulo: Companhia de Letras, 1997), 292–335; p. 310.

[20] Amy Chazkel, "The Crônica, the City, and the Invention of the Underworld: Rio de Janeiro, 1889–1922," *Estudios Interdisciplinarios de América Latina y el Caribe*, 12: 1 (2001), 79–105.

in which we disguised ourselves in lower class clothing; clogs without socks, old denim pants, shirts with rolled up sleeves, paper hats and pipes in our mouths."[21]

O Cortiço suggests that Portuguese (and other) immigrants could never become the kind of "Brazilians" that Azevedo admired. Throughout the novel, immigrant characters were objects of mockery. A shrimp peddler from China acted like a child while a Jewish character is described as an ugly cheapskate.[22] Immigration and exploitation were linked through the main character of João Romão. This Portuguese immigrant lived with a former slave and used her income from a small store to help expand and profit from the slum. Romão was an exploiter in every way:

> João Romão never took a day off, nor did he attend mass on Sundays. Everything from his tavern and Bertoleza's [his companion, a freed slave] stand went straight into his strongbox and whence to the bank. Their savings grew so fast that when some land behind the tavern was put up for auction, he bought it and immediately set to work building three two-room houses.
>
> What prodigies of cunning and frugality he realized in their construction! He was his own bricklayer; he mixed and carried mortar; he cut the stone himself – stone he and Bertoleza stole from the quarry at night, just as he robbed all the nearby construction sites.
>
> Those robberies, painstakingly planned, were always successful.[23]

As the number of Portuguese immigrants grew in the late nineteenth century, the stereotypes expanded. Unlike many other immigrants, they were not subsidized and thus had a higher level of mobility and freedom of action than those bound by labor contracts. This frequently caused resentment among the working and middle classes and anti-Portuguese sentiment became an important aspect of Brazilian national identity. The so-called Revolta da Armada (Naval Revolt) in September 1893 against

---

[21] Pardal Mallet, "O Cortiço," *Gazeta de Notícias*, May 25, 1890.

[22] Aluísio Azevedo, *The Slum: A Novel*, translated from the Portuguese by David Rosenthal (New York: Oxford University Press, 2000), 70, 47. An analysis of immigration and whiteness in the novel can be found in Bletz, *Immigration and Acculturation in Brazil and Argentina*, pp. 29–44.

[23] Azevedo, *The Slum*, p. 4.

Brazil's second president, Marshal Floriano Peixoto, brought these negative sentiments to politics. While the motives for the attempted coup had nothing to do with immigration, Peixoto claimed that the perpetrators wanted to return Brazil to colonial status under the Portuguese king. Another strategy used by Peixoto and his allies was to characterize the revolt as "cosmopolitan" since this was the word used by many Luso-Brazilians to suggest that they had a level of sophistication, both culturally and economically, that other Brazilians did not. Peixoto and his supporters even spread rumors that Portuguese merchants were financing the rebellion, although there is no evidence to support this claim.

The Jacobins, an anti-immigrant movement that grew in influence at the time of the attempted coup, supported Peixoto's Luso-phobic positions. Members of the group came from a range of economic classes and advocated a strong central regime. The Jacobins focused most of their wrath on "galegos," as they called Portuguese and other immigrants. Like many of Peixoto's supporters, they used the Naval Revolt to shift blame for inflation and rising food prices away from the government and toward the Portuguese of all classes. They blamed the rich for exploiting the national economy and the lower middle class for exploiting the poor. When the Naval Revolt ended in March 1894, the insurgents fled to two Portuguese ships that were by chance anchored in the Rio de Janeiro harbor. When the ship's captain refused to hand over the rebels, Marshal Peixoto broke diplomatic relations with Portugal, further increasing anger at immigrants.

Portuguese immigrants were and are often linked in the popular imagination to the city of Rio de Janeiro. Yet they were also small farmers in the Northeast and factory workers in the southern and south-central regions. Like other immigrants, they participated as labor activists with the result that a new ethnic slur, "Portuga," emerged in the nineteenth century. The O Jacobino newspaper "endlessly spewed forth highly colored versions of the traditional image of the Portuguese as a greedy, rough, but hard-working burro who returned home to Portugal laden with ill-gotten gains from Brazil." One editorial story told of the biblical Adam's desire to speak with animals: Adam asked God for an interpreter and was given the Portuguese as "the animal who most resembles human beings."[24] Even today, the single most popular category of jokes

[24] June E. Hahner, "Jacobinos versus Galegos: Urban Radicals versus Portuguese Immigrants in Rio de Janeiro in the 1890s," *Journal of Interamerican Studies and World Affairs*, 18: 2 (May 1976), 125–154; p. 134.

told in the public sphere involves Portuguese. Punch lines often end with Brazilian national problems resulting from colonization by the Portuguese, rather than the Spanish, English, or French.

One response to the anti-Portuguese sentiments was the growth of Luso-Brazilian institutions that promoted traditions like dances, fado music, and food, starting in the late nineteenth century. Cinemas advertised films by focusing on their "Portugueseness," just as they used other identity tropes when targeting Italian, Jewish, or Japanese audiences. Typical was a pamphlet for the Portuguese film *The Condemned*, which insisted that viewers would remember why "Love is so different in Portugal" by watching this "Genuinely Portuguese Film."[25] (See Figure 4.2. A 1923 poster-flyer from the Cine Odeon in São Paulo.) Portugal's special relationship to Brazil was also important in the creation of "Lusotropicalism," developed by the Brazilian scholar Gilberto Freyre in the 1930s. Lusotropicalism was based largely on the claim (today considered false by many) that Portugal and Brazil were part of a uniquely race-blind multicultural and multicontinental community marked by miscegenation. While Freyre hailed what he considered the positive aspects of different racial and ethnic groups, he also firmly believed in racial hierarchies. As a result, his ideas became key for those who believed simultaneously that Brazilian national identity was one without racism *and* one that needed to be improved by immigrants.

The tight, yet awkward, relationship between Luso-Brazilian ethnicity and Brazilian national identity continued into the 1960s, during which time the Brazilian government was an ardent supporter of Portuguese colonialism in Africa. Then, in 1975, Brazil's dictatorship became the first government to recognize the Marxist MPLA (Movimento Popular de Libertação de Angola, the People's Movement for the Liberation of Angola) as the government of Angola. Three decades later, as Angola exploded in civil war, Brazilians took part in United Nations peace-keeping missions and Brazil accepted almost two thousand refugees.[26]

More recently, Brazilian has become the official linguistic standard for all of the world's Portuguese speakers. In Portugal, natives complain about the loss of "their" language and the growth in the number of Brazilian products (both cultural and material) consumed in the small European country. Today, anti-Brazilian prejudice in Portugal is as common as anti-Portuguese sentiment in Brazil.

---

[25] My thanks to Lena Suk for sharing this advertisement with me.
[26] Jerry Dávila, *Hotel Trópico: Brazil and the Challenge of African Decolonization, 1950–1980* (Durham, NC: Duke University Press, 2010), 244–245.

AZEVEDO & Company
SÃO PAULO

CINE ODEON

R. Domingos de Moraes 121
121 VILLA MARIANNA

Today – **Attention!!** Today

2–Shows–2

First Show at 7:15
Second Show at 9:15

We will present a film that speaks to the soul of Portuguese and Brazilians

A film that everyone should see because it shows how much this Cinema wants to serve its public

IT IS THE MOST PORTUGUSE FILM EVER PRODUCED

THE CONDEMNED

Come and see "The Condemned"

A drama that shows the "Rural Life of Portugal"

....

The only performance by the great actress VIRGINIA, of the wonderful actress Anna Pereira, of the great comic actor from the National Theater of Lisbon, Joaquim Costa, of the futurist painter Alma Negredos, of the lovely actress Maria Sampaio

....

In this film all Portuguese will have the chance to relive a part of their land and some of its customs. In that corner of Europe all Europeans together will have a chance to see the best in art, in history and in architecture.

A beautiful story of love! Of beauty! Of feelings and art!

Love is so Different in Portugal...

A GENUINELY PORTUGUESE FILM
Costumes, Clothing, and Regional Dances –
Portuguese Music

A Cinematic Happening
Sentimental love
Delicate love
Oh, how the Portuguese
Know love
Near or far anywhere
It is in my heart
It is my fate to love you
Fate it is

Come and See THE CONDEMNED

TO BRAZILIANS: A prologue, 7 acts and an epilogue taken from the celebrated show originally performed at the National Theater of Lisbon

....

The sound of Ave-Marias! Maria do Rosario, the beautiful country girl who enchants nobles and villagers.
The condemnation of an innocent who is sent by boat into exile

....

The imposing and traditional
Festa dos Tabeleiros

....

The most Portuguese film ever produced

Figure 4.2. A 1923 poster-flyer from the Cine Odeon in São Paulo aimed at immigrants and their children.

Source: Cine Caixa 14, Grupo Cinemas 24, Arquivo Histórico Municipal Washington Luís, January 30, 1923, Processo number 2009-0.115.821-2. Courtesy of Lena Suk.

Unexpected Catholics: Spanish Immigration

Portuguese immigrants represented Brazil's colonial foundation, a challenge to the desires of landowners and politicians to use immigrants as rural workers, and a confusing case of racial identity. At the same time, they were indisputable building blocks in postcolonial Brazilian national identity. Yet the Portuguese were not the only Iberian immigrants to Brazil; Spaniards arrived, too, although they were not part of the immigration plan, in the sense that most elites expected correctly that the majority would settle in Spanish America. The surprise that any Spaniards at all immigrated to Brazil is made clear in the Brazilian use of the term "galego" as slang for foreigners, with no clear national target. What a difference from the use of the same term in the Spanish Americas and Spain, where it frequently meant the natives of the Spanish Galicia region and their language.

Spanish immigrants had experiences more like those of the Italians and Japanese than of the Portuguese. They were also less visible than the smaller groups of Japanese, Germans, or European Jews. Indeed, the numbers of Spanish ethnic institutions like newspapers, cultural centers, or restaurants were quite low. High rates of intermarriage between Spanish immigrants and Brazilians or other immigrants reinforced low visibility.

As we have seen repeatedly, immigration and emigration are two sides of the same coin. Between 1882 and 1947, about five million people emigrated from Spain, with movement highly concentrated between 1900 and 1924. Almost four million of the emigrants returned to Spain, and the numbers of permanent settlers are likely in the 750,000 range for Argentina and the 300,000 range for Cuba, with around 300,000 others divided almost equally between Brazil and the United States. The Latin American totals show the largest groups in Argentina (thirty-six percent), Cuba (twenty-five percent) and Brazil (twelve percent) (see Table 4.3 for gross immigration totals).

Spaniards often lived in rural poverty in their homelands and were "sold" on Brazil through aggressive propaganda campaigns. For the struggling owners of tiny plots in Galicia, or for rural sharecroppers in Andalucía, the sales pitches and offers of free passage were attractive. Spanish emigrants to Brazil were poorer than those who went to other countries, and many came from the region near Málaga where Brazil established a recruiting office in 1896.

Spaniards were more likely than Italians or Portuguese to arrive with agricultural experience, and they settled overwhelmingly on the

Table 4.3. *Spanish Immigration (gross)*

Dates	Brazil	Argentina	USA
1871–1880	4,667	24,706	5,266
1881–1890	40,799	134,492	4,419
1891–1900	157,119	73,551	8,726
1901–1910	104,496	488,174	27,395
1911–1920	169,994	181,478	68,611
1921–1930	76,013	232,637	28,958
1931–1940	9,937	11,286	3,258
1941–1950	8,101	110,899	2,898
1951–1960	98,457	98,801	7,894
1961–1970	21,281	9,514	44,659
Total	690,864	1,380,140	202,624

Sources: Brazil totals from Maria Stella Ferreira Levy. "O papel da migração internacional na evolução da população brasileira (1872 a 1972)]," *Revista da Saúde Pública*, supplement, 8 (1974), 49–90; Table 1, pp. 73–74. Argentina totals from R. A. Gomez, "Spanish Immigration to the United States," *The Americas*, 19: 1 (July 1962), 59–78, and Hebert Klein, *A Imigração Espanhola no Brasil* (São Paulo: Editora Sumaré, 1994), Table 2.2, p. 37. U.S. totals from *Historical Statistics of the United States Millennial Edition Online*, available at: http://hsus.cambridge.org/HSUSWeb/table/continuedownload.do?id=Ad106–120&changeSeries=false&isTopmostOn=true.

coffee plantations in São Paulo. In fact, between 1904 and 1915, more Spaniards arrived than Italians, and of the more than one hundred thousand who passed through São Paulo's Hospedaria dos Imigrantes in those years, eighty-five percent came with subsidized passages. They were primarily farmers, and the low index of urban residence was similar to that of the Japanese, with rural placements of almost ninety percent through the 1940s. Like Middle Easterners, Spanish immigrants to Brazil and the rest of the Americas had high levels of return to the home country. Like Middle Easterners and Japanese, Spaniards settled heavily in São Paulo State.

Spanish immigrants fit official Brazilian desires by being more likely than other European immigrants to arrive in family units. The percentage of women and children who came to Brazil was higher than in other countries in the Americas, with the number of children under fourteen years of age double that of Argentina.[27] These large numbers of families with children were similar to the percentages among Japanese and European and Middle Eastern Jews. Families meant male/female ratios

[27] Hebert Klein, *A Imigração Espanhola no Brasil* (São Paulo: Editora Sumaré, 1994), 36–39.

different from the norm: Spaniards had the lowest male/female ratio among major immigrants groups, 112 men:110 women (the national average for immigrants in Brazil was 122:100).

Spaniards working on coffee plantations fared no better than other immigrants who were unaware of the implications of the labor contracts they had signed. The few Spanish-language newspapers in Brazil reported actively on the maltreatment, and these reports flowed back to Spain. In 1909, the Spanish government sent Inspector Gamboa Navarro across the Atlantic to evaluate the situation. Navarro accompanied a contingent of immigrants from Almeria as they traveled by train from Santos to the Hospedaria dos Imigrantes and then to the plantations. His report was extremely negative. The inspector complained that signed contracts were only "illusory" because they were not respected. He noted that the immigrants lived in tiny houses and slept on the floor until they were able to collect enough corn leaves to use as mattresses. Abuse of the workers was frequent, and he documented the assassination, without repercussions to the owner, of a Spanish worker on a coffee plantation.[28]

Navarro's experiences became part of a longer report by Spain's Emigration Council that concluded that ninety-eight percent of the Spaniards in Brazil would return if they could. With the publication of the report, proposals for a ban on subsidized Spanish emigration to Brazil began bubbling to the surface. Italy and Germany already had such policies, and Portugal was suggesting that its emigrants go to countries other than Brazil. On August 26, 1910, Spain's King Alfonso XIII issued a decree prohibiting subsidized emigration to Brazil.

Spaniards, like all others working on plantations, tried to get out of their contracts as quickly as possible. Some were able to buy small plots of land in semiurbanized areas of São Paulo's coffee zone, and as these plots grew in size and productivity, they competed with established plantations. In 1905, about 1.1 percent of the land in São Paulo's central coffee zone was owned by Spaniards, but more important than quantity was its value. In 1920, the value of Spanish-owned land was higher per hectare than that owned by Italian and Japanese immigrants and more than triple that of native-born Brazilians.

---

[28] Elda Evangelina González Martínez, "O Brasil como país de destino para os migrantes espanhóis," in Boris Fausto, *Fazer a América: A Imigração em Massa para a América Latina* (São Paulo: Editora da Universidade de São Paulo, 1999), 239–272; p. 253.

Spanish immigrants also moved into cities, where they were over-represented in leadership positions in socialist and anarcho-syndicalist movements. One famous case involved Spanish-born anarchist leader Manuel Campos. His deportation orders tell us much about both Spanish activism and lack of visibility. In 1908 he was deported as a *Portuguese* activist since the authorities, apparently, never considered that a Spanish immigrant might be involved in labor movements. The lack of awareness by the police meant that when Campos was arrested seven years later after sneaking back into Brazil, "he was again expelled, this time as a Spaniard!"[29] Spanish immigrants were also involved in urban small business. Starting in the 1960s, Spanish restaurants, like Portuguese and Japanese ones, represented elegance, in contrast to the Italian cantina, which became so much a part of Brazilian middle-class life.

CONCLUSION

The experiences of Italian, Portuguese, and Spanish immigrants help us to understand many of the broad tropes of the immigrant experience in Brazil: poor treatment and labor activism, rural to urban migration, the creation of new ethnic identities via a commitment to whiteness, and new Brazilian national identities. Southern Europeans arrived in huge numbers and brought with them ideas about modernity, urbanization, labor, race, and ethnicity. Their European, Catholic background made them seem desirable to elites, even if the real immigrants often challenged that perception.

Stepping into one of Brazil's thousands of "Italian" cantinas today hammers home how different a European national identity is from a Euro-Brazilian one. Nothing in these restaurants is Italian in the contemporary national sense of the word, and eating in a cantina is not like having a meal in Italy. Yet everything reminds Brazilian patrons of an immigrant past and a national-identity present. Cantinas are often decorated with futebol team banners and shirts. In São Paulo, the centerpiece team is always Palmeiras (formerly the Palestra Italia). Other decorations are from teams in Venice and Rome and Florence. Together these images create Italo-Brazilians and Italy in Brazil. Nothing like

[29] Sheldon L. Maram, "Labor and the Left in Brazil, 1890–1921: A Movement Aborted," *Hispanic American Historical Review*, 57: 2 (May 1977), 254–272; p. 261.

this exists in the real Italy, where team allegiance is still city based and where it would be heretical to root for Milan while sitting in a Roman establishment.

Yet in Brazil, as elsewhere, immigration has an impact far beyond the generation that arrived from abroad. It was so for Southern European immigrants and for all the "Others" who began to fill the Brazilian imagination starting in the late nineteenth century. It is they who are the focus of the next two chapters.

APPENDIX

Document 4.1. *Report of an Italian consular official following a visit to an Italian immigrant settlement in Bahia, 1907*

In general the young people from Germany and England are educated and endowed with the necessary preparation for migration. They scatter across the world in search of new avenues through which to channel their country's commerce, creating new sources of prosperity and wealth. Italian emigrants, on the other hand, go with indifference to North or South America, Australia or Egypt. They go without support, without ideas and without means.

Humble by necessity, timid by ignorance, solely pushed by the desire to make a living, they stop speaking their native language and end up forgetting it. They do not bother to make their children learn [Italian] and they easily adopt the local customs, even the strangest and least hygienic. But this does not detract from their precious qualities of patient energy, of endurance to the physical suffering caused by these hostile climates. This emigration makes one think of the ways in which raw materials are exported before being transformed into new products.

The three or four thousand Italians scatted in the interior of the state of Bahia live in these kinds of moral and intellectual conditions. They make progress without ideals; they rarely ask for the assistance of the R(oyal) Consulate and they are, for the most part, virtually assimilated to the indigenous population due to the not infrequent unions that they form with local women.

Given this, the work of a Consular Agent is necessarily limited to purely administrative tasks. This writer tried, at a reception offered with expensive pomp by the Italian Charitable Society of Bahia, to convince its members that the most useful, the holiest expenditure which that society could have made, would have been to establish a school where the children of Italians could learn their own language and draw inspiration from the glories of the fatherland. [I told them] that I would draw the attention of the King's Government to such an initiative in order to obtain some aid. But my proposal seemed to generate wonder, rather than interest, and further solicitations came to nothing.

Source: Italy, Commissariato Generale dell'Emigrazione, *Emigrazione e Colonie. Raccolta di Rapporti dei RR. Agenti Diplomatici e Consolari*. Vol. III: *America; Parte I: Brasile* (Rome: Cooperativo Tipografica Manuzio, 1908), 15–16.

Document 4.2. *Police report on a violent encounter between a Brazilian mason and an Italian peddler, 1895*

Description of the Defendant

Name: Anastácio Cosme
Gender: Male   Age: 21 Years
Residence: Tietê   Nationality: Brazilian
Color: Black   Civil State: Single
Literate?: Yes   Profession: Mason
Length of residence in S. Carlos?: 12 or 13 years
Were you intoxicated at the time of the crime?: No

Interrogation of the Defendant

Date: May 30, 1895
Interviewer: Officer Philippe Ladeira de Faria

[Anastácio Cosme] responded that today, at 3:00 PM, he was working on Belém Street, when two Italian peddlers began walking on the sidewalk that he was repairing. Seeing that they were on the wet pavement, he said to one of them, named Jorge Muzzi, that he should not walk there because the stones had not set and if they shifted he could get hurt. The Italian turned to Anastácio Cosme and asked if he was a Judge. Anastácio Cosme responded that he was not a Judge but that Muzzi should not walk on the wet pavement as it would ruin the sidewalk. The Italian then said that Anastácio Cosme was not a Christian but was a black donkey. (The Italian also said) that if the sidewalk was ruined it was Cosme who would have to repair it and that one hundred men like Cosme did not scare him.

Anastácio Cosme then threatened the Italian with a piece of metal. The peddler started to put down his bags for a fight and as they hit the ground Cosme whacked the Italian who fell and then did not move....Some time later a person appeared saying the Italian was dead.... Anastácio Cosme turned himself in to authorities. He said that he did not have a feud with the Italian who he only knew vaguely and, when he hit him, there was no intension of killing him, only of scaring him.

Source: Fundação Pró-Memória de São Carlos, "Processos Criminais," box 286, number 37, 1895. My thanks to Karl Monsma for sharing this document.

CHAPTER FIVE

How Arabs Became Jews, 1880–1940

JUDEU: "a knowledgeable and ambitious businessman: an exploiter"
JUDIA: "a very white and pink-cheeked (i.e., does not become dark in the sun) woman, but without charm" (see definition for Alemoa, Chapter 2)
TURCO: "the same as Jew, with respect to business"
From Felisbelo da Silva (Police Investigator), *Dicionário de Gíria* [Dictionary of slang] (São Paulo: Editora Prelúdio, 1974), 69, 107.

Unexpected Immigrants

The previous chapter told one kind of immigrant story. Southern European Catholics, so desired from afar, became increasingly problematic for elites once they began to settle in Brazil. Politicians and the landowners they supported expected Italian, Spanish, and Portuguese immigrants to lead an easy transition from slave to wage labor and from a largely African-descended population to a Europeanized one. The immigrants, however, did not fulfill all those expectations. They were no more likely than slaves to be productive on plantations when poorly treated. Their ambitions for personal and communal success were often at odds with the exploitative labor conditions created by the planters who encouraged and often sponsored their entry. Tensions between immigrants and natives often exploded into violence. By the late 1920s, elite concerns about immigrant-led labor agitation were strong. A common characterization of the government approach was the phrase, often misattributed to President Washington Luís Pereira de Sousa (1926–1930), that the "the social question [i.e., the labor movement] is a matter for the police."[1]

The same forces – poverty, political upheaval, land pressures – propelling European Christians toward the Americas in the nineteenth and early twentieth centuries were felt in other places and among other groups. These included immigrants from the Middle East, for the most part but not exclusively Christian, and Jews, for the most part but not exclusively European. While contemporary images place Arabs and Jews in oppositional categories, we must be careful not to read the present into the past. A number of factors, some specific to Brazil, make it logical to examine them together. Both groups were unsubsidized and thus unexpected, challenging the elite's belief that immigration policy alone would create a new kind of Brazil. Furthermore, members of the Portuguese-descended elite linked Jews and Arabs for historical reasons. Jewish life had flourished in Iberia under Islamic rule (the eighth to twelfth centuries), and some influential Brazilians believed that Arab and Jewish "blood," for better and for worse, was a component of Portugal's, and thus Brazil's, national character. As a result, Arabs and Jews had a special place among the elite as both friend and enemy, exotically different yet somehow familiar.

Brazilian intellectuals focused on Arabs and Jews together as part of a broad nineteenth-century trend toward pseudoscientific interpretations of race. Teófilo Braga's influential *The Portuguese Fatherland: Territory and Race* (1894) argued that Mozarabs, Christians and Jews who adopted Muslim clothes and spoke Arabic in Al-Andalus (the Moorish name for their Iberian territories), were the product of the miscegenation of Roman-Goths, Arabs, and Jews. He insisted that Brazil's Portuguese colonizers were Semites and that the "Turanian" language/cultural group (which included all languages in Asia and Europe that were neither Semitic nor Aryan) linked Semites and America's indigenous peoples. For Braga and many other scholars, a biologically determined bond tied Portuguese colonizers to Tupí natives in Brazil.[2]

Other scholars claimed that the indigenous peoples of Brazil were a lost tribe of Israel or a lost tribe formed by Arab voyagers. One French crackpot theory accepted among many intellectuals in Brazil was that

---

[1] John French, *Drowning in Laws: Labor Law and Brazilian Political Culture* (Chapel Hill: University of North Carolina Press, 2004), Chapter 7.

[2] Teófilo Braga, *A Pátria Portugueza. O Território e a Raça* (Porto: Lello e Irmão, 1894), 283–293.

King Solomon was the "ancestor of the Syrians" and sailed the Amazon River making Quechua an offshoot of ancient Hebrew.[3] In the twentieth century, Brazilian national identity makers who looked to Portugal for self-understanding, like Gilberto Freyre or Luís da Câmara Cascudo, wrote fervently about the Arab and Jewish aspects of their own miscegenated Brazilian national identities.[4] In the twenty-first century, one of Brazil's most influential newspapers has suggested that Dom Pedro II's 1876 visit to Lebanon had a direct linkage to a (falsely) claimed population of eight million Brazilians of Middle Eastern descent.[5]

The Arab-Jewish-Portuguese-Mozarab-Tupí-Brazilian link settled deeply into the psyches of many learned Brazilians. It made real Arab and Jewish immigrants in the Republican-era both insiders (for their Judeo-Christian faith) and outsiders (while not "black," they were not considered "white"). Arabs and Jews met elite goals by succeeding economically, while infuriating the same elites by not working the land and seeming uninterested in blindly accepting Euro-Brazilian culture.

Religion is important to an understanding of Arab and Jewish settlement in Brazil. As we saw in Chapter 1, early-nineteenth-century immigration policy debates often revolved around a simple bipartite distinction between Catholic and non-Catholic Christians. Prior to the 1880s, virtually every non-Catholic immigrant was considered to be a white, European Protestant. As hundreds of thousands of unexpected Jewish and Arab immigrants arrived, policymakers pondered the kind of future Brazilians and Brazil that they would produce.

Scholars of immigration seem perplexed at Arab and Jewish arrivals, usually mentioning the groups only in passing. One reason is the lack of clear documentation. Many Middle Eastern immigrants (Christian,

---

[3] Vicomte Enrique Onffroy de Thoron, *Voyages des flottes de Salomon et d'Hiram en Amerique: Position geographique de Parvaim, Ophir & Tarschisch* (Paris: Imp. G. Towne, 1868). Viriato Correia, "O Rei Salomão no Rio Amazonas," in Salomão Jorge, *Album da Colônia Sírio Libanesa* (São Paulo: Sociedade Impressora Brasileira, 1948), 471–479. As we will see in Chapter 6, Japanese immigrants were not to be outdone, and in the 1930s, some intellectuals asserted that Brazil's indigenous people were a lost tribe of Asians.

[4] Gilberto Freyre, *The Masters and the Slaves: A Study in the Development of Brazilian Civilization*, 2d English-language ed., trans. Samuel Putnam (Berkeley: University of California Press, 1986), 208–220. Luís da Câmara Cascudo, *Mouros, Franceses e Judeus (Três Presenças no Brasil)* (Rio de Janeiro: Editora Letras e Artes, 1967), 17–52.

[5] "Exposição mostra tour de D. Pedro pelo Líbano," *O Estado de S. Paulo*, 24 November 2011.

Muslim, and Jew) entered Brazil as part of a broad category called *Turco* ("Turk" – referring to those with travel papers issued by the Ottoman Empire). European Jews arrived as nationals of many countries and were often recorded at the ports only as "non-Catholic." A second reason is that scholars who link the size of an immigrant group with its importance often ignore Jews and Arabs because their numbers were smaller than those of Italians, Portuguese, or Spaniards. Finally, scholars often wrongly imagine Jews and Arabs to be closed communities and thus outside of the parameters of Brazilian national identity. While this is untrue by almost any measure (marriage, education, residence), popular and elite language often defines Portuguese, Italians, and Spaniards as automatic Brazilians and Arabs and Jews as non-Brazilians.

This tendency to assume that some immigrants could never become Brazilians can be seen in the files of the Department of Political and Social Order (Departamento de Ordem Política e Social, or DOPS) a federal and state police force that existed from 1924 to 1983. DOPS officers spent much of their energy repressing subversives, including labor leaders, leftists, and political militants, groups that often included immigrants and their descendants. When the São Paulo DOPS files became public at the end of the twentieth century, researchers discovered that they were divided into two categories, one for "Brazilians" and another for "non-Brazilians." More remarkable was that the terms were not linked to citizenship. Rather, the DOPS marked those with Arab, Jewish, and Japanese names as "non-Brazilian," even if the person under investigation was a Brazilian citizen. The "Brazilian" category, on the other hand, was filled with noncitizen immigrants from Portugal, Italy, and Spain.

Arab Jews

While contemporary readers may think of Arabs and Jews in distinct categories, this is not historically the case. For centuries many Jews lived in Arab lands, and among the first non-Christians to immigrate voluntarily to Brazil were Moroccan Jews. The story begins with the outbreak of the Spanish-Moroccan War (1859–1860) when many Jews, especially those who were economically successful, began to wonder if their futures lay elsewhere. Emigration seemed a realistic option since Moroccan Jews were often multilingual; they spoke Arabic and Spanish for business, French and Hebrew at school, and Haquitia (a unique language based in both Hebrew and Moroccan Arabic) at home. During the war, a few hundred Moroccan Jewish families migrated to Brazil, primarily to Rio de Janeiro.

By the late nineteenth century, Jews were leaving Morocco in growing numbers. In the 1880s, ninety-five percent of the boys who completed their education at one of Morocco's Jewish schools were migrating to South America. About one thousand of them chose the state of Pará, in Brazil's Amazon region, where the rubber economy was booming and cities like Belém, at the mouth of the river, were filled with peddlers and small merchants. Brazil was also attractive to Moroccan Jews because naturalization certificates were fairly easy to obtain. Returning to their birthplaces as Brazilians meant that they were subject to Moroccan laws that gave special protection to foreigners. For nineteenth-century Moroccan Jews, Brazilian passports served the same roles that additional passports today hold for tens of thousands of Latin Americans who actively seek out second citizenships in order to increase their mobility (as we will see in the Epilogue).

Mimom Elbás was typical. He emigrated to Belém from Tangier at the end of 1892 and after a year moved to Rio de Janeiro. Six months later he was naturalized and returned to Morocco, leading the Brazilian consul in Tangier to complain that Elbás "does not know how to speak any language but Arabic which is typical of the Hebrews from the Eastern ports."[6] This complaint was the first of many by Brazilian diplomats unsure of how to treat new Brazilians who were not as desirable as white Europeans and North Americans.

By the first years of the twentieth century, there were more than six hundred naturalized Brazilians living in Morocco, all of whom looked to Brazil for protection, especially in times of crisis. Simon Nahmiash had moved to Pará in 1879 when he was twenty-three years old. Three years later he requested a naturalization certificate, claiming a "firm intention to continue residing in the Brazilian Empire and to adopt it as my fatherland." Nahmiash, however, did return to Tangier, Brazilian citizenship in hand. He set up an importing business and in 1901 became engaged in a legal dispute with a local Muslim merchant. He lost the case and was charged with contempt of court, an offense punishable by prison. As the police arrived to make an arrest, he raised the Brazilian

---

[6] José Daniel Colaco (consul) to Carlos de Carvalho (minister of foreign affairs), September 18, 1895, 02- RepartiçõesConsulares Brasileiras, Tangier – Ofícios – 1891–1895–265/1/11, Arquivo Histórico Itamarati, Rio de Janeiro (hereafter AHI-R).

flag over his home, but to no avail. Nahmiash immediately contacted the Brazilian consul, who was obligated to defend the Brazilian citizen and work for his release. The consul was annoyed and urged new policies with regard to naturalized citizens. In 1900, an informal rule allowed only Moroccans naturalized before 1880 to be considered Brazilians. In 1903, Brazil closed its diplomatic offices in Morocco so that they would not have to defend naturalized Brazilians. [7]

Moroccan Jewish migration to Brazil was not simply a legal matter. The primarily male migrants often married indigenous Amazonian women and a story is told of how those relationships were formalized:

> *The Jews arrived without women or rabbis. Many began relationships with indigenous women and wanted to marry, yet there was no rabbi among the immigrants to conduct conversion ceremonies. The leader of the immigrants appointed the most learned member of the group to teach all the fiancées about Judaism, emphasizing one principle – that there was only one God. The day of the marriage the bride-to-be was brought into a room blindfolded and told that a spoonful of molten gold would be put in her mouth. If she really believed that there was only one God, the gold would taste as sweet as honey. And every woman believed, and the gold always tasted like honey.*[8]

Today, Jewish tombs and small cemeteries can be found along the Amazon River. Local non-Jews often attribute special powers to the immigrants buried there and have turned them into contemporary worship sites. Most famous is the tomb of Rabbi Shalom Emmanuel Muyal, who died in 1910 and was buried in the São João Batista Municipal Cemetery in Manaus, today a city of two million. Reports of miracles taking place at his tomb can be found as early as 1930, and Rabbi Muyal is often called the "Santo Judeu Milagreiro de Manaus" (Holy Jewish Miracle Worker of Manaus). His tomb has become such an important part of local culture that in 1980, Jewish community leaders refused a request from his nephew for reburial in Israel.

FARMERS AND PEDDLERS

Morocco's Arab Jews were the first of many Jews and Arabs who immigrated to Brazil in the late nineteenth and early twentieth centuries.

[7] *Al-Shogreb-Al Aksa* (Tangier), 27 August 1902, in 02 – Repartições Consulares Brasileiras, Tangier – Ofícios – 1900–1925–265/1/13, AHI-R.
[8] Interview by author with Sr. J., Belém do Pará, April 13, 1994.

While most came independently, a small group of European Jews began to settle in South America via an organization created by Baron Maurice de Hirsch, a Bavarian-born philanthropist living in Brussels. Wanting both to help refugees and to ensure that Eastern Jews would not remain in Western Europe, he decided "to stake my wealth and intellectual powers ... to give a portion of my companions in faith the possibility of finding a new existence, primarily as farmers and also as artisans, in those lands where the laws and religious tolerance permit them to carry on the struggle for existence."[9] In 1891, the Baron founded the Jewish Colonization Association (Yidishe Kolonizatsye Gezelshaft – or ICA). In 1893, the colony of Moisesville, Argentina, was opened and boatloads of ICA-sponsored Jews arrived in the country. In early 1901, the organization began to investigate expansion into Brazil's southernmost state, Rio Grande do Sul, where local elites were eager for new European colonies alongside the nineteenth-century German ones.

Between 1904 and 1924, the ICA established two agricultural colonies on the frontier of Rio Grande do Sul. The Eastern European Jews who settled in Brazil never amounted to more than a few thousand people, but together they challenged elite images of Jews as a closed group, uninterested in becoming citizens of countries where they resided. The two farming colonies were the first step in the regular and organized migration of Jews to Brazil.

Rio Grande do Sul's politicians and large landowners were happy to support any European group that would work the land in frontier regions. A strong relationship thus developed between the ICA, committed to Jewish resettlement, and those who had been encouraging and subsidizing agricultural colonization for almost a century. When the state government decided to promote immigrant colonization at the St. Louis International Exhibition of 1904, the official English-language *Descriptive Memorial of the State of Rio Grande do Sul* singled out the Jewish colonies as examples of the positive recent results of colonization in the area.[10] (See Document 5.1: An image of Jewish immigrants, 1904, in the chapter Appendix.)

[9] Maurice de Hirsch, "My Views on Philanthropy," *North American Review* 153 (July 1889), 2.

[10] Eugenio Dahne, ed., *Descriptive Memorial of the State of Rio Grande do Sul, Brazil* (Porto Alegre: The Commercial Library, 1904), 29.

At the same time that Jewish farming colonies were being established in Rio Grande do Sul, Arab immigrants were settling in rural
Brazil. These Middle Easterners arrived not as farmers but primarily as part of a new small merchant class. Unlike the waves of Italian,
Spanish, and Portuguese immigrants who were actively pursued by
planters and politicians seeking to change Brazil's social composition
with cheap European labor, Syrians and Lebanese came on their own.
Thus, they had a different impact than did those sponsored by the government or its allies.

It is hard to say with precision how many Middle Easterners settled in Brazil. Changing national categories in the Middle East, as well
as modifications in the way that immigrant entries were counted by
the Brazilian government, means that statistics from different sources
rarely coincide. Entry statistics from the Brazilian government suggest
around 110,000 (see Table 5.1). French consular reports during the
1920s suggest almost twice that number, with 130,000 in the cities of
São Paulo and Santos, 20,000 in the state of Pará, 15,000 in the city of
Rio de Janeiro, 14,000 in the state of Rio Grande do Sul, and more than
12,000 in the state of Bahia.[11] A scholar working with emigration statistics from Lebanon and Syria for the period 1921–1926 came to a similar
conclusion, suggesting that almost 180,000 Middle Easterners were in
Brazil, compared to almost 200,000 in the United States, 110,000 in
Argentina and other significant populations in Mexico, Cuba, Canada,
and Venezuela.[12]

Middle Eastern immigrants rarely worked in agriculture. Rather, the
prototype of Arab economic integration in Brazil was peddling. Known
popularly as *mascates*, the peddlers often supplied household and dry
goods to colonos on the coffee plantations or to urban dwellers in the
lower socioeconomic classes. Legends about them abound. One of my
favorite unconfirmed stories is about a town called Marataízes in the
state of Espírito Santo, in the coastal center of Brazil. Today, Marataízes
is the second largest city in the region, with almost 35,000 residents,

[11] "Discriminação por nacionalidade dos imigrantes entrando no Brasil no período
1884–1939," RIC, 1: 3 (July 1940), 617–642; RIC, 1: (October 1940), 617–638.
Clark S. Knowlton, "Spatial and Social Mobility of the Syrians and Lebanese in
the City of São Paulo, Brazil," Ph.D. diss., Vanderbilt University, 1955, 58–59.
[12] Kohei Hashimoto, "Lebanese Population Movement, 1920–1939: Towards a
Study," Table A.1, in Albert Hourani and Nadim Shehadi, eds., *The Lebanese
in the World: A Century of Emigration* (London and New York: I. B. Tauris and
St. Martins Press, 1992), 89, 91.

Table 5.1. *Middle Eastern Immigration to Brazil, 1884–1939*

	1884–1893	1894–1903	1904–1913	1914–1923	1924–1933	1934–1939	Total
Algerians	*	*	*	*	1	0	1
Armenians	*	*	*	1	821	4	826
Egyptians	*	51	42	190	335	27	645
Iranians	*	*	*	12	107	10	129
Iraqis	*	*	*	*	10	0	10
Lebanese	*	*	*	*	3,853	1,321	5,174
Moroccans	*	192	31	35	47	23	328
Palestinians	*	*	*	*	611	66	677
Persians	*	*	*	*	374	9	383
Syrian	93	602	3,826	1,145	14,264	577	20,507
Turks	3	6,522	42,177	19,255	10,227	271	78,455
Total	**96**	**7,367**	**46,076**	**20,638**	**30,650**	**2,308**	**107,135**

Source: "Discriminação por nacionalidade dos imigrantes entrando no Brasil no período 1884–1939," *Revista de Imigração e Colonização*, 1: 3 (July 1940), 617–638.

but in the early twentieth century it was much smaller, according to the following legend:

There once was a group of peddlers who sold their wares in the interior of Espírito Santo, going from place to place by mule. One of the peddlers was named Aziz, and his wife (the colloquial Arabic word for "wife" is marat) *was considered the leader of the women who stayed behind as the men went out to sell their goods. These women went out every day to a certain place to wash clothes, and the town that grew up around that place came to be called Marataízes in honor of the "marat" of Aziz.*

The motives for emigration from the Middle East were as varied as were the reasons for the choice of Brazil over the United States or Argentina. As was the case with European Jewish and Christian emigrants, a combination of population pressures, economic dislocations, religious and political persecution, and an imagined better life abroad created the conditions for potential exit. Emigration agents traveled throughout the region, encouraging young men (one scholar suggests one-quarter of Lebanon's population by 1915) to leave.[13] Beginning

[13] Charles Issawi, "The Historical Background of Lebanese Emigration, 1800–1914," in Albert Hourani and Nadim Shehadi, eds. *The Lebanese in the World: A Century of Emigration* (London and New York: I.B. Tauris and St. Martins Press, 1992), pp. 13–31.

in the mid-nineteenth century, steamships regularly plied the oceans between the Middle East and Brazil (with stops in Europe) making it easy, and over time faster and cheaper, to migrate.

Although statistics for religious background are incomplete, most Lebanese and Syrians entering Brazil through the port of Santos between 1908 and 1941 were Melkite Christians or Marronite Catholics (sixty-five percent) or Greek Orthodox (twenty per cent of the total, but the majority of those who entered as "Syrians"). Another fifteen percent were Muslim.[14] These variations often led to confusion among Brazilians about the different ethnic categories in which Middle Easterners placed themselves. Most who entered before World War I had Ottoman passports and were called "Turcos," even though they were fleeing the Ottoman Empire. In Pará, Arabs were frequently referred to as "Jews" while in Ceará they were deemed "galegos" the general derogatory term for Southern Europeans discussed in Chapter 4. A widely repeated comment spoke to the confusion: Although newly arrived immigrants were "Turcos," a first steady job transformed them into "Syrians," and shop or factory ownership changed them into "Lebanese."

Peddlers also became a kind of postal service, delivering information between colonos, who were often prevented from leaving the plantations where they worked. As new rail lines opened throughout Brazil, the words *mascate* and *Turco* became synonymous, and many peddlers began to settle near the tracks and open small shops or factories. Syrian and Lebanese store or factory owners (about ten percent of the Middle Eastern immigrant population in Brazil in 1900) would sell piece goods or housewares on credit to other Middle Easterners to peddle. Personal relationships based largely on hometown of origin or extended family ties allowed Syrian and Lebanese peddlers to establish credit with shop and factory owners. This credit was then extended to clients, a radical innovation in a country that had only recently moved from slave to wage labor.

Rural peddlers used mules while those from urban areas carried their goods by hand (see Figure 5.1). Salt, cloth, and hats made up much of the stock. Since most plantation hands had little cash, bartering was common. Items like handmade goods, preserves, and dried agricultural

---

[14] "Entradas de imigrantes pelo porto de Santos, segundo a religião, 1908–1936," Secretaria da Agricultura, Indústria e Comércio, *Boletim da Directoria de Terras, Colonização e Imigração*, 1: 1 (October, 1937), 64; *Boletim do Serviço de Imigração e Colonização*, 2 (October, 1940), 155, and *Boletim do Serviço de Imigração e Colonização*, 4 (December, 1949), 11 and 53.

Mascate 1928

Figure 5.1. An immigrant peddler.
Source: Photo courtesy of the Arquivo Histórico Judaico Brasileiro, São Paulo, Brazil.

products were then resold in urban areas. Peddlers often grossed twice the average daily wage, and some began to invest their profits in the manufacturing sector. The early decades of the twentieth century saw Syrian and Lebanese immigrants move to urban areas where they often grouped their shops together in inexpensive neighborhoods, living on the upper floors of the buildings they owned or rented for shops or factories. These areas were often strategically located between markets and the railroad stations so that shoppers had to pass through them when returning home from work.

One of the paradoxes of elite and popular responses to immigrants (as we saw with the Portuguese) was that they were often accused of both stealing jobs and being lazy. An angry 1888 editorial in the newspaper *Mariannense* (Mariana, Minas Gerais) warned readers to be on the look-out for throngs of "Turkish vagabonds": "Lock the doors so that they do not infiltrate our organism [bringing] instead of strong blood, the evil virus of an indolent people." The Sociedade Central de Imigração's (see Chapter 3) newspaper *A Immigração* took the same position, applauding Alfredo d'Escragnolle Taunay for an anti-Arab speech in the Senate that argued for legislation to "impede the entrance of people whose only habits are vagrancy and laziness."[15] In 1908, an alderman in the city of Rio Preto (São Paulo State) tried to erase all traces of "foreign interference in public life" by proposing (unsuccessfully) that those who spoke Arabic within earshot of a Brazilian be fined on the spot.[16]

In spite of the racism, Arab immigrants often prospered. Extended families expanded and consolidated urban businesses, and new communal institutions sprang up. The Arabic-language press, like the Italian press discussed in Chapter 3, helped to maintain premigratory culture and to aid integration. Brazil's first Arabic newspaper was founded in the city of Campinas in November 1895, and another was founded less than six months later in Santos. By 1902, there were three different Arabic-language newspapers in São Paulo and two more in Rio de Janeiro. In 1914, fourteen different Arabic-language newspapers circulated in São Paulo, and one study noted the existence of ninety-five different Arabic newspapers and magazines in Brazil prior to 1933.[17] As with all immigrant newspapers, advertisements were often in Portuguese and helped to integrate Middle Easterners into both the language and culture of Brazil (see Figure 5.2).

By the early 1920s, Syrian and Lebanese immigrants and their descendants were heavily concentrated in small-scale textile production and sales and in the dry goods trade in most major Brazilian cities. As with European immigrants, many sent remittances home. The literary scholar Philip Hitti reports that forty-one percent of Lebanon's total income in the early 1900s came from remittances and that by the 1950s, virtually

---

[15] *A Immigração – Órgão da Sociedade Central da Immigração* (Rio de Janeiro), 5: 43 (March 1888), 3.
[16] A. Tavares de Almeida, *Oeste Paulista: A Experiência Etnográfica e Cultural* (Rio de Janeiro: Alba Editora, 1943), 171–173.
[17] Joseph L. Love, *São Paulo in the Brazilian Federation, 1889–1937* (Stanford, CA: Stanford University Press, 1980), 91.

Figure 5.2. The advertisement (for a shop selling silk) in *Al-Afkar* [Ideas] is typical of immigrant newspapers in Brazil in that the text is in both Portuguese and the premigratory language. My thanks to Dr. Nate Hofer for the translation of the Arabic.

every village had "a red-tile roofed house built by money from abroad."[18] Money was followed by people, and statistics from Santos show a high out-migration rate of almost 46 percent for Middle Easterners (43,596 entries and 19,951 exits of "Turcos" and "Syrios").[19] The high levels of Arab return mirror those of Spanish immigrants from Brazil and Italian golondrinas from Argentina. The Beirut neighborhood of Al-Sufi had its own "Avenida Brasil," and a priest visiting Lebanon in 1925 reported that the Brazilian national anthem was sung spontaneously in his honor.[20] A Brazilian journalist who visited the region in 1926 was stunned to discover that the *jogo do bicho* (a hugely popular and illegal game of chance that is widely played in Brazil to this day) was so popular among Middle Eastern returnees that the Rio de Janeiro results were wired to Beirut each evening.[21] In the mid-1930s, some seventy percent of the inhabitants of the Lebanese city of Zahle spoke some Portuguese.[22]

SETTLING IN CITIES

If Arab migration to Brazil was marked by return to the Middle East, Jewish entry was notable for its permanence. This was the result of a combination of push-and-pull factors. For most Jewish emigrants, return to Europe or the Middle East became increasingly dangerous over the course of the twentieth century. The upheavals created by the reconstitution of Poland in 1918 sent Jews fleeing in large numbers. The same was true in some Arab countries where Jews often found anticolonial movements unwelcoming. Brazil, on the other hand, seemed to have open arms throughout the 1920s. The economy was growing. There were few immigration restrictions and no official quotas. This was different than in the United States and Canada, which sought to limit

[18] Philip K. Hitti, *Lebanon in History: From the Earliest Times to the Present* (London: Macmillan and Company, 1957), 474–475.

[19] "Movimento migratório pelo porto do Santos, 1908–1936," *Boletim da Directoria de Terras, Colonização e Immigração*, 1: 1 (October, 1937), Table A-4, 54. After 1923, Turkish Jews made up a significant part of the emigration of "Turcos."

[20] "Como os brasileiros foram recebidos no Líbano – Uma admirável impressão do Padre José de Castro," in Amarilio Júnior, *As Vantagens da Immigração Syria no Brasil: Em Torno de uma Polêmica entre os Snrs. Herbert V. Levy e Salomão Jorge, no "Diário de São Paulo"* (Rio de Janeiro: Off. Gr. da S. A. A Noite, 1925), 135–156.

[21] *Brazilian-American*, 21 August 1926.

[22] Sadalla Amin Chanem, *Impressões de Viagem (Libano-Brasil)* (Nichteroy: Graphica Brasil, 1936), 24–25, 83.

Table 5.2. *Jewish and General Immigration to Brazil, 1872–1972*

Period	General	Jewish
1872–1879	176,337	500
1880–1889	448,622	500
1890–1899	1,198,327	1,000
1900–1909	622,407	5,000
1910–1919	815,453	5,000
1920–1929	846,647	30,316
1930–1939	332,768	22,452
1940–1949	114,085	8,512
1950–1959	583,068	15,243
1960–1969	197,587	4,258
1970–1972	15,558	450
1872–1972	**5,350,859**	**93,231**

Sources: Maria Stella Ferreira Levy, "O papel da migração internacional na evolução da população brasileira (1872–1972)," *Revista de Saúde Pública*, supplement, 8 (1974), 72. Jacob Lestschinsky, "Jewish Migrations, 1840–1956," *The Jews: Their History, Culture and Religion*, ed. Louis Finkelstein, 2 vols., 3d ed. (New York: Harper and Brothers, 1960), II: 1536–1596; p. 1554. Instituto Brasileiro de Geografia e Estatística, Censos demográficos de 1940, 1950, 1960, 1980, e 1991 (Rio de Janeiro: IBGE), various volumes. U. O. Schmelz and Sergio DellaPergola, "The Demography of Latin American Jewry," *American Jewish Year Book* (New York: The American Jewish Committee, 1985), 51–102; p. 74.

Jewish entry with highly restrictive quotas in the twenties. At around the same time Argentina began to issue visas to applicants only in their country of birth, meaning that Jewish refugees who had fled their places of birth in Europe could rarely make legal requests.

Between 1924 and 1934, Eastern European immigration to Brazil increased almost ten times to more than 93,000 people. By the mid-1920s, more than ten percent of the Jews emigrating from Europe chose Brazil as their destination, and by the early 1930s, the Jewish population of Brazil had approached 60,000. Jews made up forty-five to fifty percent of the new Eastern European arrivals (see Tables 5.2 and 5.3). They represented almost forty-two percent of all Poles who settled in Brazil between 1926 and 1937 and 77.7 percent between 1931 and 1935.[23]

The Eastern European Jews who arrived in Brazil after World War I settled primarily in the states of São Paulo, Rio Grande do Sul, Minas

[23] Jacob Lestschinsky, "National Groups in Polish Emigration." *Jewish Social Studies*, 5: 2 (April, 1943), 110–111.

Table 5.3. *Jewish Immigration to Brazil by Date and Country of Origin*

Country	1925–1929	1930–1934	1935–1939	1940–1942	Total
Poland	6,961	6,518	3,549	348	17,376
Germany	0	1,198	6,188	410	7,796
Other	2,595	2,389	1,961	848	7,793
Total	**9,556**	**10,105**	**11,698**	**1,606**	**32,695**

Sources: "Les juifs dans 1'histoire du Bresil," Rapport d'activite pendant la periods 1933–1943, HIAS-Brazil, folder 1, YIVO-NY. "Discriminação por nacionalidade dos imigrantes entrando no Brasil no Período 1884–1939," *Revista de Imigração e Colonização*, 1: 3 (July 1940), 617–638.

Gerais, and Rio de Janeiro. Like the success of the Middle Eastern immigrants, theirs came largely because they worked in peddling and textiles, and were *not* plantation workers. Since most Jews were refugees, they settled in urban areas where relief was most available, including everything from help with housing to small loans. Being a refugee also meant few remittances because entire extended families had fled. Extra money was reinvested locally, leading to higher family incomes and the ability to support communal institutions. Synagogues, schools, and youth groups sprang up quickly, leading still more Jewish immigrants to have confidence in a Brazilian future.

Most Jews arriving in Brazil in the 1920s came from Poland. Comprising a little over ten percent of Poland's population, Jews were relatively urbanized and concentrated occupationally in manufacturing and as tailors, mechanics, and shoemakers. About thirty-five percent of the Jews arriving in Brazil had no profession or salable skills and thus entered the life of the *clientelchik* (Brazilian Yiddish for "peddler"; the Brazilian Portuguese equivalent term, as noted previously, was *mascate*), an occupation that did not demand a large initial capital investment. Clientelchiks sold cloth, clothing, and sewing implements and often purchased goods wholesale from Syrian and Lebanese former peddlers who had become wholesalers. By the late 1930s, fifty-four percent of the industries in Luz, a São Paulo district with a high percentage of Jewish residents, were producing textiles.

One of the striking features of Jewish and Arab economic integration in interwar Brazil was ethnic banking and rotating credit. Ethnically based loan societies provided newcomers with the initial funds to purchase goods for peddling or to help open a small shop or factory to take advantage of a growing urban lower middle class with new consumption patterns. The economic interactions with Brazilians made Arabs and Jews stand out, and as Professor Everado Backheuser, a technical consultant to the National Council of Geography who studied immigration, explained, "Jews are Turks who sell on credit."[24]

RACISM AND REACTION

There were many similarities in the patterns of Arab and Jewish social and economic integration in Brazil. Peddling was common and often led to the capital accumulation needed to purchase a small shop or factory. This enabled immigrants to send for other family members and thus expand the business. These patterns also meant that Jews and Arabs were frequently concentrated in inexpensive neighborhoods, making them particularly visible to other urban dwellers. The combination of Arabs and Jews being unexpected, ascending economically, and concentrating residentially often led members of the elite to attack these immigrants together as "one of the causes of unemployment ... [who] frequently contribute to an increase in economic disorder and social insecurity."[25]

While there was little elite concern about the neighborhood concentrations of Christian European immigrants, areas with large numbers of Arabs and Jews caused more comment from the press, policymakers, and academics than would be expected given their modest numbers. One of the most widely read provocations came from the well-known cultural critic Guilherme de Almeida. In 1929, he wrote a series of eight satirical articles on his "impressions of our diverse foreign neighborhoods" for the mass circulation newspaper *O Estado de S. Paulo*. The articles about the Arab and Jewish neighborhoods were strikingly similar. Almeida's comments on a neighborhood with a high Jewish concentration dehumanized the immigrants with their focus on facial hair: "I found myself face to face with the first face [I saw] in the São Paulo ghetto. Face? Beard: beard and nose. The first Jew."[26] His article on a Middle Eastern neighborhood was entitled "The More Than Near East." In it, Arabs were not people but "mustaches, only mustaches.

---

[24] Everado Backheuser, "Comércio ambulante e ocupações de rua no Rio de Janeiro," *Revista Brasileira de Geografia*, 6: 1 (January-March 1944), 14.

[25] Decree 19.482, December 12, 1930, *Collecção da leis da República dos Estados Unidos do Brasil de 1930*, Vol. II: *Actos da Junta Governativa Provisória e do Governo Provisório (Outubro a Dezembro)* (Rio de Janeiro, 1931), 82.

[26] Guilherme de Almeida, "'Cosmópolis: O 'Ghetto,' *O Estado de S. Paulo*, 31 March 1929, 4.

Contemplative mustaches ... hopeful mustaches ... smoky mustaches ...
sonorous mustaches. Mustaches." A street of Syrian-Lebanese–owned
shops became a space where "wholesalers sell giant bundles from giant
plantations, with giant men with giant mustaches." The nearby residential neighborhood had "Mustaches, only mustaches." He mocked Arabs
with an image straight from elite Euro-Brazilian bar culture: "What's
the recipe for 'a Turk': Take the 25 de Março Street [a street with a high
concentration of Arab-owned businesses] cocktail shaker and put in a
Syrian, an Arab, an Armenian, a Persian, an Egyptian, a Kurd. Shake it
up really well and – boom – out comes a Turk."[27]

Brazilian stereotypes led Jews and Arabs to negotiate their Brazilian
national identities in similar ways, but ones very different from European
Christians. Community leaders often played on the elite belief that the
original Portuguese settlers and/or the indigenous people were in fact
Jewish or Arab. In doing this, they could claim that Brazilian national
identity had as much of a Jewish or Arab origin as a European or
African one. This strategy can be seen clearly during the 1922 centen-
nial of Brazilian independence, when leaders of the Arab community
decided to build a monument to the Syrian-Lebanese community of
Brazil.[28] The sculptor could have been a nobody, and the statue could
have been stuck at the end of a little street. But that is not what happened. Instead, wealthy Arab-Brazilians commissioned Ettore Ximenes,
a renowned Italian sculptor whose work was associated with Brazilian
nationalism, to build a monument that would be placed in São Paulo's
Dom Pedro II Park, the most prestigious government area in Brazil's
largest and most powerful city.

For everyone involved, a monument by Ximenes in the Dom Pedro II
Park meant success. Entitled *Amizade Sírio-Libanesa* ("Syrian-Lebanese
Friendship"), it was a fifty-foot tower of bronze and granite (see
Figure 5.3). The base was divided into four sections. Each of three sides
contained reliefs representing "Syrian" contributions to world culture:
the Phoenicians as pioneers of navigation, Haitam I's discovery of the
Canary Islands, and the teaching of the alphabet; the fourth side was
the "symbol of Syrian penetration in Brazil," represented by the "the

[27] Guilherme de Almeida, "Cosmópolis: O Oriente Mais Próximo," *O Estado de
S. Paulo*, 19 May 1929, 6.
[28] São Paulo, Prefeitura Municipal, *Catálago das Obras de Arte em Logradouros
Públicos de São Paulo: Regional Sé* (São Paulo: Dept. do Patrimônio Histórico,
1987), 39.

Figure 5.3. *Amizade Sírio-Libanesa*, São Paulo, 2011.
Source: Photographs by Aron Shavitt Lesser.

commerce [that has led to] great prosperity." The top of the monument
was composed of three life-sized figures. At the back stood a female figure representing the Brazilian Republic, "whose glory is the glory of the
Brazilian pátria"; in front of her a "pure Syrian maiden" offers a gift to
her "Brazilian brother," an indigenous warrior, "with the same love with
which she was welcomed upon arriving in this land blessed by God."[29]
The message was clear: Ancient Arab greatness changed the world,
allowing Brazil to be "discovered" and then prosper. By suggesting that
Arabs were Brazil's original colonizers, and by asserting that the three
figures at the top of the monument were siblings, leaders of the Syrian-
Lebanese community were suggesting that Brazilian national identity
was biologically and originally Arab.

The 1928 public dedication of *Amizade Sírio-Libanesa* was a huge
event. The ceremony celebrated "the traditional friendship that unites
the hardworking Syrian community to the Brazilian people," and
included a parade by two thousand soldiers and a speech by the mayor.
Basílio Jafet, a wealthy industrialist and president of the commission
that had raised funds for the statue, was given the honor of opening
the ceremony in the name of the president of Brazil. In a remarkable
display of collective ahistorical memory, the "Syrians and Brazilians" in
the crowd "exchanged expressions of the ancient friendship that unites
them."[30] Nagib Jafet, the vice president of the monument commission,
gave a keynote speech in which he asserted that the Phoenician was
"the father of the colonizers who came later, the Greek, the Roman,
the Portuguese, the Spaniard and the English." Thus, Jafet remade
Syrian and Lebanese immigrants and their descendants into Brazil's first
colonizers.

The story of the monument shows how leaders of the Middle
Eastern immigrant community used stereotypes to negotiate their
Brazilian national identity. The significance was not lost on activists
in the Afro-Brazilian community, who used the Arab example in their
own attempts to raise funds for a statue of Luiz Gama, an important
Afro-Brazilian leader.[31] Jews did the same, and this helps to explain why
Zionism and Arab nationalist movements were often accepted by elites
as part of their Brazilian ethnic identities. Albert Einstein visited Brazil

[29] Ettore Ximenes, quoted in *O Estado de S. Paulo*, 3 May 1928.
[30] *O Estado de S. Paulo*, 4 May 1928.
[31] Kim D. Butler, *Freedoms Given, Freedoms Won: Afro-Brazilians in Post-Abolition São
      Paulo and Salvador* (New Brunswick, NJ: Rutgers University Press, 1998), 100.

twice in the twenties to promote Zionism; Brazil's most noted scientists formed a welcoming committee and important journalists printed long interviews with the scholar.[32]

Zionist activity was matched by Arab nationalism. This was especially visible in the political work of the Sa'adih family of Greek Orthodox intellectuals from Lebanon. Dr. Khalil Sa'adih (a physician best known for editing the first English-Arabic dictionary in 1911), moved to Brazil in the late 1910s. There, he published *Al-Jarida*, a weekly newspaper, and the monthly *Al-Majallah*. Antun Sa'adih joined his father in São Paulo in 1920 (at the age of sixteen after spending a year in the United States) and started writing articles in favor of an independent Syrian state that he hoped would stretch through much of the Middle East. Following the 1925 "Great Revolt" against the French Mandate in Syria, Antun founded a nationalist organization while teaching Arabic language and literature at a Syrian-Brazilian school in São Paulo. His nationalist ideas took hold among many Arab émigrés in South America, and in 1929 Sa'adih returned to the Middle East. In 1932, he secretly founded the Syrian Social Nationalist Party in Beirut, and today he is remembered as the father of Syrian nationalism, much as Einstein is remembered for his strong Zionism.

RESTRICTION

In the mid-1920s, negative stereotypes about Jews and Arabs led politicians to begin to wonder if Brazilian immigration policies should emulate restrictions in place in Argentina, the United States, and many other American republics. Nativism reached a peak in the late twenties, when, in the midst of a presidential campaign, two economic crises hit Brazil. A bumper crop of coffee forced prices to decline and the New York Stock Exchange crashed at the end of October 1929. Coffee prices dropped to half of what they had been just a year before. Following the 1930 presidential election, the accusation of widespread fraud led the loser of the election, Getúlio Vargas, to stage a coup d'état that became known as the Revolution of 1930.

The new regime was as interested in immigration as the previous ones, but in some different ways. Now, the government and its supporters increasingly used the discussion of immigration to express nationalist and nativist positions. Many in the new regime were attracted to

[32] *A Noite* (Rio), 21 March 1925; *O Jornal* (Rio), 22 March 1925.

racist forms of national regeneration popular in Europe at the time and, thus, had ideological reasons for limiting foreign entry. These leanings dovetailed with the attitudes of a small but growing urban middle class that desired economic and social mobility without immigrant competition. As urban unemployment grew in the early 1930's, immigrants became easy scapegoats.

It was in this highly charged atmosphere that Brazilian politicians shifted their discourse on immigration and immigrants in dramatic ways between 1930 and 1935. Attacks on immigration became part of the government agenda, and old ideas about the "whitening" of Brazil were reenvisioned as federal policies aimed at "Brazilianization." Three aspects of the new legislation deserve particular attention. The first used the class of ship passage to the country to define one's legal status as tourist or immigrant, making all third-class passengers into immigrants who were now limited in entry. Second, the poor became officially undesirable since all needed to show proof of financial independence in order to enter Brazil with a third-class ticket. A third innovation was the creation of *cartas de chamada*. Chamadas, as they were generally known, were official forms that allowed residents of Brazil to "call" their relatives by providing them with an affidavit of support and a prepaid ticket. The chamada system functioned to increase bureaucratic hurdles inasmuch as the forms had to be approved by the police and then legalized by the Immigration Department of the Ministry of Labor, Industry and Commerce. Many people gave up "calling" relatives out of frustration. Those who persisted found that the information could be used by the police and the federal government for political reasons.

Foreign entry to Brazil was cut by more than half between 1930 and 1931, with the figure remaining below the 1930 mark until 1951. The shift from inclusionary to exclusionist meant that finding immigrants useful to Brazil's agricultural growth was no longer the priority. Rather, the main concern was that undesirable immigrant groups were to be identified and kept away. The rise of totalitarianism in Europe also contributed to the transformation of Brazil's intellectual discourse and policies on immigration. Intellectuals, diplomats, politicians, and military leaders closely tied to the Vargas regime often took fascist-leaning positions and began to lobby against the entry of "unassimilable ethnic elements," such as Jews, Arabs, and Japanese.

Immigration and assimilation featured prominently in the debates on a new constitution that began in 1933. Many in the government and dominant classes were committed to changing Brazil's national identity from within, even while maintaining racial hierarchies. The Constitution of 1934 thus reflected the xenophobia that had become widespread in urban Brazil. The document appealed to the same urban middle and working classes by guaranteeing free elections while centralizing and expanding the government's social and economic roles.

Immigration was an important part of the new constitution. An annual quota of two percent of the number from each nation who had arrived in the previous fifty years was fixed, and the national government now had total authority "to guarantee the ethnic integration and physical and civic capacity of the immigrant." Licensed businesses now needed a majority of native-born Brazilians on their boards of directors. Liberal professions were restricted to citizens or those who had been naturalized *and* had served in the Brazilian armed forces.[33]

For some elites, the Constitution of 1934 did not go far enough. In 1937 President Getúlio Vargas used the excuse that immigrants and overseas foreign forces were planning to take over Brazil to create an authoritarian regime called the *Estado Novo* ("New State"). In that same year a secret order banned "Semites" from entering Brazil, although both Arabs and Jews continued to do so because others in the dominant classes saw them as critical to Brazil's modernization both economically and culturally (see Figure 5.4). The Vargas regime also created a *brasilidade* ("Brazilianness") campaign that targeted immigrants over issues of national integration. All foreign-language newspapers were banned in 1941, a policy that hit hard at the active Yiddish, Arabic, and Japanese press. By the early 1940s, immigration to Brazil was only a trickle due to the outbreak of World War II. Even so, one of the remarkable ironies of the Estado Novo was that ethnic institutions thrived in Brazil, even as immigrants were increasingly prohibited from entry.

Soon after World War II ended, President Vargas was deposed in a military coup, democracy returned, and many of the antiforeigner laws were repealed. Jews and Arabs continued to be linked as a single group, but this time as one whose presence was critical to Brazil's international power. Arabs and Jews, in many ways, had become the "best" of all Brazilian immigrant groups (along with Japanese, as we will see in Chapter 6). An anecdote that has come down to us with the title "Getúlio and the Two Semites" makes this clear:[34]

---

[33] Constituição de 16 de Julho de 1934. Article 5, para. 19, g; Article 121, para. 6; Article 133; Article 136, para. a.

[34] Queiroz Júnior, *222 Anedotas de Getúlio Vargas: Anedotário Popular, Irreverente e Pitoresco, Getúlio no Inferno, Getúlio no Céu* (Rio de Janeiro, 1955), 179.

Figure 5.4. Jewish immigrants arriving in 1937 *after* the secret restrictions on "Semitic" entry.

Source: Photo courtesy of the Arquivo Histórico Judaico Brasileiro, São Paulo, Brazil.

One day in 1954, Federal Deputy Aziz Maron, the leader of Bahia's Partido Trabalhista Brasileiro, was talking to a journalist in the Press Room of the Palácio Tiradentes (Brazil's Presidential Palace). Suddenly President Getúlio Vargas appeared (after being overthrown as dictator in 1945, he was elected democratically as president in 1950). The reporter took the opportunity to ask Vargas if he had been wise to have Ricardo Jafet, a Brazilian of Lebanese descent and president of the Bank of Brazil, and Horácio Lafer, the son of European Jewish immigrants and minister of the interior, working together in two related and critical positions. What was it, Getúlio asked, that the journalist found so strange about Jafet and Lafer working together? The man responded, "But Your Excellency, an Arab and a Jew. They will be warring with each other constantly. You will have a real Palestine in your government."

"Don't get scared," counseled Getúlio. "In the end it's all the same. Both are Semites, Lafer and Jafet. Arabs and Jews fight for the largest booty and after that they understand each other."

This tale shows a linkage of Arabs and Jews on two counts. The first is expected. In the early 1950s, when this conversation purportedly took place, the partition of Palestine and the establishment of the State of Israel in 1948 had made Jews and Arabs seem like enemies for life. Yet the response of Vargas in the story is not one that hinged on contemporary battles in the Middle East. Rather, it shows the well-developed idea of Jews and Arabs as one race committed to Brazil, as members of a single people more similar than different, and Vargas wants them fighting in order to increase national "booty."

A Surprising Epilogue

Arabs and Jews were unexpected immigrants. They often faced discrimination and hardship, both as a matter of policy and of cultural expectations. Within two generations, however, many became members of Brazil's dominant classes in part because they arrived during a moment of industrialization and urbanization. Both groups had the advantage of not being plantation workers and not being considered black. Arabs and Jews were able to strategically manipulate ideas about race, for example, by changing their names, making money, and passing as "typical" Brazilians. Even so, members of both groups were, at different times, barred from entering Brazil.

A different scenario, however, took place in 1932 when the League of Nations began to expend considerable energy in helping twenty thousand Assyrian refugees leave Iraq. The Assyrians were Chaldean members of the Nestorian Christian Church who lived in a legally separate and semiautonomous community within the Ottoman Empire. Two British-led Assyrian battalions had fought Iraqi nationalists, and upon independence in 1932, the new Muslim-dominated regime refused citizenship to the Assyrians, making them refugees within their own country. In October of that year, a British colonization company proposed to settle the entire Assyrian population on an enormous plot of land in Paraná, some sixty kilometers from the city of Londrina in an area of Austrian, Czechoslovak, German, Italian, Japanese, and Polish immigrants.[35]

---

[35] "Protection of Minorities," Monthly Summary of the League of Nations, 14: 1 (January, 1934), 17; "Report by the Committee for the Settlement of the Assyrians of Iraq, Submitted to the Council on May 17th, 1934," League of Nations – Official Journal, 6: 1 (June, 1934), 545.

The Vargas regime identified a number of advantages to accepting the Assyrian refugees. The group's settlement would help populate a relatively deserted area in Paraná where rail lines were being laid. The Assyrians, religiously devout Christians arriving in family groups, also seemed to fit with the regime's desire to return to a more traditional society. Raúl do Rio Branco of Brazil's delegation in Geneva emphasized that they "are all Catholics ... headed by a patriarch recognized by the Holy See," repeating similar comments made by the British who boasted that the Assyrians had maintained their Christian religion in spite of "the fact that they have lived among somewhat lawless and turbulent people of an alien religion." Indeed, Rio Branco drew a sharp distinction between the "Christian" Assyrians and the majority of "Muslim fanatic[s]" who lived in Iraq.[36]

Over the next few years, Brazilian and League of Nations diplomats worked on the plan, eventually agreeing to transfer funds to the government to help with the settlement and to ensure that repatriation of the Assyrian refugees could take place. Yet when the plan became public, an uproar ensued in Brazil. The Vargas regime, which saw the scheme as a way of populating a frontier area at virtually no cost, became the target of nativists, who claimed that the Assyrians were unassimilable "nomads and Mohammedans."[37] News reports on the topic inflamed passions through the use of provocative headlines like "A grave danger to remove: You only have peace with an Assyrian after he dies" and "An Undesirable Immigration."[38] A letter to the minister of foreign affairs attacked the Assyrians as "semi-barbarians who will only disturb order and cause the Brazilian race to degenerate."[39]

Leading members of the Syrian-Lebanese community, rightly fearing that attacks on the Assyrians would carry over to all of Middle Eastern descent, often confirmed the charges in Arabic-language newspapers.

---

[36] Memo of Raúl P. do Rio Branco (Geneva) to Afrânio de Melo Franco, 20 November 20, 1933: 6(04).0034 Lata 401, maço 6048, AHI-R. Sterndalle Bennett to Lopez Olivan (president of Assyrian Committee of the League of Nations), April 6, 1934: FO371/17836, E2209/l/93, PRO-L.

[37] Military Attache Sackville to U.S. ambassador in Brazil, December 28, 1933: 832.5593/1, National Archives and Record Administration, Washington (hereafter NARA-W).

[38] *Correio da Manhã*, 28 March 1934; *Diário de Notícias*, 2 April 1934.

[39] Letter of the president of the Associação dos Agrônomos e Médico Veterinários do Paraná to minister of foreign affairs, March 1, 1934: 15/5 6(04).0034, Lata 401, maço 6048, AHI-R.

The official visa application label changed from the positive "Assyrian immigrants" to the much less desirable "Immigration of Refugees from Iraq" or "Assyrian Refugees from Iraq." The wording was critical since proponents of the plan had gone to great pains to distinguish between "fanatic" Iraqi Muslims and Christian Assyrians. Assyrian Christian immigrants were thus transformed into Iraqi Muslim refugees and eventually banned from entering Brazil.

The decision to ban Assyrians from settling in Brazil had a surprising precedent. A decade earlier, the Brazilian diplomatic corps had been thrown into turmoil when a group of United States citizens of African descent decided to apply for immigrant visas. According to Brazilian law, U.S. citizens had a legal right to enter and settle in Brazil. What Brazilian policymakers had never considered was that the legislation denying Africans (and Asians) immigration rights did not specifically prevent those in the African diaspora from settling. The legislation banning nonwhites from Brazil was written in geographic terms (African and Asian) that recognized neither that all blacks were not African nor that all Africans were not black.

Ironically, the development of a myth of racial democracy made Brazil appear a haven for just those blacks whom policymakers wished to exclude. This view was reinforced by numerous African Americans who visited Brazil in the early twentieth century but, because of their social status, did not experience the kind of segregation and open racism that they did in the United States. Perhaps the most famous African American to have had the mistaken impression that Brazil was a racial paradise was the intellectual and civil rights activist W. E. B. Du Bois. He used his newspaper, Crisis, to promote emigration for blacks after the Brazilian American Colonization Syndicate (BACS), a land-development company owned by a group of African Americans from Chicago, set out to purchase land and set up a colony in 1920 in Mato Grosso, a large state that borders Bolivia (see advertisement in Figure 5.5). The BACS mistakenly believed that the active Brazilian promotion of immigration did not have racial undertones. Its directors were unaware that Brazil's immigration legislation was meant to exclude all blacks, African and non-African.

Brazilian policymakers now had an unexpected problem on their hands: How to control the entry of potential immigrants of black African descent who were not African and not legally barred from entering Brazil. Unlike Arabs and Jews who had entered as Europeans or Turks and faced discrimination after arrival, African Americans, whom

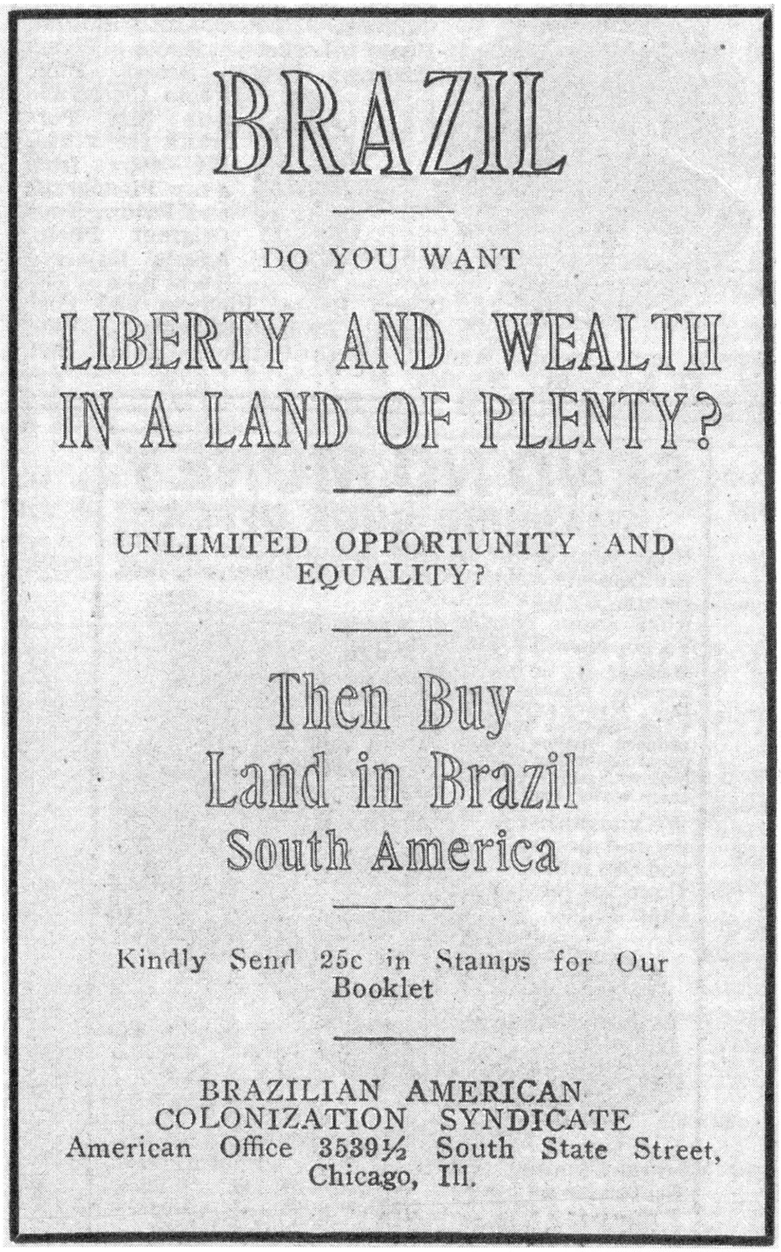

Figure 5.5. BACS advertisement from *Crisis* (March 1921).
Source: Courtesy of the Carter Woodson Papers, Manuscript, Archives, and Rare Book Library, Emory University.

policymakers considered racially undesirable, would not be allowed to set foot in Brazil. Thus, when the BACS visa applications arrived at Brazil's Ministry of Foreign Relations (known as the Itamarati) for approval, the foreign minister sent panicky instructions to the embassy in Washington, as well as to the consulates in the United States and elsewhere, not to give visas to "black emigrants destined to Brazil."[40] Concurrently, Brazilian policymakers wanted to project an image of racial harmony, which they believed was necessary in order to attract white immigrants and foreign investment. The Itamarati's solution was to reject the visas but give no reason for the refusal other than that it was "inconvenient."[41]

Refusing visas without explanation did not make the problem go away. The confidential instructions to consulates and embassies were read by employees in Brazilian and U.S. telegraphic agencies and then leaked to newspapers. This prompted the Brazilian American Colonization Syndicate to send lawyers to the embassy with a Brazil–United States treaty in hand, which seemed to suggest that all U.S. citizens had the right to immigrate. Now, the Itamarati had a complicated and embarrassing legal problem. The original framers of the 1890 ban on African and Asian immigrants never imagined that a group of influential, educated, U.S. citizens of African descent would try to set up a colony in Brazil. Furthermore, they never anticipated that a group of foreign (or, for that matter, Brazilian) blacks would know how to confront the government on its own terms. The Itamarati was forced into a legal and diplomatic corner.

The BACS's legal argument was based on a statement in the 1828 treaty that "the citizens and subjects of each may frequent all the coasts and countries of the other, and reside and trade there." In addition, the treaty specifically noted the statement's application "throughout their possessions and territories respectively, without distinction of persons or places."[42] This treaty had been reaffirmed a number of times after

---

[40] Telegram number 18, Azevedo Marques to Brazilian Embassy (Washington), March 15, 1921, in Adriano de Souza Quartin (Itamarati), "Emigração de Negros para o Brasil": Maço 9691/92 (629), p. 1, AHI-R.
[41] Teresa Meade and Gregory Alonso Pirio, "In Search of the Afro-American Eldorado: Attempts by North American Blacks to Enter Brazil in the 1920's," *Luso Brazilian Review*, 25: 1(1988), 85–110.
[42] "Treaty of Peace, Friendship, Commerce, and Navigation," December 12, 1828, Article 1, in Charles I. Bevans, 1970. *Treaties and Other International Agreements of the United States of America, 1776–1949*, Vol. 5 (Washington: Department of State Publications, 1970).

1828, and African Americans and all other U.S. citizens appeared to be entitled to settle in Brazil.

Not surprisingly, the Itamarati's legal team had a different interpretation. They asserted Brazil's right to make domestic decisions without foreign comment. The response was meant to put the U.S. government on the defensive by linking the Brazilian policy with existing racist immigration legislation in the United States. Pointing to the U.S. prohibition on Chinese immigration in the late nineteenth century, which became legal only after the United States had revoked a previously signed treaty with China, the Itamarati argued that its policy mirrored that of other American republics. Brazil's refusal to grant visas had thus simply followed a precedent set by the United States, a precedent that linked the exclusion of blacks to that of the Chinese (both undesirable immigrants, respectively, according to Brazilian and U.S. elites), without actually entering into a discussion of race.

The Itamarati also suggested that the Brazilian American Colonization Syndicate was politically radical and that its members would "bring subversive ideas" from the United States that might encourage the spread of black militancy in Brazil. The possibility of insurrection would be an accepted, and acceptable, explanation for the denial of the visas, or so the Brazilian government hoped. As one Itamarati legal memo put it, "it is not the condition of being Negro" that determined the ministry's refusal to grant visas since "happily we have no racial prejudice in our country." Rather, Brazil had the legal right and social responsibility to "lock our doors to all foreigners – white, black or yellow, who come to bring social problems."[43]

The Itamarati's diplomats and lawyers were wrong in thinking that denying visas would end African American attempts to settle in Brazil. In early April, 1922, Hélio Lobo, consul-general in New York, refused Clara L. Beasley a visa to visit Rio de Janeiro. Lobo initially told Beasley that her visa was rejected because "she could not explain why she was going to visit Brazil." The following day, according to the consul-general, she reappeared at the consulate with a "white, American man," claiming that she was his fiancée. Their joint application was rejected again, this time "because she should be treated as a woman of black color." Beasley contacted the National Association for the Advancement of Colored People (NAACP), and soon an uproar ensued.

[43] "Informação" of A. Alves de Fonseca, June 11, 1921: Maço 9691/92 (629), 2,4, AHI-R.

The NAACP was *much* more influential than the BACS. Brazilian diplomats were ordered to keep the restriction against granting visas to blacks confidential and to respond to questions "evasively." Since it was colonization, not tourism, that Brazilian diplomats feared, Consul Lobo suggested "the possibility of granting [tourist] visas, in sporadic cases when it was judged that this was the best thing to do."[44] In other words, the prohibition against the entry of African Americans would remain unless an applicant could potentially muster the political force to embarrass Brazil by exposing its racist policy. In these cases, tourist, not immigrant, visas would ensure that African Americans stayed only temporarily.

Throughout the 1920s, the Brazilian government continued to feel pressure with regard to its visa policy for U.S. citizens of African descent. In 1923, Robert S. Abbot, owner-publisher of *The Chicago Defender* visited Brazil. He created pandemonium when he told the press that Brazilian race relations were so advanced that he wanted to organize large-scale African American colonization. The Rio de Janeiro newspaper *O Paiz* roared, "We thank [him] for his kind comments about our people ... but this is an idea to be combated. It will be one more serious problem to be resolved in the future if the Negroes are permitted to immigrate to Brazil."[45] Diplomats feared a barrage of visa applications and made sure that most were rejected.

Abbot hoped that that the United States would force Brazil to interpret the treaty in a way favorable to African American emigrants. His efforts were unsuccessful, and as the complaints mounted, Du Bois decided to press the issue. In 1926, he wrote directly to President Washington Luís asking if "the government of Brazil discriminated between American citizens who wish to visit their country, and that no person of Negro descent is allowed to make such a visit." Du Bois pointed out that many African Americans were "authors, writers and scientists in America, and in business and commerce. Many of them travel each year; quite a number visit Europe and I am sure some would

---

[44] Helio Lobo to Azevedo Marques, April 19, 1922, Confidential Letter 80, "A prohibição de immigrantes de côr preta para o Brasil": Maço 9691/92 (629), 1, AHI-R.

[45] *O Paiz* (Rio de Janeiro), 11 May 1923; Micol Seigel, *Uneven Encounters: Making Race and Nation in Brazil and the United States* (Durham, NC: Duke University Press, 2009), Chapter 5.

like to see the West Indies and South America if they could be assured of the treatment usually accorded gentlemen and ladies."[46] Du Bois's letter never received a reply, and in early 1927, he made a formal complaint to the U.S. ambassador to Brazil, Edwin Morgan. The ambassador already knew that "not only colored persons of American citizenship but also all colored individuals regardless of nationality" would not be allowed to immigrate to Brazil.[47] Constant pressure from Du Bois and others did lead U.S. diplomats to question (very gently) Brazil's immigration policy. Even so, the restrictions remained. In 1928, the U.S. Department of State was untruthfully told by the Itamarati that "[y]ou may respond [to U.S. citizens of African descent] that the Brazilian immigration laws do not distinguish by color, blacks are selected [for immigration visas] subordinate to the general conditions which regulate immigration."[48] Although the U.S. government realized that this was not the truth, it accepted the Brazilian statement and passed it on to all who asked.

Brazilian immigration officials saw the attempts at African American colonization as a wake-up call. They quickly began to create new policies to prevent those deemed nonwhite from entering. In 1930, a group of five hundred already-contracted rural laborers from India were suddenly barred because, according to the National Population Department, Brazil "has always been opposed to the Hindu immigrant [who] is undesirable ... because of his physical incapacity, as well as other defects, that make assimilation difficult, or perhaps impossible."[49] That same year, the aforementioned Assyrians were banned, and one Brazilian diplomat urged Itamarati "not to give visas to Chinese or Negroes."[50]

Brazilian immigration policy was never straightforward. Sometimes secret policies were more important than official ones. At other times,

[46] W. E. B. Du Bois to Washington Luís, November 16, 1926: Maço 9691/92 (629), AHI-R.
[47] Telegram of Edwin V. Morgan to secretary of state, March 24, 1926, Records of the Foreign Service Posts of the Department of State, Brazil (Rio de Janeiro Embassy), 1926 (X), 855 (immigration), National Archives, Washington, D.C.
[48] Adriano de Souza Quartin (Itamarati), "Emigração de negros para o Brasil": Maço 9691/92 (629), 4, AHI-R.
[49] Octavio Pacheco to Cavalcante de Lacerda, March 10, 1932: Maço 29.625/29 (1291), AHI-R.
[50] Gabriel de Andrade, (Brazilian Consulate, Chicago) to Minister of Foreign Affairs Octavio Mangabeira, July 30, 1930: Maço 9691/92 (629), AHI-R.

as was the case between 1937 and 1940, secret prohibitions (like those on Semites) led to surprising results, like an increase in Jewish entry. One of the greatest challenges to the policies, and the Brazilian elite belief in remaking the country through immigration, emerged with Japanese immigrants who had started entering in 1908. They became one of Brazil's largest immigrant groups at a moment when the country seemed to be shutting its doors. As we will see in Chapter 6, a combination of racial reinterpretation, power politics, and capitalist desires would help to make Brazil the country with the globe's largest population of Japanese descent.

APPENDIX

Document 5.1. An image of Jewish immigrants, 1904

The first colonies were founded by German emigrants, introduced by the government, who conceded them free passages, pecuniary subsidies and many favors, and privileges. This system of offering free passages and subsidies was continued until 1895, when the public lands and colonization service was by the central government handed over to the States. The State-Government, finding that the old system led to innumerable abuses and useless waste of public funds, abandoned it and now every encouragement and protection is given to voluntary emigrants, but no more free passages and subsidies.

In the beginning the colonists were almost exclusively Germans. Then a number of Italians were introduced and in the last years also Spaniards, Portuguese, Austrians, Poles, Russians, Swedes, and other nations. The German and Italian element however predominates by far and forms the main population of the colony districts. They make the best colonists, and after the first few years of hard work, the lot of every new settler, they commence to enjoy comforts and prosperity that they never dreamt of in their native country.

Thus out of the 1,350,000 inhabitants of Rio Grande do Sul, more or less 400,000 may be taken to represent the foreign agricultural element. But notwithstanding that colonization has been going on now for some 60 or 70 years, there still exist extensive tracts of rich uninhabited forest lands, which are being surveyed and little by little, colonized, peopled and developed by the continuous efforts of the government, at the same time that many private undertakings have likewise and are still, continually acquiring tracts of unpopulated land from the government, to colonize on their own account. Thus only a few months ago the "Jewish Colonization Association", the concession of Baron Hirsch, bought a large tract of land on the railway between Santa Maria and Cruz Alta, and is now colonizing the same with Jewish families from south-eastern Europe.

Source: Descriptive Memorial of the State of Rio Grande do Sul, Brazil, organized by order of the president, Dr. Antônio Augusto Borges de Medeiros, for the 1904 St. Louis International Exhibition, p. 29.

CHAPTER SIX

ASIANIZING BRAZIL

NEW IMMIGRANTS AND NEW

IDENTITIES, 1900–1955

Figure 6.1. 1974 stamp celebrating the arrival of Japanese immigrants.

Avenida Paulista is São Paulo's Fifth Avenue. In the evening, tens of thousands of people walk up and down the sidewalks alongside the imposing boulevard. Many of them stop at the small carts that sell yak-isoba (a Japanese fried noodle dish) for a quick bite or a take-home dinner. The immigrants who sell the noodles speak Portuguese with a heavy accent, often blaming their linguistic mistakes on their recent arrival from Japan. There is, however, a hitch. These "Japanese" immigrants are from China. They are selling what they know as lo mein, a Chinese fried noodle dish. In Brazil, they have rebranded the dish after learning that that their sales, and their status, would improve if they insisted that they were Japanese.

Turning Japanese makes perfect sense in Brazil. Japanese-Brazilians (often referred to as Nikkei) and "Japanese" cultural references are

Table 6.1. *Japanese Emigration, 1899–1941*

Country of Destination	Number
United States	87,848
Hawaii	165,106
Canada	31,052
Brazil	188,209
The Philippines and Guam	53,120
Others	93,023
Total	618,358

Source: Koji Sasaki, "Between Emigration and Immigration: Japanese Emigrants to Brazil and Their Descendants in Japan," Yamashita et al., eds., *Transnational Migration in East Asia, Senri Ethnological Reports*, 77 (2008), 53–66.

ubiquitous, the result of a twentieth-century mass migration (as the chapter-opening Figure 6.1 can attest). Why did so many Japanese immigrants settle in a country seemingly committed to whiteness? How did the Japanese, and the 1.5 million people who today define themselves as Nikkei, come to be seen in elite and popular culture as model immigrants and Brazilians par excellence? The answers to these questions tell us much about shifts in Brazilian national identities.

JAPANESE EMIGRATION

The year 1868 marks one of the two beginnings of Japanese settlement in Brazil. The end of the Tokogawa Shogunate (1603–1868) led to a period of modernization known as *Meiji*, which would last until 1912. Industrialization and westernization became hallmarks of the Meiji era, and as the rural population grew, the peasants became hungry and restless. State-encouraged emigration was aimed at relieving pressure on the land while creating colonies abroad that would grow food for export back to Japan. Initially, the Japanese government aimed its emigrant streams at Asia and the United States, but soon policymakers looked toward other parts of the world (see Table 6.1). Brazil, with its agricultural economy and seemingly endless need for immigrants, was on the radar.

Brazilian elites were also interested in Japan. Attempts at Chinese contract labor had ended in failure. Fazendeiros and their political allies were unhappy with Europeans, who appeared to spend more time fighting for their rights than "whitening." Jews and Arabs seemed to be everywhere except on the plantations. With the Meiji Restoration, however, Japan had become a modern and powerful nation. National elites often promoted Japan as Asia's "white" country, and this piqued Brazilian interest. A diplomat who visited Japan in 1882 summed up the sentiments: "[T]hirty years ago Western geographers and publicists considered the Japanese a despicable race, [but now] this people is amazing us with their power to assimilate everything from European civilization in letters, in science, in art, in industry, and even in political institutions."[1]

In the early 1890s, on the heels of the establishment of the republic and the growing entry of European and Middle Eastern immigrants, the Brazilian and Japanese governments began negotiating an agreement. The Brazilian diplomat in charge, José de Costa Azevedo, extolled the ability of the Japanese "to receive the civilization and customs of civilized people ... [since they] have, in general and naturally, qualities never considered in the Chinese."[2] Henrique Lisboa, another statesman working on the project, was equally enamored: "When I think of the delicious fatherland of 'Mme. Chrysanthemum,' my imagination can only see it covered with colored and sweet flowers and inundated with happy rays of sunshine."[3]

In 1894, the Japanese diplomat Sho Nemoto arrived in Brazil to move negotiations forward. In a self-penned front-page article in the influential newspaper Correio Paulistano, he wrote of his "enchantment" with Brazil, where Japanese immigrants "could be perfectly settled" and where "we can improve our standard of living, buy property, educate our children, and live happily."[4] Japanese immigrants were presented as everything that Europeans were not: quiet, hardworking, and eager to become Brazilian. Within a year the treaty was signed, and in 1897 Brazil opened diplomatic offices in Tokyo and Yokohama. Lisboa, now the minister plenipotentiary, could barely contain his excitement:

During the two months I have been here, I am already convinced of the positive results that would come to Brazil by establishing a

[1] A. Jaceguay (Barão Artur da Motta Silva), O Dever do Momento: Carta a Joaquim Nabuco (Rio de Janeiro: Typ. Levzinger, 1887), 11–12.
[2] Relatório apresentado ao Presidente da República dos Estados Unidos do Brazil pelo Ministro do Estado das Relações Exteriores Carlos Augusto de Carvalho em Maio de 1895 (Rio de Janeiro: Imprensa Nacional, 1895), 44–45.
[3] Henrique C. R. Lisboa, Os Chins do Tetartos (Rio de Janeiro: Typographia da Empreza Democratica Editora, 1894), 149, 152.
[4] Correio Paulistano, 20 October 1894.

Figure 6.2. Brazilian postcard of the Kasato-Maru docked at the Port of Santos, 1908.

Japanese emigration stream and direct commercial relations.... I am certain that Japanese workers can contribute more to our development than various other cultures among us who don't use scientific and economic methods. The character of these people is unbeatable in terms of the desire to do perfect work.... Everything the Chinese do not have, the Japanese do: initiative and the spirit of invention and adaptation that allow them to do efficiently and with excellence what the Chinese cannot without an enormous loss of time and energy.[5]

THE IMMIGRANTS ARRIVE

On an early morning in mid-June 1908, the Kasato-Maru completed its fifty-one day, 12,500-mile journey from Japan. As the ship docked at the Brazilian port of Santos (see Figure 6.2), the first 781 members of what would become the largest Japanese-descent community outside

[5] Henrique Lisboa (Legation in Tokyo) to Dionisio E. de Castro Cerqueira (Itamarati), November 1, 1897: 01- Missões Diplomáticas Brasileiras, Tóquio – Ofícios – 1897–99 – 26 /232/2/1. Arquivo Histórico Itamarati, Rio de Janeiro [hereafter AHI-R].

of Japan began descending the gangplank.[6] The effects of Japan's self-promotion as a "white" country were clear. Many influential politicians and intellectuals treated the newcomers as non-Asians, in a hierarchic position equal to or above Europeans.[7]

São Paulo's inspector of agriculture, J. Amândio Sobral, met the immigrants as they disembarked. He was impressed that almost seventy percent of the colonists were literate and that "in flagrant contrast ... with our workers" did not seem poor. He was equally amazed that the immigrants wore "European clothing [that] had been purchased in Japan and made in Japanese factories." They had "combed hair that was perfectly in harmony with their ties." The living and eating quarters on the Kasato-Maru were in an "absolute state of cleanliness" and everyone had "clean clothes," "clean bodies," and carried kits with toothbrushes, hairbrushes, and razors, something that only the wealthiest Brazilians did when they traveled. "The race is very different, but it is not inferior," Sobral gushed.[8]

Many of the immigrants were equally pleased: a strange twist of fate put the docking during a festa junina celebration (an annual Brazilian festival associated with Saint Anthony, Saint John the Baptist, and Saint Peter), leading the newcomers to believe that the fireworks had been arranged in their honor.[9] Even in the early twenty-first century, the arrival of the Kasato-Maru is remembered as bringing important building blocks for modern Brazilian national identity. (See Document 6.1: A memory of the Kasato-Maru, 1994, in the chapter Appendix.)

Newcomer Japanese were citizens of a world power, and other immigrant groups paid attention. The antifascist Italian-Brazilian newspaper Fanfulla had three different reports in its edition following the arrival of the Kasato-Maru. One editorial worried that "we have already had the German Peril and the Italian one as well. Now it's the Yellow Peril." In a different article in the same issue, entitled

---

6   Secretaria da Agricultura – Diretoria de Terras, Colonização e Immigração, June 30, 1908. File: Wilson, Sons and Co. Ltd., no. 121, pp. 3–7. Setor Manuscritos – Secretaria da Agricultura – Requerimentos Diversos. Ano – 1908: Maço – 38, Caixa – 39, Ordem – 7255. Arquivo do Estado de São Paulo [hereafter AESP].

7   Correio da Manhã (Rio de Janeiro), 30 November 1908.

8   J. Amândio Sobral, "Os japonezes em S. Paulo," Correio Paulistano, 25 June 1908.

9   Teijiro Suzuki, secretary of the Hospedaria dos Imigrantes, quoted in Tomoo Handa, Memória de um Imigrante Japonês no Brasil (São Paulo: T. A. Queiroz/ Centro de Estudos Nipo-Brasileiros, 1980), 80.

"A Revelation," readers were told to "Be Calm" because the "most terrifying of the ancient fighters, and most fortunate of the modern one, the little Japanese," were in Brazil to grow new products, not compete with other immigrants.[10]

Federal Deputy Nestor Ascoli linked the 1905 Japanese military victory over the Russian Empire with Brazil's modernization: "[T]he small and ugly Japanese recently sneered and did what he had to do, beating the tall and formidable Russian. The Japanese is now a better element of progress than the Russian and other European peoples." According to Ascoli, the introduction of Japanese "blood" into the Brazilian racial mix "will have a better result with our national population than [the introduction of] black blood or that of any other nonwhite." By harping on the idea that "intellectually the Japanese is frighteningly superior," Ascoli was suggesting that Brazil would soon begin to match the production levels of Japanese industry.[11]

As we have seen repeatedly, immigrants rarely met the unrealistic expectations of the elites. This case was no different. Fazendeiros hoping for docile colonists found that poor treatment was no more acceptable to Japanese workers than to others. Newcomers who thought they would become rich felt tricked, and some remigrated to Argentina where salaries were higher. Some fled from plantations to urban areas in the states of Minas Gerais, Paraná, Rio de Janeiro, and São Paulo. Others moved into railroad construction, and Campo Grande, a large city near the Bolivian border, is still renowned for the size of its Okinawan-descended population (Okinawa is one of Japan's provinces, with a culture distinct from the rest of the country). Those immigrants came with the railroad in the early twentieth century, and Okinawa soba, a noodle dish, is marketed throughout the country as a typical western *Brazilian* meal.

Nineteen-year-old Riukiti Yamashiro was typical of the first arrivals from Japan. He emigrated from Okinawa in 1912, having learned about Brazil from neighbors whose family members had already emigrated. After spending a week at São Paulo's Hospedaria dos Imigrantes, Yamashiro, his wife, and fifteen other families were sent to a fazenda where they worked alongside Spanish immigrants. Only a few months later, Yamashiro and his friends left for the port city of Santos in hopes

---

[10] *Fanfulla* 19 June 1908.
[11] Nestor Ascoli, *A Immigração Japoneza na Baixada do Estado do Rio de Janeiro* (Rio de Janeiro: Edição da "Revista de lingua portuguesa," 1924), 22.

of earning more as dockworkers.[12] His experiences were summed up in a song popular among immigrants: "It was a lie when they said Brazil was good: the emigration company lied."[13] Another immigrant, Shuhei Uetsuka, wrote a *haiku* about early-twentieth-century plantation life:

Nightfall: in the shade I cry picking coffee
I think about the migrant that fled; starlight on dry meadow.[14]

A Different Kind of Colonization

Although the Japanese suffered like all other immigrants, they had a more powerful protector regime than most others. The Japanese government made sure that life on ships was well organized, with plenty of food and medical care on board. Children had a regular school schedule, while adults participated in gymnastics and morale boosting. Films were shown about what to expect on arrival (not unlike the films shown today on airplanes explaining how to pass through customs) and about life in the colonies.[15] One Japanese ship captain was so embarrassed that his crew did not help a passenger whose luggage was stolen at the port of Santos that he made a public apology.[16] What a difference from what had happened a century earlier when, as discussed in Chapter 2, a German ship captain executed passengers who had complained about his actions.

When Italian, Spanish or Portuguese workers were treated poorly, the best their governments could do was ban further subsidized exit. Japanese government officials, wanting to insure that immigrants

---

[12] Part of Riukiti Yamashiro's handwritten diary was translated into Portuguese by his son. José Yamashiro, *Trajetória de Duas Vidas: Uma História de Imigração e Integração* (São Paulo: Aliança Cultural Brasil-Japão/Centro de Estudos Nipo-Brasileiros, 1996), 20–31.

[13] Tomoo Handa, *O Imigrante Japonês: História de Sua Vida no Brasil* (São Paulo: T. A. Queiroz: Centro de Estudos Nipo-Brasileiros, 1987), 164.

[14] Masuji Kiyotani and José Yamashiro, "Os Imigrantes do *Kasato-Maru*," in Comissão de Elaboração da História dos 80 anos da Imigração Japonesa no Brasil, *Uma Epopéia Moderna: 80 anos da Imigração Japonesa no Brasil* (São Paulo: Editora Hucitec, 1992), 73. Portuguese translation from the Japanese in the original. The translation to English is from a free translation to Portuguese and does not attempt to follow the poetic style.

[15] L. H. Gourley to Secretary of State, March 3, 1927: 894.5632/2, National Archives and Records Administration, Washington [hereafter NARA-W].

[16] Notes of an interview by Hiroshi Saito with K. Nakagawa, October 10, 1953, Donald Pierson Papers (Box 8), Smathers Library, University of Florida.

remained in Brazil, took a very different approach. When a wage strike hit the powerful Prado family's Fazenda São Martinho in 1908, a Japanese diplomat personally handled the negotiations between owner and workers and arranged to move the strike leaders and their families to another plantation. When a government commission discovered that over fifty percent of all immigrants were fleeing plantations within a year of arrival, Japanese public–private firms worked with the São Paulo government to create Japanese-only colonies. These large plots were placed in regions considered unusable by Brazilian planters whose focus was on coffee and cotton. By 1917, large Japanese immigrant colonies in São Paulo and Paraná were growing new products, such as silk and fruit. In 1908, the rice crop in Brazil was not sufficient for national consumption, but fifteen years later it had become an export crop.

Foreign government–sponsored colonies were a new approach to rural settlement. On the Brazilian side, costly subsidization of laborers who often fled plantations was replaced by land grants in regions with little agricultural development. For the Japanese, state-directed colonies meant an end to headaches with landowners, who often acted as if abolition had never taken place. With a focus on settlement and production, the new colonies produced profits that flowed largely back to the immigrants, discouraging their return to Japan and encouraging more emigration as news of success in Brazil spread. This was markedly different from the general case on plantations where permanence seemed a sure path to poverty.

School systems were active in Japanese colonies where education for boys and girls was universal. The curriculums were modeled on Japanese imperial ones, and the government sent most of the printed materials. Schooling and reading helped the Brazilian-born children of immigrants move into dominant positions since educational opportunities and literacy were far from universal. A comparison of book imports from Italy and Japan highlights the differences. By the mid-1930s, the gross numbers of Japanese materials far exceeded those from Italy, the source of vastly larger numbers of immigrants.[17]

Newspapers were critical in establishing local identities for all immigrants and this was no different among the Japanese. The *Shûkan Nambei* [South American weekly], founded in January of 1916, was the first of three newspapers published for Japanese and Japanese-Brazilians,

---

[17] Laurence Hallewell, *Books in Brazil: A History of the Publishing Trade* (Metuchen, NJ: The Scarecrow Press, 1982), Table 40, 432.

eighty to ninety percent of whom lived in rural areas. The *Nippak Shinbun*, founded six months later, published three times a week and claimed a circulation of thirty thousand by the late 1920s. In 1929, the *Nippak Shinbun* also began to publish some pages in Portuguese for the growing number of Brazilian-born children who were unable to read Japanese. These newspapers often included translated information from Portuguese-language newspapers, providing a window on life in urban areas.

FIGHTING STEREOTYPES

Japanese immigrants and their descendants faced many of the same challenges as other groups, be they expected Southern European Catholics or unexpected Arabs and Jews. For every important intellectual and politician in favor of Japanese settlement there was one against. Dr. Arthur Neiva, the microbiologist who directed São Paulo's health services, believed that "if we look for a solution to the problem of the lack of labor with scientific care and an eye to the future of Brazil, we will see that the Oriental races are unassimilable ... and the Hindu and Japanese immigrants will create fatal ethnic cysts among us."[18]

Such attacks did not go without responses from the Japanese government. Diplomats wrote newspaper columns rejecting anti-Japanese claims. Internationally respected scholars traveled to Brazil to meet with members of the academic elite. Dr. Mikinosuke Miyajima, a specialist in infectious diseases, even invited the aforementioned Dr. Neiva and his wife to a fully paid study trip to visit the Kitasato Institute for Infectious Diseases in Tokyo. They were happy to accept the offer, and as a result, Neiva's language about Japanese immigrants changed significantly.[19]

In 1924, the number of Japanese entries to Brazil jumped to almost 5,000 per year, and in the next decade approximately 130,000 would arrive (see Table 6.2). In the decade after 1924, only Portuguese immigrants entered more frequently than Japanese, who themselves outnumbered Italian and German arrivals by about 2:1 and Spanish by

---

[18] Arthur Neiva, "Discurso na inauguração do Horto Oswaldo Cruz," São Paulo, 1918, cited in Vivaldo Coroacy, *O Perigo Japonês* (Rio de Janeiro: Jornal do Comércio, 1942), 140–141.

[19] M. Miyajima (Tokyo) to Arthur Neiva, November 11, 1919; S. Kitsato to Arthur Neiva, November 20, 1919. Papers of Artur Neiva [hereafter AN] 16.11.27, Centro de Pesquisa e Documentação de História Contemporânea do Brasil, Fundação Getúlio Vargas, Rio de Janeiro [hereafter CPDOC-RJ].

Table 6.2. *Japanese Immigration to Brazil, 1908–1941*

Years	Number
1908–1914	15,543
1915–1923	16,723
1924–1935	141,732
1936–1941	14,617
Total	188,615

Source: Hiroshi Saito, "Alguns aspectos da mobilidade dos Japoneses no Brasil," *Kobe Economic and Business Review 6th Annual Report* (1959), 49–59; p. 50.

about 2.5:1.[20] Japanese made up 2.3 percent of all immigrants to São Paulo in 1923, 4.0 in 1924, 8.7 in 1925, and 11.6 in 1928.

There are a number of factors that explain the dramatic increase in Japanese entry beginning in the midtwenties. One was United States immigration policy, culminating with the 1924 National Origins Act that closed the country's doors to most Asians. Brazilian interest in Japan's booming economy was equally important, and diplomats from both countries tied trade to migration. In early 1925, the Japanese Foreign Office sponsored an exhibition of *sixty tons* of Brazilian produce in Tokyo, including coffee, cocoa, cotton, iron, and steel, even as a similarly sized Japanese product shipment was being prepared for show in Brazil.

Emigration was usually carried out by the public–private Kaigai Kogyo Kabushiki Kaisha (Overseas Development Company, or KKKK), which in 1920 managed most of the Japanese colonies in Brazil. In Japan, the KKKK targeted the second and third sons of farmers whose tiny plots meant poverty for most in the family. Municipal and local governments regularly sponsored public lectures on Brazil, hailing emigrants for their contributions to international harmony.[21] Government grants helped to pay for travel costs. Ken-ichi Nakagawa, who came to Brazil from Hyogo province in 1926 as a twenty-four-year-old, remembered tales of sweet potatoes "so large that they fed children for an

[20] The exact numbers were as follows: Portuguese – 242,381; Japanese – 131,354; Italians – 72, 684; Germans – 65,357; and Spanish – 53,384. "Discriminação por nacionalidade dos imigrantes entrando no Brasil no Período 1924–1933 e 1934–1939," *Revista de Imigração e Colonização*, 1: 3 (July 1940), 633–638.

[21] See translated advertisement in Document File from Mr. Woods (U.S. Embassy, Tokyo) to Secretary of State, May 22, 1924: 832.5594/29, NARA-W.

entire day."[22] Advertisements about Brazil were equally fantastic. "Let's Go! Take Your Family to South America," urged a colorful 1923 poster that showed a muscular young man pointing to Brazil with a hoe and with his family in his arms, a child waving a Japanese flag. Another poster featured a large map of South America dotted with photos of colonial life. Superimposed was a boat of immigrants sailing into Rio de Janeiro's Guanabara Bay, with the Sugarloaf posed gorgeously overhead.

In 1927, a new public–private enterprise, the Brasil Takushoku Kumiai (Brazil Colonization Corporation), was founded, and two years later it bought four huge plots of land in São Paulo and Paraná. Emigrants were offered the chance to make a down payment in Japan, receive their passage and a twenty-five hectare lot, and pay back the loan as the land was developed. By the end of the twenties, passenger ships carrying about eight hundred immigrants each regularly made the forty-five-day journey between the port cities of Kobe and Santos. Brazil's Japanese immigration population rapidly increased from 49,400 in 1925 to 116,500 in 1930 and almost 193,000 in 1935 (see Table 1.1 source).

Among the immigrants, of course, were con artists. The most infamous was Mitsuyo Maeda, remembered today as Count Koma, teacher of the Gracie family who "founded" the Brazilian jiu-jitsu style that has become a global fad. His story shows how the perception of Japanese power, diligence, and honesty by Brazilians granted authenticity to lies. Koma arrived in 1914 and went to Belém do Pará, the same city at the mouth of the Amazon where many Moroccan Jews had settled in the late nineteenth century. By 1915, he was a member of an acrobatic troupe that included jiu-jitsu as part of the show. He soon began giving martial arts lessons, but he also had a side "job," successfully convincing locals and a gullible U.S. diplomat that he was Japan's unofficial consul in Brazil. Gerald Drew (the diplomat) even believed Koma to be a secret operative preparing a Japanese plot to occupy the Amazon.[23]

---

[22] Notes of an interview by Hiroshi Saito with K. Nakagawa, October 10, 1953, Donald Pierson Papers (Box 8), Smathers Library, University of Florida.

[23] Memorandum of Gerald A. Drew, vice-consul of the United State in Brazil to Dr. Munroe, June 27, 1930: 832.52 J27/68, NARA-W. Edwin L. Neville, charge d'affaires, U.S. Embassy, Tokyo to Secretary of State, February 26, 1931: 832.52 J27/69, NARA-W.

The Uses of Visibility

The 1920s marked a decade of increasing Japanese entry into Brazil. While most newcomers settled in rural areas, the urban immigrant population grew steadily, especially in cities like São Paulo and Curitiba (the largest city in the state of Paraná). The numbers, and the world economic crisis, led to growing anti-Japanese sentiment among the elites and working classes, who often saw all immigrants as nonassimilable and as job stealers. Japanese imperialism was one area of particular anxiety. While it was rare for nativists to claim that weak countries like Italy or Spain or Syria were going to take over Brazil, Japan's military might led some elites to fear that it might colonize their country. In spite of the loud outcry, other elites favored continued entry because of the success of agriculture in the Japanese colonies. In the twenties, rice production rose by four hundred percent, cotton by thirty percent, and sugarcane by one hundred percent.

Japanese immigrants used economic success as a way to negotiate their places in Brazil. They also used cultural approaches. One theory suggested that the Amazonian indigenous people were a lost tribe of Japanese (recall how Syrian-Lebanese leaders built a monument suggesting that Arabs and Brazil's indigenous peoples were siblings). The lost tribe theory was also used by immigrants in the Andes, and as recently as the 1990s, former Peruvian President Alberto Fujimori would dress as both a samurai and an Inca as part of his political campaigns.

The hypothesis that Brazilian Indians and Japanese immigrants were of the same biological stock, and thus that assimilation was assured, found support among some Brazilian elites. Professor Bruno Lobo of the Rio de Janeiro Medical School asserted that "Mongolian blood ... incontestably exists in Brazil through the Indians and their descendants of mixed parentage."[24] Edgar Roquette-Pinto, an anthropologist and professor at Brazil's National Museum, went a step farther. He argued that the modern Japanese people had emerged from the mixing of whites (Ainus as Europeans), yellows (Mongols as Indians), and blacks (Indonesians as Africans), thus mirroring Brazil's tripartite "racial" development.[25] These national identity assertions were important. Over the course of

[24] Bruno Lobo, *Japonezes no Japão: No Brasil* (Rio de Janeiro: Imprensa Nacional, 1926), 151–152, 157.
[25] Edgar Roquette-Pinto, *Ensaios de Antropologia Brasileira*, 2d ed. (São Paulo: Editora Nacional, [1933] 1978), 103.

the twentieth century, Japanese immigrants were often seen as building blocks of a modern Brazil.

Elite belief that Japanese immigrants were uniquely able to integrate and improve Brazil reached a wider public in numerous ways. Japanese intellectuals and policymakers frequently exhorted emigrants to con-vert to Catholicism, and public mass baptism ceremonies in Brazil were frequent. By 1930, there were more "Japanese" Catholics in Brazil than in Japan (this, of course, included those Brazilian-born children of Japanese parents).[26]

Another approach was the publication of photographs of "Brazilian"-looking children who were, at least ostensibly, of Japanese and Brazilian or European parentage.[27] The pictures were usually in books and pamphlets published with the financial support (both open and hidden) of the Japanese government. All showed Japanese men married to white Brazilian women (or white European immigrant women) who had produced white children. The symbolism of these photographs was an aggressive statement of assimilability and of same-ness. Japanese, like European, immigrants would produce obviously white children.

Another way of expressing a special Japanese ability to become Brazilian was via gambling. Brazil's famed *jogo do bicho* (animal game), a widely played but officially prohibited game of chance based on choos-ing animals to which numbers correspond, was often used as evidence. Whether immigrants won at the jogo do bicho more than anyone else is doubtful, but stories of Japanese proficiency at the game were legend-ary. The following story is not only about an immigrant striking it rich but also about joining together two quintessential national foods, the Brazilian banana and the Japanese rice, to create success:

> One day a Japanese immigrant, unsure of the animal on which he should place his bet, was eating a banana to which a grain of rice was stuck. The immigrant realized that the ideogram for rice could be decomposed into three parts, one of which represented the number 88.

---

[26] Lobo, *De Japonez a Brasileiro*, 142–144, 183. Kaigai Kogyo Kabushiki Kaisha, *Aclimação dos Emigrantes Japonezes*, 41–45.

[27] *Folha da Manhã* (São Paulo), 5 July 1934; Lobo, *Japonezes no Japão: No Brasil*, 159; Calvino Filho, ed., *Factos e Opinões Sobre a Immigração Japoneza* (Rio de Janeiro: np, 1934), 17, 33, 97, 112; *Cruzamento da Ethnia Japoneza: Hypóthese de que o Japonez Não se Cruza com Outra Ethnia* (São Paulo: Centro Nipponico de Cultura, 1934).

*The number 88 in the jogo do bicho represented a tiger, and the immi-
grant won handsomely with his bet.*[28]

A widespread story suggesting that Japanese were uniquely Brazilian
emerged in mid-1932. The armed forces of the state of São Paulo,
with much popular support, began an unsuccessful and short-lived
"Constitutionalist Revolution" in favor of presidential elections that
President Getúlio Vargas had been delaying. Many immigrants joined
the revolutionary forces, and two young Japanese-Brazilians emerged as
folk heroes. Cassio Kenro Shimomoto had arrived from Japan as a baby
and was a student at São Paulo's São Francisco Law School when he
volunteered along with a Brazilian-born student, José Yamashiro. Both
were hailed for their decision after Shimomoto declared to a journalist
from the *Diário de S. Paulo* that he was "before anything ... a Brazilian."[29]
Yamashiro's moment of fame came when a letter from his father was
translated for the pro-revolutionary newspaper *O Estado de S. Paulo*. The
father played on Japan's highly nationalistic culture in order to show that
Nikkei like his son were uniquely Brazilian: "[A]s a Brazilian and Paulista,
you obeyed the natural impulse to pick up arms to defend your State."[30]
Who was a better Brazilian than one whose loyalty was natural?

In spite of the Japanese-Brazilian revolutionaries, the federal government even called a truce so that a shipload of Japanese immigrants
could pass the tight naval blockade around the port of Santos. Although
the revolution was a failure, its memory in the state of São Paulo is
still strong. On a state holiday every July 9, businesses and schools shut
down and the failed uprising is commemorated by eating pizza. Linking
pizza to state's rights shows the importance of Italian immigrants, but
the types of pizzas show how deeply immigrant groups have touched
national culture. In the twenty-first century, popular pizzas include the
"Portuguesa," which includes olives, ham, and eggs, and the "Shitake-
Shimeji," based on mushrooms from Japan.

QUOTAS

Immigration was hotly debated during the 1933 Constitutional Con-
vention (see Chapter 5). Delegate speeches boiled down to two rather

[28] Handa, *O Imigrante Japonês*, 185.
[29] *Brasil e Japão: Duas Civilizações que se Completam* (São Paulo: Empreza Graphica
da "Revista dos Tribunaes," 1934), 238–240.
[30] *O Estado de S. Paulo*, 19 September 1932.

simple positions. Those in favor portrayed the Japanese as biologically superior to Brazilians of African or mixed backgrounds. They
focused on levels of production (in 1933, Japanese farmers produced
forty-six percent of the cotton, fifty-seven percent of the silk, and
seventy-five percent of the tea in Brazil even though they comprised
less than three percent of the population) and on the modernity of
the Japanese. [31] Those who opposed Japanese entry used nativist arguments about stealing jobs and land, racist arguments about biological
pollution, and militarist arguments suggesting that Japanese imperial
aspirations in Asia would soon move toward Brazil.

The constitutional debates show how deeply immigration was linked
to Brazilian national identity by the 1930s. They also show the unusual
support that Japanese immigrants received from their home government. The KKKK placed large advertisements in major newspapers promoting the high levels of production.[32] Diplomats and businesspeople
in Japan and Brazil worked to make sure that trade and immigration
would not be affected. Even so, the strategies were not wholly effective. A clause of the constitution of 1934 created immigration limits
modeled on the U.S. National Origins Act of 1924. An annual quota
was fixed at two percent of the number of immigrants from each nation
who had arrived in the previous fifty years, giving farmers preferential
treatment. The national government gained total authority over immigration.[33] While the article appeared to sharply restrict Japanese immigration, the Brazilian government wanted to cause "as little offense as
possible" because Japan was a buyer of large quantities of cotton, wool,
manganese, and nickel and many elites saw the new arrivals as changing Brazil for the better.[34]

The official Japanese immigration quota for 1935 was under 3,000, a
marked drop from the 23,000 who had entered in 1933. Yet in a nod to
Japanese power and Brazilian flexibility, officials on both sides created
innovative ways of circumventing the strictures. Oscar Correia arrived

---

[31] J.F. Normano and Antonello Gerbi, *The Japanese in South America: An
Introductory Survey with Special Reference to Peru* (New York: The John Day
Company, 1943), 39.
[32] *Folha da Manhã*, 5 July 1934; 28 March 1935.
[33] Constituição de 16 de Julho de 1934, Article 5, para. 19, g and Article 121,
para. 6.
[34] Report of Joseph C. Grew (U.S. Embassy, Tokyo), August 4, 1934: 739.94/2,
NARA-W. John M. Cabot, third secretary, U.S. Embassy, Rio de Janeiro to
Secretary of State, May 31, 1934: 832.55/94, NARA-W.

in Kobe in 1934 as Brazil's consul general just as the constitution was passed. He dismissed the quotas as he stepped off the ship, saying to the local press: "I should think that a way will eventually be found out of this delicate situation."[35] Japanese Foreign Minister Hirota was equally confident. During a visit to New York, he asserted that "Japan may send almost as many settlers from now on as in the past, since there is reason to believe that the amendment will not be enforced to the letter."[36]

The diplomats were correct. In spite of the 3,000-person quota, 10,000 Japanese settled in Brazil in 1935. This was a fifty percent reduction from the previous year but three hundred percent more than the quota allowed. In 1936, the official quota rose to 3,480, the result of adding to the Japanese base unfilled portions from countries that sent few immigrants. More than 8,000 Japanese entered that year, and relations between Japan and Brazil seemed to have survived the crisis. In total, more than 50,000 Japanese immigrants entered in the eight years after 1934, more than double what the quota officially permitted.

By 1937, a new sense of urgency regarding Japanese entry was felt in the Brazilian Foreign Ministry, the Itamarati. Oswaldo Aranha, the pro-United States foreign minister (and former ambassador to Washington), believed that Japan was plotting to divide South America into colonies. The United States pressured Brazilian military officials stationed in Japan to minimize contact with locals.[37] In early November 1937, the Imperial Japan/Nazi Germany Anti-Comintern Pact (an agreement against the Soviet Union–supported Communist International) was extended to include Italy. Brazil was now filled with immigrants from all three prominent Axis military powers, and four days later President Vargas ended Brazil's limited democracy with the imposition of the dictatorial Estado Novo.

Beginning in April 1938, new decrees sought to diminish foreign influence in Brazil, modifying the ways in which immigrant communities operated. A wide-ranging *brasilidade* ("Brazilianization") campaign began to target Japanese and German immigrants, along with Jews, Arabs, and other groups. This homogenization program sought to eliminate distinctive elements of immigrant and minority culture. It

---

[35] *The Osaka Mainichi and The Tokyo Nichi-Nichi Shinbun*, 29 May 1934.
[36] *The Osaka Mainichi and The Tokyo Nichi-Nichi Shinbun*, 29 September 1934.
[37] Jefferson Caffery (U.S. Embassy, Rio de Janeiro) to Secretary of State, July 11, 1938: 732.94/4 LH. Confidential Memorandum of Lt. Colonel Harry Creswell (U.S. military attache, Tokyo), June 1, 1939: 732.94/7 LH, NARA-W.

strictly controlled entry and prevented foreign residents from congregating in residential communities, such as ethnic colonies. By decree, all schools were required to have native-born Brazilians as directors, and all instruction had to be in Portuguese and include "Brazilian" topics. In early 1939, Brazil's justice minister decided that all foreign-language publications had to be accompanied by Portuguese translations. The Ministry of War began drafting children of foreign residents into the army and stationing them outside the regions of their birth. Speaking foreign languages in public was banned, and the Brazilian children of foreign residents were prohibited from international travel.[38]

In spite of the brasilidade campaign, neither the Brazilian nor Japanese governments desired to break relations. Commercial ties were intense, and many in the Vargas regime looked with envy on Japanese fascism. In late 1939, the Conselho de Imigração e Colonização (the Immigration and Colonization Council, or CIC) sent two of its members to Japanese and German (but not Italian) colonies in the states of São Paulo, Santa Catarina, and Paraná. Arriving at the Japanese colony in Bastos (today a city of more than twenty thousand residents) in early 1940, they found that the library had only two books in Portuguese, one of which was a Japanese-Portuguese dictionary that no one could find. The only Portuguese-language newspaper in the colony was used to keep dust off a chessboard. Marriage registration was at the Japanese consulate rather than at a Brazilian government office. The "clandestine" Japanese school system was operating openly.[39] Even so, the CIC representatives focused on the intense economic activity in the colonies and recommended that no action be taken. None was.

The repression became more intense in early 1941. The Vargas regime banned all foreign-language newspapers, shutting down four Japanese-language dailies with a total circulation of about fifty thousand. When a local official in a rural town decided to enforce the brasilidade measures to the letter, he ended up arresting almost every Japanese resident. Even so, until the end of 1941, Vargas sought to maintain relations with both the Allied and Axis powers. After the attack on Pearl Harbor in December, however, Brazil moved fully into the Allied camp. In March 1942, Brazil ruptured diplomatic relations

[38] Decree Law 1.545 (August 25, 1939), Articles 1, 4, 7, 8, 13, 15, 16.
[39] Aristóteles de Lima Câmara and Arthur Hehl Neiva, "Colonizações Nipônica e Germânica no Sul do Brasil," *Revista de Imigração e Colonização*, 2: 1 (January 1941), 39–120.

with Japan. Five months later, German U-boats began sinking ships off the coast, and suddenly Brazil was at war. The Vargas regime started attacking immigrants from Axis countries at every opportunity. Wild and untrue stories of "fifth column" activity spread throughout the country. The police were ordered to round up Japanese and German (but not Italian) citizens and remove them from strategic locations. Jews were threatened for speaking Yiddish (presumed by the police to be German) in public.

A young immigrant named Tomoo Handa remembered being arrested with a group of friends as they were fishing off the coast. A police unit suddenly appeared at the water's edge with a Japanese flag and ordered the youngsters to grab it. When they refused, an officer pulled a gun and forced them to stand in front of the flag. An immigrant photographer whom the police had kidnapped was compelled to snap a picture of the "traitors," who were then turned over to authorities as spies. Japanese government officials in Brazil regularly complained not only of false arrests but also about Brazilian policemen who were stealing merchandise and cash from Japanese-owned stores.[40] After President Vargas ordered the property of Axis companies and individuals seized, all Japanese colonies were placed under government supervision, a move that reportedly netted the regime at least a hundred million dollars.[41]

With Brazil's entry into the Allied camp, all those appearing Asian had a good chance of being branded as Japanese infiltrators. Two non-Japanese businessmen in the city of Belo Horizonte even placed a sign in their shop window saying "Attention: We are Chinese." Such confusion was embarrassing since China was now a Brazilian ally. One attempt to solve the problem came from the political police, who began circulating crude sheets on appearance and ethnicity. Germans could be distinguished from other Europeans because they "tolerated adultery" and had "almost no sexual morals."[42] Another tip sheet, called "How to tell a Chinese from a Japanese," had pictures and helpful hints: "The Chinese are racially less complex than the Japanese.... [T]he Japanese

[40] Handa, O Imigrante Japonês, 635. Page 1 article "Brazil Warned For Treatment of Immigrants" in The Japan Chronicle and The Japan Mail, 27 September 1947.
[41] New York Times, 12 April 1942; 4 and 29 October 1943.
[42] "Atividades Nazistas no Brasil, especialmente no Distrito Federal, Minas Gerais, e Santa Catarina," Polícias Políticas, Alemão: Caixa 1, Relatório 21.5.1940 (May 21, 1940), Arquivo Estadual do Rio de Janeiro. My thanks to Glen Goodman for sharing this document with me.

are bad, the Chinese are good; the Japanese are false, the Chinese are sincere; the Japanese are mean, the Chinese are nice."[43]

World War II was more difficult for Japanese and their descendants than for immigrants from other Axis countries. They did not, however, suffer internment in concentration camps as did Japanese immigrants and their U.S. citizen descendants in the United States. Furthermore, Brazil did not deport Japanese to the United States as happened in Peru and Bolivia.[44] These decisions, however, had nothing to do with human rights. Rather, the choice was a result of two fears among Brazilian policymakers and military officials: that the population was too large and well armed to intern or deport without creating a rebellion, and that Japan might attack (and defeat) Brazil if Japanese citizens were rounded up.

JAPAN "WINS" WORLD WAR II

Historians love to use grand political events (like world wars) as temporal markers, but sometimes reality does not conform to chronology. The story of Brazilian immigration thus includes an unusual tale that began in 1942 and ended only in 1950. It involved World War II but in a very different way than you might imagine.

Beginning in the early 1940s, some immigrants in Brazil began to strike out at the regime's brasilidade campaign by emphasizing their Japanese identities. Many had been educated with ideas about Japan's invincibility, and emperor worship became important. The underground Japanese–language press (recall that only Portuguese–language newspapers and radio stations were officially allowed) exploded with denunciations of immigrants who did not show their loyalty to Japan. Rumors spread like wildfire about babies born fully grown, speaking Japanese and predicting that Japan was about to win the war.[45] Yet the monster babies (I have found no traditional historical evidence of their existence) pale in comparison to the secret societies that emerged at the end of the World War II era. These groups first came to the public's attention in

---

[43] Undated DOPS translation of report from agent "Nagai" to agent "Hayão." "Como distinguir um Chinez de um Japonez," February 22, 1943. Pasta I. Arquivo Público do Estado – Rio de Janeiro, Time, December 22, 1941.

[44] C. Harvey Gardiner, Pawns in a Triangle of Hate: The Peruvian Japanese and the United States (Seattle: University of Washington Press, 1981). For an update on this story, see Tim Golden, "Held in War, Latins Seek Reparations," New York Times, 29 August 1996.

[45] Handa, O Imigrante Japonês, 640.

Figure 6.3. The cartoon reads, "Tell me what street you are on and I will tell you who you are."
Source: *Folha de Manhã*, 15 October 1944, p.15. Image courtesy of the Arquivo Histórico Judaico Brasileiro, São Paulo.

1942 when they destroyed some Japanese-immigrant-owned silkworm farms, believing that the silk was being sold to the United States Army for parachutes.[46]

What triggered a massive expansion of Japanese secret societies was President Vargas's decision in July 1944 to send twenty-five thousand troops to Italy as part of the Allied forces. The Brazilian Expeditionary Force included many soldiers of immigrant descent, Nikkei among them. Yet their arrival in Europe generated immense nationalist sentiment, xenophobia, and anti-Axis feeling in Brazil. The Bela Lugosi film *Yellow Peril* played to large crowds in major cities, and popular music often included anti-Japanese lyrics. Belmonte, one of Brazil's most famous political cartoonists, linked blacks and immigrants as outsiders (see Figure 6.3). In this cartoon, the groups are Arabs, Japanese, Afro-Brazilians, Portuguese, Italians, and Jews. Note how both Jews and Japanese are linked via their daughters and how facial hair is emphasized as an indication of otherness, just as Guilherme de Almeida had done two decades earlier, as we saw in Chapter 5.

Brazil's late entry into World War II came just a few months before the Allies were clearly on their way to victory in Europe. Nevertheless, Brazil declared war on Japan in May 1945. Now, the U.S. military could continue to use bases in the Northeast to refuel Allied planes on their way to Africa. Since Italy and Germany had surrendered, Japanese immigrants were suddenly the last "enemy aliens" in Brazil.

---

[46] *New York Times*, 15 November 1942; *O Estado de S. Paulo*, 16 December 1942.

The largest secret society to emerge in Brazil was the Shindo Renmei (Way of the Subjects of the Emperor's League). This group became particularly important *after* World War II ended and after Vargas's Estado Novo was toppled in a 1945 coup. The leaders of the society were immigrants who had retired as Japanese army officers. Their goals were to maintain a permanent Japanized space in Brazil through the preservation of language, culture, and religion, as well as the reestablishment of Japanese schools. The Shindo Renmei posited that Japan had *won* World War II, and by December 1945, the group could claim fifty thousand members.[47]

Critical to the growth of the Shindo Renmei was its monopoly on information because of the ban on the foreign-language press. The group's circulars and secret newspapers mixed fact and fiction. Reports of Japan's defeat in the Brazilian press were described as U.S. propaganda. Rio de Janeiro's newspapers were said to have announced the Japanese victory and that General Douglas MacArthur had been imprisoned as a war criminal.[48] Photos of President Harry Truman bowing to Emperor Hirohito were circulated, along with reports of Japanese troops landing in San Francisco and marching toward New York. Getúlio Vargas was rumored to be on his way to Tokyo to sign surrender documents.[49] Just a week after Emperor Hirohito broadcast his real surrender message over shortwave radio on August 15, 1945, the Shindo Renmei released its own version of the event:

Emperor Hirohito has been forced to abdicate in favor of a Regent because he accepted the conditions imposed by the Potsdam Declaration. The Imperial combined fleet has been given the order for immediate action, and in a furious battle in Okinawan waters the Japanese Navy and Air Force destroyed about four hundred Allied warships, thus deciding the course of

[47] See translation of Shindo Renmei objectives and statutes in report of João André Dias Paredes to Major Antonio Pereira Lira (state police chief, Paraná), April 30, 1949. Secretaria de Estado de Segurança Pública, Departamento da Polícia Civil, Divisão de Segurança e Informações, No. 1971, Sociedade Terrorista Japonesa, Arquivo Público Paraná, Curitiba.
[48] The documents were found in a raid on Shindo Renmei headquarters in Santo André and published in translation in Herculano Neves, *O Processo da "Shindo-Renmei" e Demais Associações Secretas Japonesas* (São Paulo: n.p., 1960), 288–290.
[49] *O Estado de S. Paulo*, 26 March 1946; *Correio da Manhã*, 6 April 1946; *A Noite*, 13 April 1946.

the war. The Japanese employed for the first time their secret weapon, the "High Frequency Bomb." Only one of the bombs killed more than one hundred thousand American soldiers on Okinawa. [This led to the] unconditional surrender of the Allies [and] the landing of Japanese expeditionary forces in Siberia and the United States.[50]

Along with the false reports came opportunities for con artists. One scam was to say that a Japanese prince was en route to Brazil and that immigrants should contribute funds to celebrate as the contingent went from the port at Santos to various Japanese communities. In some towns, all of the red and white cloth disappeared from stores as immigrants bought material to make banners in the "prince's" honor. A "secret agent" sold worthless war medals by saying that the funds were for the Japanese soldiers coming to occupy Brazil. Other con men sold faked photographs of Allied generals accepting defeat aboard the USS *Missouri*. Most common, however, was the trafficking of worthless one hundred yen notes, false tickets for passage to Japan, and plots of land in the countries that had been "conquered" by the "victorious" Japanese.[51]

The con men were not, however, killers. But murders did become part of the Shindo Renmei strategy. The assassinations began in early March 1946. That was when Japanese immigrants divided into two camps: the *kachigumi* ("victorist") and *makegumi* ("defeatist"). The Shindo Renmei denounced "traitors" and put evil spells on defeatists. Fanatical youth were recruited to gun down those who spoke of Japanese defeat.[52] Kidnappings took place, with the ransom a promise never to speak of Japan's conquest.

Between March and September 1946, sixteen immigrants were assassinated for insisting that Japan had lost World War II. Thirty makegumi were seriously injured in kachigumi attacks. Hundreds of others received death threats marked by the Shindo Renmei's trademark skull and crossbones. Numerous silk, cotton, and mint farmers had their homes and fields destroyed. Brazilian authorities were stunned by these developments, especially when one captured kachigumi told police that

[50]   Reprinted in the *Paulista Shinbun*, 29 April 1947.
[51]   José Yamashiro, "Algumas Considerações sobre o fanatismo japonês," *Paulista Shinbun*, 29 April 1947; *A Noite* (Rio de Janeiro), 25 May 1946.
[52]   Interview by Jeffrey Lesser with Masuji Kiyotani, July 27, 1995, at the Centro de Estudos Nipo-Brasileiros (São Paulo).

"Japan did not lose the war. As long as there is one Japanese on earth, even if he is the last, Japan will never surrender."[53] Japan's postwar government sent documents to Brazil proving the Allied victory, but the kachigumi dismissed them as false.[54]

The police raided Shindo Renmei headquarters in early 1946. There they found piles of propaganda materials, a mimeograph machine used to produce the organization's weekly newspaper, and a list of 130,000 members. Four hundred leaders were arrested and eighty were scheduled for deportation to Japan. Then something remarkable happened before full-scale violence could erupt. Brazilian government representative José Carlos de Macedo Soares (a former foreign minister) invited police, military officials, and secret society members, including those in jail, to a meeting at the São Paulo governor's mansion.

Some six hundred people gathered that night, the majority Shindo Renmei members. Macedo Soares begged for the violence to end. He called Japanese immigrants "a treasure" and "the most important part of the Brazilian population." Because Japan did not have diplomats in Brazil following World War II, it was represented by a Swedish diplomat, who also hailed the immigrants in the room. The irony of the meeting was not lost on Jorge Americano, the rector of the University of São Paulo and an important cultural commentator: "I don't know if the tall, ruddy, and blond [Swedish] 'representative of Japan,' speaking English and fixing his blue eyes on the squinty black Japanese eyes, I don't know if he was able to convince them that Japan lost the war any more than he, Swiss, tall, ruddy, blond, blue-eyed, speaking English, was able to convince them that he was the defender of the interests of the Japanese in Brazil."[55] The meeting ended as Shindo Renmei leader Sachiko Omasa lectured Macedo Soares and the Swedish representative to the delight of her colleagues: "[W]e Japanese do not believe ... in Japan's defeat. If Your Excellency wants to end the disputes and terrorist acts, begin by spreading word of Japan's victory and order that all false propaganda about defeat be stopped."[56]

[53] Handa, O Imigrante Japonês, 673.
[54] "As atividades das sociedades secretas japonesas e a ação repressiva da polícia de São Paulo, publicadas pela imprensa," Arquivos da Polícia Civil de São Paulo, 12: 2 (1946), 523–530.
[55] Jorge Americano, "Shindo Renmei (1946)," in São Paulo Atual, 1935–1962 (São Paulo: Edições Melhoramentos, 1963), 186–187.
[56] Information on the meeting from Correio Paulistano, 20 July 1946; Diário de São Paulo, 20 July 1946; A Gazeta, 20 July 1946; Jornal de São Paulo, 20 July 1946.

Macedo Soares did almost exactly what Omasa wanted. He prohibited Brazilian newspapers from publishing news of Japan's defeat and ordered the term "unconditional surrender" taken out of all official communications. The high court ruled that those convicted of the murders could not be deported. However, Shindo Renmei leaders saw the gentle treatment as evidence of Japan's victory and thus took even firmer positions. When a Shindo Renmei member said in a bar in the city of Oswaldo Cruz (state of São Paulo) that he would "kill three or four Brazilians" who insisted that the Allies had won the war, a riot took place. Three thousand Brazilians hunted down immigrants, screaming "Lynch the Japanese." When the army was called in to calm the situation, Shindo Renmei activists engaged them in a shoot-out.[57]

In 1947 the secret societies were still growing. They collected firearms and circulated hit lists. One hundred and fifty members of São Paulo's Kokumin Zenei-tai (National Vanguard Unit) were arrested with bombs, guns, and surveillance photos of their intended victims' homes. Shindo Renmei propaganda frequently linked the Brazilian government to "the Jews in Rio" (recall that anti-Jewish immigration restrictions had been put into place by Vargas) as they sought to discriminate between insiders and outsiders by using economic and ethnic language. Those who denied Japan's victory were interchangeably "Western capitalists," "Communists," "Jews," or "Chinese."[58]

The end of the secret societies came only in 1950. That was when Japanese Olympic swimming champion Masanori Yusa arrived in Brazil with his team the "Flying Fish." Six thousand people crowded into Congonhas Airport in São Paulo to meet the athletes. An exhibition match at the Pacaembu Stadium (a major futebol arena) was a sellout and included music by the State Military Police Band and the presence of the governor. During an interview, members of the Flying Fish expressed shock when presented with the idea that Japan had *won* World War II. Soon the kachigumi began claiming that the swimmers were Koreans masquerading as Japanese. Immigrants and their children

[57] *Revista Cruzeiro* (Rio de Janeiro), 31 August 1946.
[58] Unsigned confidential São Paulo DOPS report, "Atividades atuais no seio da colônia japoneza sobre rearticulação do movimento fanático-terrorista-chantagista," March 1950. Secretaria da Segurança Pública do Estado de São Paulo – Departamento de Ordem Política e Social #108981-Ordem Política/ Shindo Remmey – Vol. 1, AESP.

were offended, and the Brazilian government's indictment of two thousand Shindo Renmei members was met with relief.[59]
It was 1950. World War II had finally ended in Brazil.

CONCLUSION

This chapter emphasizes a number of important global and local perspectives in linking immigration to Brazilian national identity. Changes in Japan's economic structure during the Meiji era created rural population pressure. Relief would come through emigration at a moment when Brazilian elites began to believe that Japanese immigrants could resolve the problem of rural work created by their disappointment with the labor activism of European immigrants. Yet as we have seen repeatedly, the planter's poor treatment always led to the same outcomes, flight and revolt. The difference was that Japanese immigrants left traditional fazendas to form their own agricultural communities. This reinforced a vision among many in the elite that the Japanese were more modern, and thus "whiter," than Europeans. Japanese immigrants fit national identity goals so well that their numbers would exceed the rest of the Americas combined.

Japanese migration also highlights important differences in the patterns of immigration to Brazil. Unlike most newcomers, a powerful and activist Japanese government deeply committed to immigrant success abroad made sure that return would be infrequent. Diplomats worked hard to provide disillusioned and maltreated immigrants with options other than flight. By the 1920s, few immigrants had faced abusive treatment from fazendeiros and their henchmen because they were settling in Japanese-government sponsored colonies.

Today more than 1.5 million Brazilians claim Japanese descent. The heritage of agricultural production and world power continue to lead many among the elite and the masses to see Japanese immigrants and their descendants as fundamental to the construction of a modern Brazil. Those of Japanese descent often have the cachet of being the "best" Brazilians, and this cultural attitude has helped many move into the upper echelons of society in terms of class, education, or residence. Today, Japanese-Brazilians can be found in virtually all areas of Brazilian society, from politics to the military, from the liberal professions to the arts to industry.

[59] *Folha da Noite*, 21 March 1950.

Figure 6.4. A 2008 Rio de Janeiro Carnival version of the *Kasato-Maru*, the first boat to bring Japanese immigrants to Brazil.
Source: Photo courtesy of Anna Toss (anna_t on Flickr).

Yet even positive stereotypes take a toll. As we will see in the Epilogue, Japanese-Brazilians (among others) began to emigrate in large numbers in the late twentieth century as the story of Brazilian immigration began to shift direction.

APPENDIX

Document 6.1. A memory of the Kasato-Maru, 1994

In 1994 one of Rio de Janeiro's most famous samba schools decided to make Japanese immigration to Brazil their carnival theme. One float was a replica of the *Kasato-Maru*, the first boat to bring Japanese immigrants to Brazil (see Figure 6.4). Another one was less traditional – a fifteen-foot-high bottle of soy sauce with giant plastic sushi and sashimi revolving around it. Most of the performers were non-Nikkei made up to "look" Japanese and dressed as carnivalized samurais, geishas, and sushimen. This is the song they sang "Burajiru, Meu Japão Brasileiro" [Brazil, My Brazilian Japan]:

Geishas with patterned kimonos, taught to serve and seduce with love.... Monks, warriors, samurai, the Buddha is the religious image and in judo my Brazil is champion.... From the country of soccer to the Empire of the Rising Sun, I mix sake with samba to make our people happy. I mix sake with samba to make our carnival happy.

Source: Sociedade Educativa e Recreativa Escola de Samba Unidos do Cabuçu, Rio de Janeiro Carnaval, 1994.

Epilogue

THE SONG REMAINS THE SAME

NEW POLICIES FOR A NEW ERA

Brazil changed markedly between the Great Depression and the end of World War II. Coffee, the driver of the economy since the late nineteenth century, declined as prices and market percentage dropped. Coffee plantations in São Paulo and Rio de Janeiro were abandoned, divided, or sold. Brazil's fazendas, run for centuries as family fiefdoms, often became the property of large corporations that began to harvest products like soybeans and sugarcane for local and international markets.

The changes in agricultural production, new infusions of international capital, and increasing orientation to export led to industrial growth. Some plantation owners had begun investing in factories in the nineteenth century and that trend continued. Numerous immigrants and their descendants did the same. By end of the twentieth century, industrial Brazil was producing everything from automobiles to airplanes.

Immigration patterns also changed in the years surrounding World War II. From 1942 to 1945, most ports were closed to passenger traffic and transoceanic travel became increasingly dangerous. In the United States, new permanent resident permits dropped below thirty thousand per year (during the previous forty years the average had been almost half a million per year, with many single years reaching over a million).[1] Argentina's numbers also dropped substantially. The decline was most dramatic in Brazil. Immigrant entries virtually stopped, falling below two thousand per year.

[1] U.S. Department of Homeland Security, *Yearbook of Immigration Statistics: 2009* (Washington, DC: U.S. Department of Homeland Security, Office of Immigration Statistics, 2010), Tables 1 and 5.

In 1943, with the war in Europe and Asia raging, Brazil's Immigration and Colonization Council (CIC) began to debate new immigration policies. One of the most important ideas came from Roberto Simonsen, a politician, businessman, and economic policymaker. Simonsen believed that immigration should be linked to industrial development rather than agricultural production. Only European immigrants, he believed, had the technological qualifications and the social and political culture necessary to modernize Brazil. In other words, his ideas were not so different from those put forth in the nineteenth century.

With Simonsen's concept in mind, CIC members examined four options for a new postwar immigration policy. One was an open door, based on the idea that Brazil was a melting pot that would easily assimilate all immigrants. No member of the CIC supported this position. At the other end of the spectrum was a policy vociferously represented by Ernani Reis, the secretary of the Ministry of Justice. He advocated closing Brazil to all but the Portuguese and "Mediterranean Latin" peoples, arguing that the existing population would have a large natural rate of increase and fewer immigrants were needed. A third option focused on tinkering with the immigration quotas set out in the 1934 constitution: All others would simply be banned from entering Brazil.

Most CIC members, however, supported a fourth approach. A preferential open door policy would target immigrants who were within the "ethnic composition" of the Brazilian population, "most convenient[ly] ... its European origins."[2] Africans, Asians, and their descendants would continue to be banned, following the 1890 legislation, so that Brazil would remain "the only great white country in the tropical area."[3] The enthusiasm for urban workers in postwar Brazil showed that industrialists, more than fazendeiros, were the dominant economic actors. Immigration policy in the 1940s was not that different from a century earlier when whiteness was also a critical component.

World War II ended in August 1945. The dictator, President Vargas, declared his country victorious in the fight for democracy. The irony was not lost on Brazilians, many of whom were delighted when the military deposed him in a bloodless coup in October of that year. The new

---

[2] Regulation of the Conselho de Imigração e Colonização, March 12, 1948 (revised April 30, 1948) in Brazil, Ministério da Justiça e Negócios Interiores, *Estrangeiros: Legislação, 1940–1949* (Rio de Janeiro: Serviço de Documentação, 1950), 689.

[3] Tewell to U.S. Secretary of State Cordell Hull, June 12, 1944: 832.111/319, National Archives and Records Administration, Washington.

democratic government that replaced Vargas took a position on immigration much like that of the previous one, in part because many members of the old regime remained in place (Vargas himself was elected to Brazil's senate in 1946 and as president in 1950). Not surprisingly, the preferential open door policy would define Brazil's immigration regulations over the next decade.

The War Ends

The end of World War II and the fall of the Vargas regime did not immediately change immigration patterns. The global dislocations of the 1930s and 1940s continued to have a profound impact on migratory flows. Even after Brazil began dismantling its quota system in 1945 (this was done rapidly in practice and more slowly via the legislative system), the number of entries remained low. By the early 1950s, however, things began to change. Migration was safe again. New political and economic disruptions encouraged people to consider new homes. Advances in transportation technology made movement quicker, cheaper, and easier. Brazil's cities were growing rapidly, opening up economic and cultural spaces for newcomers. Within two decades, São Paulo would be the largest city in the Western and Southern Hemispheres, and Brazil would have one of the world's ten largest populations.

A combination of generosity and imperial attitudes among the former Allied powers meant that many Axis nations were rebuilt. By the late fifties, Germany and Japan were becoming economic rather than military giants. Italy moved tentatively in the same direction. These nations had provided a large percentage of the immigrants to Brazil before the war, and their recovery renewed the migratory streams. Postwar Portugal and Spain continued their prewar fascist political leanings, with the result that immigrants to Brazil were often fleeing political persecution. Other Portuguese immigrants came from Africa as Angola and Mozambique began to seek independence from the colonial master.

Post–World War II immigration, then, in terms of European national origins, was not dissimilar to that of the sixty years before the war. A 1948 policy provided visas only to those with "good health, good conduct, no criminal records, no acts against national security and who will fit well with the ethnic composition of the Brazilian population."[4] These

---

[4] Heloisa Paulo, *Aqui Também é Portugal: A Colônia Portuguesa do Brasil e o Salazarismo* (Lisbon: Quatreto, 2000), 143–144.

policies continued until about 1960 and provided the leeway to accept unskilled workers from "desirable" ethnic backgrounds, while prohibiting all but those defined as economically useful from other groups. Put differently, Brazil's entry into World War II on the Allied side, and its postwar claims of being a "racial democracy," were not sustained in the area of immigration.

Right after the war, the flow of Portuguese immigrants was diminished because their homeland did not participate fully in the postwar European Recovery Program (ERP), known by most as the Marshall Plan. One part of the plan was to help devastated European countries send part of their populations abroad as emigrants. Portugal's unwillingness to accept many of the Marshall Plan's regulations meant that it did not receive much emigration assistance. Emigration patterns, however, changed between 1950 and 1955, as Table E.1 makes clear. The former date corresponds to Brazil's lifting of all visa requirements for Portuguese immigrants, including those born in Angola and Mozambique. The latter date coincides with Portugal's decision to promote white settlement in Angola with material incentives, leading fewer emigrants to choose Brazil.

Unlike Portugal, Italy took full advantage of the Marshall Plan and received more than ten percent of the funds allotted between 1948 and 1952. Italians suffered the highest unemployment rates in Western Europe after the war, and emigration thus promised the dual advantage of reducing the national population and injecting money into the economy via remittances. While Brazil sought industrially skilled immigrants, Italy was interested in sending agricultural workers. This difference in national interests helps to explain why a jump in Italian entry in 1952 was sustained for only a few years. In fact, many sponsored Italian immigrants to Brazil after the war were repatriated because they could not find jobs. By 1955, Brazil was no longer a desirable relocation site for Italians. This stands in striking contrast to Argentina, where three times more immigrants entered between 1950 and 1957 than in Brazil. In 1960, Brazil and Italy signed a new migration agreement in hopes of encouraging a greater flow, but as the statistics in Table E.2 suggest, this did not change the decreasing pattern.

POSTWAR ASIAN ENTRY

Japanese entry into Brazil was renewed in the mid-1950s. Japan's Emigration Bureau focused on the islands of Okinawa that had been

Table E.1. *Post–World War II Immigration*

Period	Germans	Spanish	Italians	Portuguese	Japanese	Others
1945	22	74	180	1,414	–	1,928
1946	174	203	1,059	6,342	6	5,525
1947	561	653	3,284	8,921	1	5,333
1948	2,308	965	4,437	2,751	1	11,106
1949	2,123	2,197	6,352	6,780	4	6,361
1950	2,725	3,808	7,342	14,739	33	7,296
1951	2,858	9,636	8,285	28,731	106	12,978
1952	2,364	14,898	15,207	42,815	261	12,605
1953	2,305	13,677	15,543	33,735	1,928	13,054
1954	1,952	11,338	13,408	30,062	3,119	12,369
1955	1,122	10,738	8,945	21,264	4,051	9,046
1956	844	7,921	6,069	16,803	4,912	8,257
1957	952	7,680	7,197	19,471	6,147	12,166
1958	825	5,768	4,819	21,928	6,586	9,463
1959	890	6,712	4,233	17,345	7,123	8,217
1960	842	7,662	3,341	13,105	7,746	7,811
1961	703	9,813	2,493	15,819	6,824	7,937
1962	651	4,968	1,900	13,713	3,257	6,649
1963	601	2,436	867	11,585	2,124	6,246
1964	323	616	476	4,249	1,138	3,193
1965	365	550	642	3,262	903	4,116
1966	377	469	643	2,708	937	3,041
1967	550	572	747	3,838	1,070	4,575
1968	723	723	738	3,917	597	5,823
1969	524	568	477	1,933	496	2,615
1970	535	546	357	1,773	435	3,241
1971	354	281	254	807	260	4,422
1972	635	470	535	1,095	472	5,560
1973	404	225	402	581	25	4,294
1974	641	244	478	426	75	4,902
1975	1,248	410	1,358	959	111	7,480

Source: *Brasil: 500 Anos de Povoamento* (Rio de Janeiro: IBGE, 2000), Apêndice: "Estatísticas de 500 anos de povoamento," p. 226, available at: http://www.ibge.gov.br/seculoxx/arquivos_pdf/populacao.shtm.

under direct U.S. military occupation since 1945 (and would remain so until 1972). Emigratory pressure in Okinawa was intense since the new military bases dislocated large numbers of people. The United States, however, prohibited postwar Japanese immigration, and the 1952 Immigration and Nationality Act (also known as the McCarran-Walter Act) excluded those from former Axis countries.

Table E.2. *Mass Migration to Brazil, Argentina, and Venezuela, 1950–1957*

	Italian	Spanish	Portuguese	Total	% Italians
Brazil	74,600	75,800	192,900	456,800	16.3
Argentina	220,800	129,700	15,029	439,800	50.2
Venezuela	188,400	175,100	40,800	487,800	38.6
Total	482,600	380,600	248,729	1,384,400	34.8

Source: Gloria La Cava, *Italians in Brazil: The Post–World War II Experience* (New York: Peter Lang, 1999), Table 7, p. 59.

The combination of a U.S. ban on Japanese entry and its occupation of Okinawa made Latin America a popular relocation site. In 1951, the U.S. Civil Administration of the Ryukyu Islands (the official name for Okinawa) hired an academic from the United States to do a study of Okinawan emigration to Latin America. His report was encouraging and soon new migratory streams appeared: Between 1954 and 1964, 3,200 Okinawans formed the Uruma Colony near Santa Cruz, Bolivia. Between 1953 and 1963, almost 55,000 would settle in Brazil on the heels of the 200,000 Japanese who had immigrated before the war.

Brazilian elites generally hailed postwar Japanese immigrants, just as they had fifty years earlier. The positive attitudes about the newcomers, and the fact that more than forty percent of them had relatives who had migrated prior to the war, made integration relatively smooth. There were, however, some areas of cultural tension, especially between older and newer Japanese immigrants. Longtime residents were often shocked by the attitudes of young Japanese toward everything, from the emperor to sexual relations. The newcomers were equally confused: They had trouble understanding old dialects filled with Japanized Portuguese words and wondered if earlier immigrants had become *Brasil-bokê* ("made senile by Brazil"). The new immigrants also brought religious practices that had not existed in prewar Japan. The most widespread was the Sôtô Zenshu school of Zen Buddhism, with its focus on meditation as the primary path to enlightenment. Buddhism was a community-building experience in Brazil, but the religion also spread among non-Nikkei. For them, participating in a new Japanese religion was like listening to a transistor radio – it was a way to be "modern" and a member of the "First World." In 2005, more than 250,000 Brazilians counted themselves as Buddhists, the majority non-Nikkei from urban areas.[5]

---

[5]   Cristina Rocha, *Zen in Brazil: The Quest for Cosmopolitan Modernity* (Honolulu: University of Hawaii Press, 2006).

Postwar Okinawan immigrants also began to Brazilianize their traditions by focusing on ancestor worship, often led by female shamans.
In the 1960s, a number of syncretic sects emerged that practiced ritual spirit possession, including Catholic, African, and Okinawan dei-
ties. These sects have increasingly become part of global networks
of Okinawan ethnicity. Starting in the late twentieth century, many
Okinawan-Brazilians began reburying the remains of their ancestors in
Brazil. Doing so, in effect, made Brazil into the Okinawan homeland.

The Japanization of Brazil and the Brazilianization of the Japanese
have become important tropes in Brazilian national identity. Advertisers
frequently use phrases like "our Japanese are better than everyone
else's" and "we need more Brazilians like this Japanese." Such language
harkens back to the early twentieth century when elites often considered Japanese whiter than Europeans. The prominent place of Japanese
immigrants and their descendants has also had an impact as other
Asians have settled in Brazil. The two largest groups are from Korea
and China, in both cases mirroring broader patterns of migration to the
Americas (see Table E.3).

Beginning in the mid-1950s, the South Korean government began
to use emigration to control population, reduce unemployment, and
garner foreign exchange via remittances. South Koreans hoped Brazil's
economy could absorb many newcomers, but postwar immigration policies made entry complicated. Korean immigrants, however, were not
deterred. Many went to Paraguay and Bolivia, where on-the-spot border visas for foreigners were available for a fee. They then remigrated
without formal documents to Brazil, where the economy was larger and
the high status of Asians provided cultural advantages. Perhaps two
hundred thousand Koreans migrated to Paraguay and Bolivia between
1975 and 1990, and as many as half then moved to Brazil. In 2011,
the South Korean government extrapolated a population of about fifty
thousand, based on families registered at its various consulates in Brazil.[6]
More recent nongovernmental figures put the numbers at around one
hundred thousand immigrants (not including an equally large number
of Brazilian-born children).

Today most Koreans are legal residents because Brazil regularly has
amnesty programs for undocumented immigrants. The size of Brazil's
economy and the technological sophistication of many of its economic

[6] Korean Ministry of Foreign Affairs and Trade, available at: http://www.
mofat.go.kr/ENG/countries/latinamerica/countries/20070803/1_24583.
jsp?menu=m_30_30 (accessed May 16, 2012).

Table E.3. *"Other" Immigrants to Brazil, Post–World War II*

Period	Lebanon	China	Korea	United States	Argentina	Chile	Poland
1945	4	–	–	788	99	–	44
1946	155	–	–	975	79	–	706
1947	581	–	–	732	52	–	561
1948	925	–	–	633	50	–	2,439
1949	850	–	–	825	68	–	360
1950	707	–	–	911	125	–	127
1951	1,868	–	–	–	–	–	–
1952	2,515	–	–	–	–	–	–
1953	1,704	–	–	–	–	–	–
1954	1,186	265	–	1,236	485	–	–
1955	1,518	–	–	–	–	–	–
1956	1,481	–	–	–	–	–	–
1957	900	–	–	–	–	–	–
1958	629	–	–	–	–	–	–
1959	1,061	–	–	1,462	–	–	–
1960	653	–	–	1,184	–	–	–
1961	734	–	–	1,208	–	–	–
1962	612	–	–	973	–	–	–
1963	547	–	–	971	–	–	–
1964	202	253	–	764	572	–	49
1965	188	402	–	979	515	–	47
1966	178	232	–	823	516	–	27
1967	360	766	–	1,261	462	–	21
1968	299	1,066	–	1,537	597	–	43
1969	11	432	–	406	97	–	32
1970	9	444	–	810	270	–	71
1971	9	226	1,895	675	276	–	224
1972	7	897	1,190	1,068	370	–	305
1973	46	358	204	874	628	–	860
1974				data not available			
1975	–	118	–	1,414	1,095	–	1,203

Source: *Brasil: 500 Anos de Povoamento* (Rio de Janeiro: IBGE, 2000), Apêndice: "Estatísticas de 500 anos de povoamento," p. 226, available at: http://www.ibge.gov.br/seculoxx/arquivos_pdf/populacao.shtm.

sectors often lead Koreans and their Brazilian children to see Brazil as a place of social mobility. The population at large has found new products available in the small stores owned by the immigrants, especially inexpensive technology and clothing. Korean immigrants in Brazil and throughout the Americas are often strongly committed to Protestant Christian worship. Religious affiliation functions both as a faith orientation and as a community-building exercise since rituals are often conducted in both Korean (as a maintenance effort) and Portuguese (as an acculturation effort).

The overwhelming majority (ninety percent) of Korean immigrants live in São Paulo neighborhoods that have long housed immigrants. These include Liberdade, the traditional Japanese neighborhood, and the formerly Italian neighborhood of Brás where the Hospedaria dos Imigrantes discussed in Chapter 3 was located. There is also a large Korean presence in Bom Retiro, a traditional immigrant neighborhood associated with East European Jews. In 2001, many in Bom Retiro were surprised to learn that a Korean-Brazilian student at the local Jewish school had won the annual prize as best Hebrew speaker.

Korean immigrants often hold a globalist view of their own immigration and have close family members in other countries, from Paraguay to Canada. Indeed, many Koreans are educated in one country and subsequently move to work in a family business in another. It is not unusual to find immigrants who speak English, Spanish, and Portuguese in addition to their native Korean. These patterns were made clear to me at Malcha's, a falafel shop owned by a woman said to have left Yemen to settle first in Israel and then Brazil:

Malcha's small restaurant is located in the São Paulo neighborhood of Bom Retiro, known for most of the twentieth century for its Jewish population but more recently for its Korean and Bolivian residents. Not surprisingly, the menu is written in Portuguese, Hebrew, and Korean. One day I went for lunch at Malcha's but it was closed so I entered a small Korean restaurant next door. The man at the door insisted that I would not like the food. When I refused to take no for an answer (I was hungry!), I was told in Portuguese that there was only a Korean menu available. Since I knew the Korean name of what I wanted for lunch, and could recognize the Korean characters on the menu for it, I was given a seat. After a delicious meal, the waiter came to speak with me and was surprised to discover that I was born in the United States: "Dude," the young dude exclaimed in unaccented English, "I just moved here from California." After finishing his degree at UCLA, he was sent to São Paulo to help with a family business, and was living with cousins whose children were learning Hebrew in the aforementioned neighborhood Jewish school.

Korean immigrants generally lead middle-class lives in Brazil, in large part because they arrive with some cash available to invest. This is not the case for the many Chinese immigrants who came to Brazil after World War II. As you will recall, nineteenth-century attempts to bring Chinese labor were not successful, and in this regard, Brazil is distinct from the United States, Canada, Cuba, and Peru. In the 1980s, however, Chinese immigration expanded along with Brazilian–Chinese commercial relations. While a 2005 report from the Overseas Compatriot Affairs Commission of the Republic of China's (Taiwan) put the number of immigrants at 150,000, press reports cite figures two times larger.

Chinese immigrants often enter Brazil via Paraguay and frequently move back and forth between the two countries. About seventy-five percent live in São Paulo where some of them work in the low-end clothing industry as producers, retailers, or both. Others focus on the retail and wholesale sales of inexpensive imported products like toys, writing utensils, watches, and electronics. While many enter Brazil without full documentation, they have been able to take advantage of the country's frequent immigrant amnesty programs. Like Koreans, Chinese live in significant numbers in traditional immigrant neighborhoods. Indeed, many shops in the formerly "Arab" neighborhoods of São Paulo, Rio de Janeiro, and Porto Alegre are now owned by Chinese immigrants. The newcomers have also purchased many of the *lanchonettes* ("small diners") located in city centers and around the bus stations that serve poor migrants. In those locations, customers eat "Arab" esfihas and "Chinese" wonton soup, along with the archetypically Brazilian rice and beans.

As Korean and Chinese immigrants ascend the economic ladder, still more immigrants from Asia see Brazil as a country where they can start anew. Brazil's 2010 census showed one million more people declaring their race as "yellow" than in the 2000 census. (Color is the way race is counted in the Brazilian census: In 2010, almost fifty-one percent of the population declared themselves "black" or "brown.") The total number of self-declared "yellow" respondents, more than two million, represents more than one percent of the total Brazilian population. The rise in numbers is attributed largely to Chinese immigrants and the growing number of Brazilian of mixed parentage who define themselves as Asian-Brazilians.[7] Most Chinese immigrants, like Koreans and Japanese in earlier decades, have high educational ambitions for their children, who attend schools in lower-middle-class neighborhoods in

[7] "Em 10 anos, país ganha 1 milhão de moradores que se declaram amarelos," *O Estado de S. Paulo*, 23 July 2011, A20.

increasing numbers. These children often enter universities, and with success, a new version of an old and ugly joke about Nikkei has started to circulate among the São Paulo elite: "To get a place at the University of São Paulo you have to first kill an Asian."

Other New Immigrants

Stereotypes also play a part in Jewish and Arab postwar immigration to Brazil. After the war, Oswaldo Aranha, the former foreign minister and an ex-ambassador to the United States, became president of the United Nations General Assembly that approved the plans for the creation of the modern state of Israel put forward by the U.N. Palestine Commission. Brazil and Aranha, both crucial to the decision, were considered friends of Israel and Zionism. In Tel Aviv, a street was named after Aranha, as was a cultural center in a kibbutz settled by Brazilian Jews. Even Aranha's reported comment that the creation of Israel meant that the Rio de Janeiro neighborhood of Copacabana would be returned to the "Brazilians" passed unnoticed.

Following the Suez crisis and the rise of Arab nationalism in the 1950s, about five thousand Jews from Egypt and other Middle Eastern countries immigrated to Brazil. Non-Jewish immigration patterns from the Middle East to Latin America also changed dramatically after World War II. The numbers of Lebanese and Syrian immigrants diminished and the numbers of Palestinians increased. While there are no exact figures, it appears that Brazil currently has a Palestinian population of about 50,000. This compares to 500,000 in Chile, 67,000 in the United States, and 54,000 in Honduras.[8] While some settled in Brazil after Jordan annexed what had been part of Palestine in 1948, much larger numbers arrived following the Six Day War between Israel and numerous Arab states in 1967, as well as during the Lebanese civil war that began in 1975.

Many Palestinian immigrants have settled in the south of Brazil, most noticeably in the city of Foz do Iguaçu in the state of Paraná. Unlike earlier, primarily Christian, Middle Eastern immigrants, new Palestinians are often Muslim and the city's Omar Ibn Al-Khattab mosque is the largest outside of the Middle East. One result of this new immigration is that the "triple border" where Paraguay,

---

[8] Helena Lindholm Schulz and Juliane Hammer, *The Palestinian Diaspora: Formation of Identities and Politics of Homeland* (London: Routledge, 2003); Nancie L. Gonzalez, *Dollar, Dove, and Eagle: One Hundred Years of Palestinian Migration to Honduras* (Ann Arbor: University of Michigan Press, 1993).

Argentina, and Brazil meet has been treated with international suspicion because of an unproven connection with terrorism. In an interesting local twist, some leaders of Brazil's established Arab-descent community seem uncomfortable with Palestinians. A 2000 law allowing Brazilians to marry spouses abroad and return to Brazil under a "family reunification" category was heavily criticized by influential Arab-Brazilians of the Christian faith for encouraging the creation of Muslim enclaves in Brazil.[9]

Immigration to Brazil after World War II has also been marked by the many entries from other Latin American countries, notably those in the Southern Cone (see Table E.4). Sometimes these migrations were short term, as dictatorships in one place led to refuge in another. At other times the wages available in different national settings have motivated the shifts. In 1991, the Southern Cone Common Market (Mercosul/Mercosur) was established by Brazil, Paraguay, Uruguay, and Argentina, with Chile, Bolivia, Peru, Venezuela, Ecuador, and Colombia later becoming associate members. In 2004, the Mercosur countries began to regularize migration policies, and this has led to an increased movement of people and products among Brazil, Argentina, Uruguay, and Bolivia.

Immigrants from within Latin America have posed unique challenges to Brazil's national identity. For example, hundreds of thousands of Brazilians and their descendants (estimates range from 300,000 to 450,000) have lived for more than fifty years in Paraguay, making up almost ten percent of the population. Called *brasiguayos* (*brasiguaios* in Portuguese), most migrated from areas in southern Brazil where German, Italian, and Polish settlement was heavy in the nineteenth century. They moved in the 1960s and 1970s when Paraguay's dictator offered to sell land cheaply to farmers. Today, brasiguayos own significant amounts of land and have dominant economic positions in their new homeland. Their European phenotypes and their use of Portuguese as a first (or simultaneous first) language, often while refusing to learn Guarani (one of Paraguay's two official languages), has infuriated those from more traditional backgrounds. Many brasiguayos do not have Brazilian citizenship, and so pressure on the Brazilian government to protect its "citizens abroad" often comes into conflict with the definition of descent and citizenship in international law.

[9] John Tofik Karam, *Another Arabesque: Syrian-Lebanese Ethnicity in Neoliberal Brazil* (Philadelphia: Temple University Press. 2007), 96.

Table E.4. *Latin American Migrants Resident in Brazil, 1970–2000*

Country of Birth	1970	1980	1990	2000
Bolivia	10,712	12,980	15,691	20,398
Argentina	17,213	26,633	25,468	27,531
Uruguay	13,582	21,238	22,143	24,740
Paraguay	20,025	17,560	19,018	28,822
Peru	2,410	3,789	5,833	10,841
Chile	1,900	17,830	20,437	17,131
Total	**65,842**	**100,030**	**108,590**	**129,463**

Source: Iara Rolnik Xavier, "Projeto migratório e espaço: Os migrantes bolivianos na Região Metropolitana de São Paulo," M.A. thesis, Departamento de Demografia do Instituto de Filosofia e Ciências Humanas, State University of Campinas, 2010, p. 42.

While Brazilians have moved to Paraguay, hundreds of thousands of Bolivians have come to Brazil.[10] Bolivian migration is part of a broader pattern of emigration within Latin America, notably to Argentina where many live in Buenos Aires and work mainly in construction. In Brazil, Bolivians usually settle in São Paulo where population estimates range from sixty thousand (by the Bolivian consulate) to more than two hundred thousand (by a church group working specifically with Bolivians). Other significant populations live in the Brazilian states of Mato Grosso and Mato Grosso do Sul, which are closest to the Bolivian border.

Many Bolivian immigrants to Brazil are undocumented and often work in sweatshops owned by other immigrants. American republics have dealt differently with undocumented immigrants, but Brazilian legislation is more tolerant than that in many other places, perhaps because of Brazilian national identity constructions, which assume that immigrants are "better" than natives. Brazil had amnesty programs for undocumented immigrants in 1980, 1988, 1998, and 2009. The last three programs regularized the status of more than a hundred thousand foreign residents, with more than forty thousand coming from Bolivia and almost twenty-five thousand from China. Other significant groups represented were from Lebanon, South Korea, and Peru.[11]

[10] Simone Buechler, "Sweating It in the Brazilian Garment Industry: Korean and Bolivian Immigrants and Global Economic Forces in São Paulo," *Latin American Perspectives* 31: 3 (May 2004), 99–119.
[11] Iara Rolnik Xavier, "Projeto migratório e espaço: Os migrantes bolivianos na Região Metropolitana de São Paulo," M.A. thesis: Departamento de Demografia

EMIGRATION

For most of the last two hundred years, Brazil has been a destination for immigrants. Yet in the 1980s, that began to change when a serious economic crisis hit all sectors of the population. Even at the start of the twenty-first century with an improved economy, Brazil has more emigrants than immigrants. Most Brazilians work in lower-status jobs abroad, although significant numbers are skilled and highly educated. In 2010, Brazil's Ministry of Justice estimated that four million Brazilians lived abroad, with large groups in the United States, Paraguay (see the previous discussion of brasiguayos), Japan, the United Kingdom, Portugal, Italy, Switzerland, and Angola. The numbers of Brazilian emigrants since 2000 have averaged about a hundred thousand per year, with about fifty percent coming from Brazil's southeastern states of Minas Gerais, Paraná, São Paulo, and Goiás.

Emigration from Brazil is the result of the confluence of several factors. One, of course, is wages and the desire for economic and social ascension, the same factors that motivated so many to immigrate to Brazil before World War II. Remittances thus play an important part of the Brazilian economy; in 2002, for example, 4.6 billion U.S. dollars were sent to Brazil by citizens living abroad, representing one percent of Brazil's gross national product. A second factor was that Portugal's economy grew with its entry into the European Common Market, and free flow between that country and its former colony created a large population of Brazilians in Portugal. Finally, many European countries make it relatively easy for the children or grandchildren of immigrants to get second passports. As a result, emigrants from Brazil are often the descendants of immigrants to Brazil. This phenomenon is also noticeable in Argentina, and in both countries the lines outside of Italian consulates are filled with Latin Americans eager to become European Common Market citizens.[12]

Brazilian emigration to the United States is particularly large, although the numbers are not always clear. In 2000, the Brazilian Ministry of Foreign Relations estimated that there were almost 800,000 Brazilians, whereas the United States census of that year listed the number at

do Instituto de Filosofia e Ciências Humanas, State University of Campinas, 2010, 67.

12 Arnd Schneider, *Futures Lost: Nostalgia and Identity among Italian Immigrants in Argentina* (Oxford: Peter Lang, 2000).

212,430. The 2008 population, according to the U.S. Census Bureau, was 351,914, although other estimates put the population at closer to one million.[13] Brazilians are unusual Latin American immigrants to the United States because of their high educational levels, which usually include high school diplomas.[14] They are typical in migrating in a point-to-point fashion, from one specific city to another. Thus, the Boston area has a very large number of immigrants from Minas Gerais, often from the area of Governador Valadares, where a number of New England companies had semiprecious stone operations in the 1950s. In Atlanta, most immigrants are from the state of Goiás and come via church networks.

Another focus of Brazilian emigration is Japan, where the phenomenon known as *dekasegui* (a Japanese term meaning "working away from home" that has come to define descendants of Japanese and their families who have migrated to Japan) began in force in 1990. The Brazilian population in Japan is more than a quarter of a million (see Table E.5), and initial motivations for migration to Japan were twofold. One was the stagnation of the Brazilian economy in the late 1980s. The second was an amendment to Japan's Immigration Control and Refugee Recognition Law in 1990 that allowed Japanese descendants (called *nikkeijin* in Japan) up to the third generation and their spouses to have work visas. Government officials believed that encouraging the entry of those of Japanese descent would end illegal immigration (notably from the Middle East) and provide workers for factories facing a labor shortage. While some Nikkei from Bolivia, Peru, and Argentina took advantage of the new legislation, by far the largest group was from Brazil.

---

[13] U.S. Census Bureau, "United States–Selected Population Profile in the United States (Brazilian [360–364])," 2008 American Community Survey 1-Year Estimates, available at: http://factfinder.census.gov/servlet/IPTable?_bm=y&-reg=ACS_2008_1YR_G00_S0201:519;ACS_2008_1YR_G00_S0201PR:519;ACS_2008_1YR_G00_S0201T:519;ACS_2008_1YR_G00_S0201TPR:519&-qr_name=ACS_2008_1YR_G00_S0201&-qr_name=ACS_2008_1YR_G00_S0201PR&-qr_name=ACS_2008_1YR_G00_S0201T&-qr_name=ACS_2008_1YR_G00_S0201TPR&-ds_name=ACS_2008_1YR_G00_&-TABLE_NAMEX=&-ci_type=A&-redoLog=true&-charIterations=414&-geo_id=01000US&-geo_id=NBSP&-format=&-_lang=en.

[14] Maxine L. Margolis, *An Invisible Minority: Brazilians in New York City* (Gainesville: University Press of Florida, 2009).

Table E.5. *Registered Brazilian Nationals in Japan (1989–2009)*

1989	15,000*
1990	56,000
1991	119,000
1992	148,000
1993	155,000
1994	160,000
1995	176,000
1996	202,000
1997	233,000
1998	222,000
1999	224,000
2000	254,000
2001	266,000
2002	268,000
2003	275,000
2004	287,000
2005	302,000
2006	312,979
2007	316,967
2008	312,582
2009	267,456

*Figures to the nearest thousand.
Source: Available at: http://www.moj.go.jp/content/000058065.pdf, Table 4.2, p. 122; Koji Sasaki, "A Ruptured Circuit: The Recession and the Breakdown of the *Dekassegui* System," working paper presented at the 109th American Anthropological Association Annual Meeting, New Orleans, November, 2010, used by permission of the author.

In 2005, Brazilians made up about eighty percent of the more than three hundred thousand Latin Americans in Japan. Many were well educated and often members of Brazil's middle class. In Japan, however, they worked in factories, often in medium-size cities where automotive and electronics companies experienced a loss of native workers as young people moved to larger urban settings. Brazilian workers became famous for their willingness to work at "three K" jobs: *Kitsui*, *Kitani*, and *Kiken* – hard, dirty, and dangerous. They earned a modest salary by Japanese standards, but one that represented five to ten times their Brazilian incomes. One important strategy was to work overtime hours, which were paid at a wage of 1.5 to two times the regular salary. In 2005 alone, US$ 2.65 billion was remitted from Japan to Latin America, with US$ 2.2 billion going to Brazil, US$ 365 million to Peru, and only

US$ 100 million to Bolivia, Paraguay, and Colombia combined.[15] Not surprisingly, the Brazilian remittances were directly correlated to the states that had received the most Japanese immigrants and thus today have large Nikkei populations: São Paulo received US$ 1.25 billion, Paraná US$ 650 million, Mato Grosso do Sul US$ 100 million, and Pará US$ 25 million.[16]

Brazilian migration to Japan in the 1990s was not unlike that from Europe to Brazil a century earlier. Brazilian banks opened branches that would facilitate remittances (see the advertisement in Figure E.1). Emigration brokers sold a vision of Japan that was often untrue, and scams were common. Upon arrival, Brazilian immigrants were often treated poorly both in work and social spaces. The children and grandchildren of Japanese immigrants were surprised to find that they were expected to act "Japanese" even though they were Brazilian.

As Brazil's economy grew stronger in the 2000s, and as Japan's economy weakened, the migratory trends reversed slightly. In 2006, remittances from Japan to Brazil dropped to $2.2 billion (compared to $2.7 billion from the United States and $1 billion from Europe out of a total of $6.4 billion), and the amounts have continued to fall. In 2009, only fifteen thousand new Brazilian Nikkei officially registered to work in Japan, down from the 2005 high of more than forty-six thousand. Earnings were only eighty percent of what they had been a decade earlier, and overtime work was no longer available. Even so, following in the traditional patterns of immigrant settlement, Brazilians have remained in Japan. Yet unlike in the Americas, birthplace is not linked to citizenship in Japan, and thus the generation of children born and educated there remains Brazilian, the opposite of what happened in the brasiguayos case.

In April 2009, the Japanese government created a new policy that offered Latin American immigrants a stipend of $3,000 for airfare and $2,000 for each dependent, in return for their agreement to leave permanently and not to pursue future employment in Japan. The program ended in March 2010, and of the 21,675 Nikkei who took advantage

---

[15] Inter-American Development Bank, Multilateral Investment Fund, *Remittances to Latin America from Japan* (Fact Sheet), Okinawa, Japan: April 2005, available at: http://idbdocs.iadb.org/wsdocs/getdocument.aspx?docnum=546696.

[16] Flávio Nishimori, "Remessas continuam impulsionando economia: Valor enviado pelos dekasseguis ao Brasil deve aumentar em 15% este ano," *International Press* (São Paulo) January 11, 2006, available at: http://www.ipcdigital.com/br/Noticias/Comunidade/Remessas-continuam-impulsionando-economia.

Figure E.1. An advertisement encouraging Brazilian Nikkei to have emigrant relatives in Japan send remittances: "Receba remessas do Japão pelo Itaú" (October
2006, Liberdade, São Paulo).
Source: Photograph by Koji Sasaki, used by permission.

of the program, 20,053 were Brazilian, 903 were Peruvian and 719
came from other nationalities, primarily Bolivian.[17] According to the
Japanese Ministry of Justice, the number of Brazilians living in Japan
in 2009 was still more than a quarter of a million, though significantly
lower than its high a few years earlier.

CONCLUSION

Brazil's dekasegui highlight the fact that emigration and immigration
cannot simply be linked to wage differentials. As in the past, everything from ethnicity, how individuals imagine their new lives, and the
link between personal identity and national citizenship is at play when
people decided to migrate. Like their nineteenth-century European
counterparts, Brazilian-Japanese immigrants believed that they were

---

[17] Japan, Ministry of Health, Labor and Welfare (2011), "The result of a program
to those unemployed of Japanese descent wishing to return to home country,"
available at: http://www.mhlw.go.jp/bunya/koyou/gaikokujin15/kikoku_shien.
html.

migrating temporarily in order to become wealthy and return home. Yet over time, the immigrants established new lives, had families, and remained. They often saw the old homeland as foreign and became comfortable in the new one. Natives were equally changed by immigration. Unrealistic elite expectations, as we have seen, led to a pattern of enthusiasm and then disenchantment. In Brazil, racism and discrimination existed alongside a growing belief that immigrants were creating a better country.

In the current decade, immigrants continue to be an important, and growing, part of the Brazilian population in all of the formal categories (entry, naturalizations, permanent residency). According to the Ministry of Justice, Brazil has almost one million legal foreign residents. Hundreds of thousands more do not possess formal documentation. The numbers represent both older and newer immigrant groups but do not include Brazilian-born children or naturalized citizens. The largest current foreign-born groups, according to government statistics, are Portuguese (270,000); Japanese (92,000); Italian (69,000); Spanish (58,000); Argentine (39,000); Bolivian (33,000); German (28,000); Uruguayan (28,000); U.S. (28,000); Chinese (27,000); Korean (16,000); French (16,000); Lebanese (13,000); and Peruvian (10,000).[18] Paraguayans are entering in growing numbers. So are Angolans, who began immigrating when the country became independent from Portugal in 1975, and also Nigerians, who are part of a growing diaspora found throughout the Americas.

The ebbs and flows of immigrants are particularly apparent during World Cup years, when this international soccer championship has more television viewers than any other single sporting event. In 2006, sixty million people watched Brazil defeat Croatia in the opening week of the championship. More than ten times that number watched the final game in 2010. In Brazil, numerous channels broadcast the national team games simultaneously. In many parts of the country, another phenomenon takes place. A few supporters root for the teams of their ancestors, but most cheer for Brazil. Ethnic restaurants are filled with excited fans, most opposing the team of the country whose food they happen to be eating. When the World Cup was held in Japan in 2002, some Japanese-Brazilians started wearing T-shirts with an image of the

---

[18] Available at: http://portal.mj.gov.br/data/Pages/MJA5F550A5lTEMIDBA915BD3AC384F6C81A1AC4AF88BE2D0PTBRNN.htm (accessed May 15, 2012).

rising sun and the phrase "I will never visit you." This saying made clear that Japan had no place in public expressions of national identity among Nikkei. Many fans of the Rio de Janeiro futebol team Flamengo took a different approach. Their allegiance was to the team's greatest player, Zico, who in 2002 was coach of the Japanese national team. As Japanese-Brazilians roared for Brazil, Flamengo's diehards screamed for Japan.

The story of immigration to and from Brazil is far from over.

HISTORIOGRAPHICAL ESSAY

It is surprising how little attention is paid to immigration and immigrants to Latin America in the English-language academic literature. There are a number of explanations. Scholars often treat immigrants as "foreign" and thus outside of the national experience. Many Latin American intellectuals see immigrants and their descendants in the same way. As a result, scholarly work often focuses away from immigration and immigrant ethnicity, often toward questions of race, especially among those of African and indigenous descent.

In Brazil, scholarship on immigration is widespread but frequently conducted outside of the formal academy. Much of the research is done by community historians, especially of groups that have been traditionally oriented toward education. Thus, there are as many books on Jewish and Asian immigrants in Brazil as there are on Portuguese or Italians. In all of the cases, however, the emphasis tends toward community institutions or important individuals.

Within the academy, most research is on elite discourses concerning immigrants. This often leads to the impression that the newcomers were primarily victims. It is only recently that calls for "new ethnic studies" have begun to change research models in Latin America, especially those that would suggest commonalities in the experiences of immigrant groups and their descendants. It is certain that over the next decades we will learn more about the ways in which immigrants and nonimmigrants interacted. We will see studies arguing that the descendants of immigrants should be treated as Brazilians rather than as foreigners. A broader comparative approach to immigration in the Americas is also needed. While we know something about individual nations with large numbers of immigrants (like Brazil, Argentina, Uruguay, the United

States, and Canada), we know little about similarities since studies usually emphasize the differences between countries.

Many important books and articles can be found in the footnotes to
this volume. The following pages identify other books in English available in college and university libraries or online. The bibliographies
and footnotes in these scholarly works will point readers to a wide range
of primary and secondary sources in Portuguese, Spanish, English, and
other languages. Because of the paucity of English-language secondary
sources about immigration to Brazil, some paragraphs are grouped by
"type" of emigration and include works about Latin American countries
other than Brazil.

The classic general history of Brazil is Thomas E. Skidmore, *Brazil:
Five Centuries of Change* (Oxford University Press, 1999). A very different, and equally useful, approach is Boris Fausto, *A Concise History
of Brazil* (Cambridge University Press, 1999). Other excellent broad
histories are Marshall C. Eakin, *Brazil: The Once and Future Country*
(Palgrave Macmillan, 1998), and Joseph A. Page, *The Brazilians* (Da
Capo Press, 1996). Two important demographic studies are Thomas W.
Merrick and Douglas H. Graham, *Population and Economic Development
in Brazil, 1800 to the Present* (Johns Hopkins University Press, 1979),
and Nicolás Sánchez-Albornoz, *The Population of Latin America: A
History* (University of California Press, 1974). For a sense of some
national myths about the relationship between immigration and
national identity and how they were constructed, three classics from
Brazilian scholars are available in English: José Honório Rodrigues, *The
Brazilians: Their Character and Aspirations* (University of Texas Press,
[1967] 2011); Darcy Ribeiro, *The Brazilian People: The Formation and
Meaning of Brazil* (University Presses of Florida, [1995] 2000); Gilberto
Freyre, *The Masters and the Slaves: A Study in the Development of Brazilian
Civilization* (University of California Press, [1933] 1986).

For the colonial period, the Leslie Bethell–edited *Colonial Brazil*
(Cambridge University Press, 1987) is excellent. For an examination
of the early settlers in Latin America, see Ida Altman and James P.
P. Horn, *"To Make America": European Emigration in the Early Modern
Period* (University of California Press, 1991). A book more focused on
the modern period is Robert M. Levine and John J. Crocitti, *The Brazil
Reader: History, Culture and Politics* (Duke University Press, 1999).
An overview of the transatlantic slave trade and forced migration of
Africans is found in David Eltis, *Coerced and Free Migration: Global
Perspectives* (Stanford University Press, 2002).

On the impact of slavery in Brazil prior to the advent of mass immigration, see Stuart B. Schwartz, *Slaves, Peasants, and Rebels: Reconsidering Brazilian Slavery* (University of Illinois Press, 1995), and João José Reis, *Slave Rebellion in Brazil: The Muslim Uprising of 1835 in Bahia* (Johns Hopkins University Press, 1995). An important study of the Argentine case is George Reid Andrews, *The Afro-Argentines of Buenos Aires, 1800–1900* (The University of Wisconsin Press, 1980). A superb examination of the politics surrounding slavery is Jeffrey D. Needell, *The Party of Order: The Conservatives, the State, and Slavery in the Brazilian Monarchy* (Stanford University Press, 2006). For intriguing discussions of the challenges to the established racial order in Brazil, see Laura Jarnagin Pang, *A Confluence of Transatlantic Networks: Elites, Capitalism, and Confederate Migration to Brazil* (University of Alabama Press, 2008), and David J. Hellwig, ed., *African-American Reflections on Brazil's Racial Paradise* (Temple University Press, 1992).

Immigration was critical to Brazil's shift from colony to empire to republic. During the centuries of change numerous Europeans traveled in the country, and facsimiles of many of the original publications are available on the Internet. Some of the most interesting include C. F. Van Delden Laërne, *Brazil and Java: Report on Coffee-Culture in America, Asia and Africa, to H. E. the minister of the colonies* (London: W. H. Allen & Co., 1885); the four volumes of Charles Darwin, *Voyages of the Adventure and Beagle Proceedings of the First Expedition, 1826–30, under the command of Captain P. Parker King, R. N., F. R. S* (London: Henry, 1838); John Luccock, *Notes on Rio de Janeiro and the Southern Parts of Brazil: Taken During a Residence of Ten Years in That Country from 1808 to 1818* (London: Samuel Leigh, in the Strand, 1820).

Important scholarly tomes on moments of political transition in Brazil include Kirsten Schultz, *Tropical Versailles: Empire, Monarchy, and the Portuguese Royal Court in Rio de Janeiro, 1808–1821* (Routledge, 2001); Roderick Barman, *Brazil: The Forging of a Nation, 1798–1852* (Stanford University Press, 1988); Jeffrey D. Needell, *A Tropical Belle Epoque: Elite Culture and Society in Turn-of-the-Century Rio de Janeiro* (Cambridge University Press, 1987); Neill Macaulay, *Dom Pedro: The Struggle for Liberty in Brazil and Portugal, 1798–1834* (Duke University Press, 1986); and Emília Viotti da Costa, *The Brazilian Empire: Myths and Histories* (University of Chicago, 1985). The transition from slave to wage labor is treated in works like Stanley J. Stein, *Vassouras: A Brazilian Coffee County, 1850–1900* (Princeton University Press Reprint, 1986); Warren Dean, *Rio Claro: A Brazilian Plantation System,*

1820–1920 (Stanford University Press, 1976); and Michael M. Hall, "The Origins of Mass Immigration to Brazil, 1871–1914" (unpublished Ph.D. diss., Columbia University, 1969).

For a broad overview of immigration to Latin America, see Samuel L. Baily and Eduardo José Miguez, eds., *Mass Migration to Modern Latin America* (SR Books, 2003); Magnus Mörner and Harold Sims, *Adventurers and Proletarians: The Story of Migrants in Latin America* (University of Pittsburgh Press, 1985); and Fernando DeAvila Bastos, *Immigration in Latin America* (Pan American Union, 1964).

Brazilian immigration took place in the context of the competition with Argentina in the nineteenth and twentieth centuries. The groundbreaking book in this regard is Thomas H. Holloway, *Immigrants on the Land: Coffee and Society in São Paulo, 1886–1930* (University of North Carolina Press, 1980). Works focusing on Argentina include Arnd Schneider, *Futures Lost: Nostalgia and Identity among Italian Immigrants in Argentina* (Peter Lang, 2000); Jose C. Moya, *Cousins and Strangers, Spanish Immigrants in Buenos Aires, 1850–1930* (University of California Press, 1998); Samuel L. Baily and Franco Ramella, *One Family, Two Worlds: An Italian Family's Correspondence Across the Atlantic, 1901–1922* (Rutgers University Press, 1988); and Carl Solberg, *Immigration and Nationalism: Argentina and Chile, 1890–1914* (University of Texas Press, 1970).

The comparison between immigrant experiences in Latin America and the United States is important. One excellent work is Samuel L. Baily, *Immigrants in the Lands of Promise: Italians in Buenos Aires and New York City, 1870–1914* (Cornell University Press, 1999). Professor Baily's work is debated in a fascinating "Forum" in the *American Historical Review* 88: 2 (April 1983). One of the few books on Middle Eastern immigrants to the United States that includes a Latin American comparative perspective is Sarah M. Gualtieri, *Between Arab and White: Race and Ethnicity in the Early Syrian American Diaspora* (University of California Press, 2009).

Innovative books that speak to broader immigrant experiences in the Americas and provide methods that could be applied to the study of immigration and immigrants in Latin America include Raanan Rein, *Argentine Jews or Jewish Argentines? Essays on Ethnicity, Identity, and Diaspora* (Brill, 2010); Jane Ziegelman, *97 Orchard: An Edible History of Five Immigrant Families in One New York Tenement* (HarperCollins, 2010); Anna Pegler-Gordon, *In Sight of America: Photography and* the *Development of U.S. Immigration Policy* (University of California Press, 2009); and Ronald T. Takaki, *A Different Mirror: A History of Multicultural America* (Back Bay Books, 1993).

Immigration to Brazil cannot be separated from broad questions of race and ethnic relations. On these topics see May E. Bletz, *Immigration and Acculturation in Brazil and Argentina, 1890–1929* (Palgrave Macmillan, 2010); Darin Davis and Oliver Marshall, eds., *Stefan and Lotte Zweig's South American Letters: New York, Argentina and Brazil, 1940–42* (Continuum, 2010); Nancy P. Appelbaum, Anne S. Macpherson, and Karin Alejandra Rosemblatt, eds., *Race and Nation in Modern Latin American* (University of North Carolina Press, 2003; Melissa Nobles, *Shades of Citizenship: Race and the Census in Modern Politics* (Stanford University Press, 2000); Jeffrey Lesser, *Negotiating National Identity: Immigrants, Minorities and the Struggle for Ethnicity in Brazil* (Duke University Press, 1999); Robert Stam, *Tropical Multiculturalism: A Comparative History of Race in Brazilian Cinema* (Duke University Press, 1998); Thomas E. Skidmore, *Black into White: Race and Nationality in Brazilian Thought* (Duke University Press, 1993); and Nancy Leys Stepan, *"The Hour of Eugenics": Race, Gender and Nation in Latin America* (Cornell University Press, 1991).

For an excellent overview of race relations in Latin America, see the Richard Graham–edited *The Idea of Race in Latin America* (University of Texas Press, 1990). Books that provide important, and different, views of immigrant-led industrialization are George Reid Andrews, *Blacks and Whites in São Paulo, Brazil, 1888–1988* (University of Wisconsin Press, 1991); James. R. Scobie, *Buenos Aires: Plaza to Suburb, 1870–1910* (Oxford University Press, 1974); and Warren Dean, *The Industrialization of São Paulo, 1880–1945* (University of Texas Press: 1969).

For those interested in how individual Brazilian states dealt with immigration and immigrants, see Joseph Love, *São Paulo in the Brazilian Federation, 1889–1937* (Stanford University Press, 1980); Eul-Soo Pang, *Bahia in the First Republic: Coronelismo and Oligarchies (1889–1934)* (University Presses of Florida, 1979); Robert M. Levine, *Pernambuco in the Brazilian Federation, 1889–1937* (Stanford University Press, 1978); John D. Wirth, *Minas Gerais in the Brazilian Federation, 1889–1937* (Stanford University Press, 1977); and Joseph Love, *Rio Grande do Sul and Brazilian Regionalism, 1882–1930* (Stanford University Press, 1971).

The following books focus broadly on specific immigrant groups in Brazil and Latin America:

German immigration: Krista O'Donnell, Renate Bridenthal, and Nancy Reagin, eds., *The Heimat Abroad: The Boundaries of Germanness* (The University of Michigan Press, 2005); Jürgen Buchenau, *Tools of Progress: A German Merchant Family in Mexico City, 1865–Present* (University of New Mexico Press, 2004); Dirk Hoerder and Jörg Nagler, *People in Transit: German Migrations in Comparative Perspective, 1820–1930* (German Historical Institute, 1995); Frederick C. Luebke, *Germans in the New World: Essays in the History of Immigration* (University of Illinois Press, 1990); Leo Spitzer, *Lives in Between: Assimilation and Marginality in Austria, Brazil, West Africa, 1780–1945* (Cambridge University Press, 1989); Frederick C. Luebke, *Germans in Brazil: A Comparative History of Cultural Conflict During World War I* (Louisiana State University Press, 1987); and Ronald C. Newton, *German Buenos Aires, 1900–1933: Social Change and Cultural Crisis* (University of Texas Press, 1977).

Italian immigration: Gloria La Cava, *Italians in Brazil: The Post–World War II Experience* (Peter Lang, 1999), and Warren Dean, *Remittances of Italian Immigrants: From Brazil, Argentina, Uruguay and U. S. A., 1884–1914* (New York University, Ibero-American Language and Area Center, 1974).

Portuguese immigration: Rosana Barbosa, *Immigration and Xenophobia in Early Nineteenth Century Rio de Janeiro* (University Press of America, 2008), and Marcelo J. Borges, *Chains of Gold: Portuguese Migration to Argentina in Transatlantic Perspective* (Brill, 2009).

Jewish immigration: Judith Elkin, *The Jews of Latin America* (Scholarly Publishing Office, University of Michigan Library, 2011); Sandra McGee Deutsch, *Crossing Borders, Claiming a Nation: A History of Argentine Jewish Women, 1880–1955* (Duke University Press, 2010); Jeffrey Lesser and Raanan Rein, eds., *Rethinking Jewish-Latin Americans* (University of New Mexico Press, 2008); Erin Graff Zivin, *The Wandering Signifier: Rhetoric of Jewishness in the Latin American Imaginary* (Duke University Press, 2008); Kristin Ruggiero, ed., *The Jewish Diaspora in Latin America and the Caribbean: Fragments of Memory* (Sussex Academic Press, 2005); Leo Spitzer, *Hotel Bolivia: The Culture of Memory in a Refuge from Nazism* (Hill and Wang, 1999); Sander L. Gilman and Milton Shain, *Jewries at the Frontier: Accommodation, Identity, Conflict* (University of Illinois Press, 1999); Jeffrey Lesser and Ignacio Klich, *Arab and Jewish Immigrants in Latin America: Images and Realities* (Frank Cass, 1998); David Sheinin and Lois Baer Barr, eds., *The Jewish Diaspora in Latin*

America (Garland Publishing, 1996); Katherine Morris, ed., *Odyssey of Exile: Jewish Women Flee the Nazis for Brazil* (Wayne State University Press, 1996); Jeffrey Lesser, *Welcoming the Undesirables: Brazil and the Jewish Question* (University of California Press, 1994); and Haim Avni, *Argentina and the Jews: A History of Jewish Immigration* (University of Alabama Press, 1991).

Asian immigration: Robert Chao Romero, *The Chinese in Mexico, 1882–1940* (University of Arizona Press, 2010); Jeffrey Lesser, *A Discontented Diaspora: Japanese-Brazilians and the Meanings of Ethnic Militancy, 1960–1980* (Duke University Press, 2007); Cristina Rocha, *Zen in Brazil: The Quest for Cosmopolitan Modernity* (University of Hawaii Press, 2006); Lok C. D. Siu, *Memories of a Future Home: Diasporic Citizenship of Chinese in Panama* (Stanford University Press, 2005); Wanni W. Anderson and Robert G. Lee, eds., *Displacements and Diasporas: Asians in the Americas* (Rutgers University Press, 2005); Daniel M. Masterson with Sayaka Funada-Classen, *The Japanese in Latin America* (University of Illinois Press, 2004); Lane Ryo Hirabayashi, Akemi Kikumura, and James A. Hirabayashi, eds., *New Worlds, New Lives: Globalization and People of Japanese Descent in the Americas and from Latin America in Japan* (Stanford University Press, 2002); Roshni Rustomji-Kerns, *Encounters: People of Asian Descent in the Americas* (Rowman and Littlefield, 1999); Walton Look Lai, *Indentured Labor, Caribbean Sugar: Chinese and Indian Migrants to the British West Indies, 1838–1918* (Johns Hopkins University Press, 1993); and C. Harvey Gardiner, *Pawns in a Triangle of Hate: The Peruvian Japanese and the United States* (University of Washington Press, 1981).

Middle Eastern (Arab) immigration: Jeffrey Lesser and Raanan Rein, eds., *Together Yet Apart: Arabs and Jews in Latin America*, special issue of *Latin American and Caribbean Ethnic Studies*, 6: 2 (2011); John Tofik Karam, *Another Arabesque: Syrian-Lebanese Ethnicity in Neoliberal Brazil* (Temple University Press, 2007); Theresa Alfaro-Velcamp, *So Far from Allah, So Close to Mexico: Middle Eastern Immigrants in Modern Mexico* (University of Texas Press, 2007); Christina Civantos, *Between Argentines and Arabs: Argentine Orientalism, Arab Immigrants, and the Writing of Identity* (State University of New York Press, 2005); and Albert Hourani and Nadim Shehadi, eds., *The Lebanese in the World: A Century of Emigration* (I. B. Tauris and St. Martin's Press, 1992).

Brazilian emigration: Maxine L. Margolis, *An Invisible Minority: Brazilians in New York City* (University Press of Florida, 2009); Clémence Jouët-Pastré and Leticia J. Braga, eds., *Becoming Brazuca: Brazilian*

Immigration to the United States (David Rockefeller Center Series on Latin American Studies, 2008); Jeffrey Lesser, ed., *Searching for Home Abroad: Japanese Brazilians and Transnationalism* (Duke University Press, 2003); Daniel Linger, *No One Home: Brazilian Selves Remade in Japan* (Stanford University Press, 2001); Joshua Hotaka Roth, *Brokered Homeland: Japanese Brazilian Migrants in Japan* (Cornell University Press, 2002); and Karen Tei Yamashita *Circle K Cycles* (Coffee House Press, 2001).

Many novels are centered around immigrant and immigrant-descended characters in Brazil. Among those easily available in English are Milton Hatoum, *The Brothers* (Farrar, Straus and Giroux, 2002); Jô Soares, *A Samba for Sherlock* (Vintage Books, 1998); Karen Tei Yamashita, *Brazil-Maru: A Novel* (Coffee House Press, 1992); and Jorge Amado, *Gabriela, Clove and Cinnamon* (Knopf Doubleday Publishing Group, 2006). Much of the work of Moacy Scliar has now been translated into English, and his novels give a flavor of immigrant life in southern Brazil. Two of my favorites are *The War in Bom Fim* (Texas Tech University Press, 2010), and *The Centaur in the Garden* (University of Wisconsin Press, 2003).

Films are an exciting way to get a sense of the immigrant experience in Brazil. *Gaijin* (Tizuka Yamisaki, 1980) is about the experience of Japanese immigrants, especially women. *The Year My Parents Went on Vacation* (Cao Hamburger, 2006) takes place largely in Bom Retiro, one of São Paulo's immigrant neighborhoods discussed in Chapter 4 of this volume. Three excellent films dealing with immigrants in other Latin American countries are *Un Cuento Chino* (Sebastian Borensztein, Argentina, 2011), *A Lost Embrace* (Daniel Burman, Argentina, 2004), and *My Mexican Shivah* (Alejandro Springall, Mexico, 2007). There are many documentaries on Brazilian emigration. One that is particularly good at examining the broad context for migration and resettlement is Ann Kaneko's *Overstay*, available at: http://www.annkaneko.com/overstay/.

INDEX

Abbott, Robert, 146
abolition, 20, 21, 26, 34, 47, 94
  as cause of labor crisis, 67
  enacted, 61
African Americans, 49, 142–148
African slaves, 2, 6, 11, 25, 61
  compared to Chinese, 20, 21, 47
  living conditions, 94
  as non-immigrants, 7
  productivity versus immigrants, 65
Afro-Brazilians, 26
  ex-slaves, 12
  marginalization of, 66
  separation from immigrants, 89
Arab nationalism, 136, 187
Arabs and Jews
  as excellent Brazilians, 138
  as Indigenous peoples, 117
  as similar ethnic groups, 117
Argentina, 12, 39, 72, See Brazil, compared
    to American Republics
  Bolivian immigrants to, 189
  as competitor for immigrants, 64
  conflicts with Brazil, 34
  immigration policy, 64
  Jewish immigrants, 122
Assyrians, 140–142
Azevedo, Aluísio, 103–104

Bolivians, 189
Brazil
  abolition of slavery, 27
  Census of 2010, 186
  compared to American Republics, 2, 4, 5,
    6, 7, 33, 60, 62, 65, 91, 109, 130

Constitution of 1824, 27
Constitution of 1934, 138, 164
  immigrant population, 2010, 195
  immigration policy, 12, 29, 33, 62, 69,
    136, 142, 145, 177–179
  immigration quotas, 138, 163–165, 178
  independence period, 24
  as a "Jewish" country, 173
  as multicultural nation, 3, 10, 77
  as nation of immigrants, 23, 53
  population in 1825, 22
  population in 1890, 65
  secret immigration policies, 148
  urban population. See urbanization
Brazilianization, 137, 138, 165

Chinese
  as lost tribe, 5
  debates over entry, 20–22, 46–50
  negative comparison with Germans,
    47
  Portuguese images of, 19–20
  twentieth century immigration,
    186–187
colônia
  definitions of, 83
colonies, 90
  Bastos, 166
  Blumenau, 35
  images of, 66
  Japanese, 157
  Jewish Colonization Association, 122
  Uruma, Bolivia, 182
colono, 91, 95
  definitions of, 40, 84

205

Made in the USA
Lexington, KY
17 January 2018